day trips® from toronto

help us keep this guide up to date

We would love to hear from you concerning your experiences with this guide and how you feel it could be improved and kept up to date. Please send your comments and suggestions to:

editorial@GlobePequot.com

Thanks for your input, and happy travels!

day trips® from toronto

first edition

>>> **getaway ideas for the local traveller**

barbara ramsay orr

gpp®

travel

Guilford, Connecticut

Editor: Amy Lyons
Project Editor: Heather Santiago
Layout: Joanna Beyer
Text Design: Linda R. Loiewski
Maps: Ryan Mitchell © Morris Book Publishing, LLC.
Spot photography throughout © Elena Elisseeva/Shutterstock

ISBN 978-0-7627-6462-4

Printed in the United States of America
10 9 8 7 6 5 4 3 2 1

contents

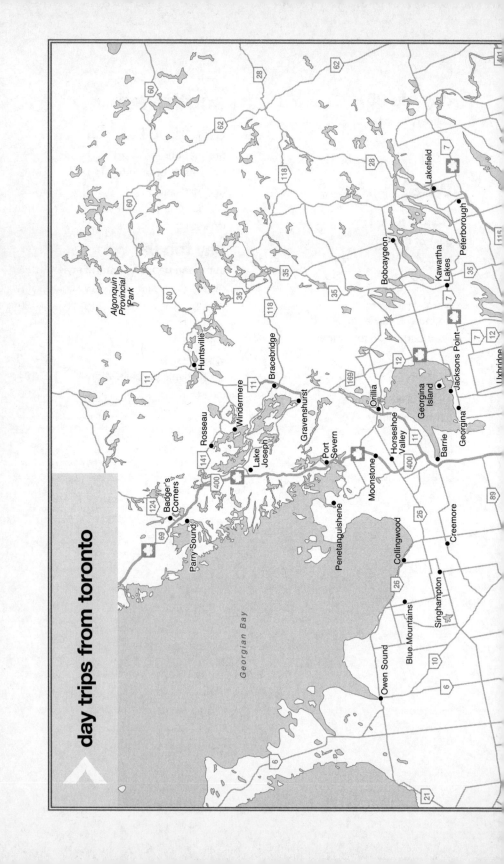

day trips from toronto

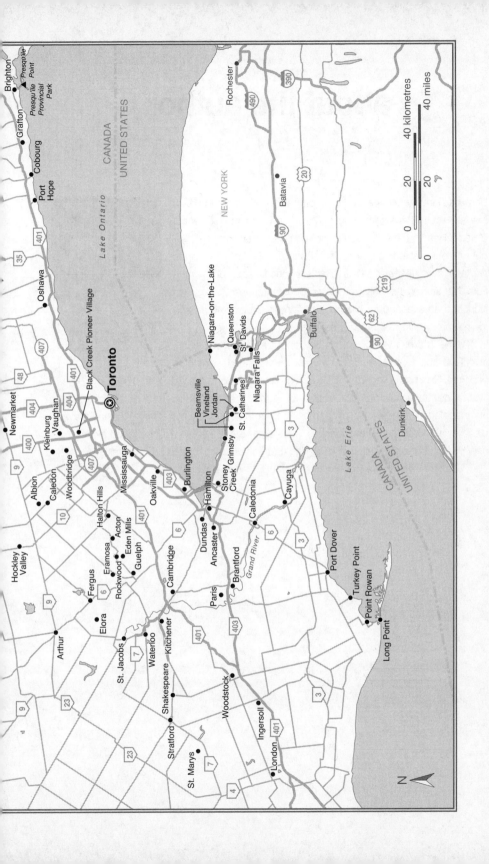

about the author

Barbara Ramsay Orr is a freelance journalist, author of the *Frommer's Guide to the Niagara Region* (Wiley) and a lifetime resident of Ontario. Her work has appeared in many national and international publications, including *Chatelaine, Canadian Living, The Globe and Mail,* and *Reader's Digest*. She is the local expert on Niagara Falls, Niagara-on-the-Lake, and Wine Country for *Nile Guides,* has launched a travel app for Niagara Falls and is developing an app for international food and wine festivals.

While she has visited and written about exotic destinations, from Thailand to Norway, her heart belongs to her hometown province. She has biked the trails of Niagara, swooned to the actors at the Stratford Festival, and fattened up on artisan cheeses at the Mennonite markets in St. Jacobs. She's an unapologetic foodie who loves to search out the special gems at farmers' markets and discover authentic cafes and wineries in the area. She's also an accomplished award winning photographer as well as a struggling (but enthusiastic) watercolour painter.

You can follow her adventures at www.upperendtravel.com.

>> introduction

I was one of six kids and growing up, the only trips my family could afford were car trips. We would all squeeze into the backseat, where the mood would swing from squirming battles to giggle fits. In an effort to keep us quiet, Mom would begin *I Spy with My Little Eye* or *Pediddle* or one of those songs that gets more complicated with each repeated verse. And in case of complete meltdown there would suddenly appear a large bag of popcorn that she would have made the night before for emergencies.

While these trips may have taught me about co-existence, they taught me more about the joy of the day trip and the many pleasures that could be found around the twists and turns of the roads around our Ontario home.

We went to "Pick Your Own" farms, kite festivals, fall fairs, nature parks, the zoo, and historic villages. We tramped over old battlefields, dropped in on a pig roast, and kept up a continual search for the best ice cream stand in the province. (It's in Stoney Creek!) Those are family memories I will keep forever. And the car trips gave me a wanderlust that has stayed with me. Although I have lived in this province for most of my life, except for a few years away at university, I have yet to exhaust the pleasure of discovering a new corner of Ontario.

There are almost too many corners to explore within a two-hour drive of Toronto.

Don't get me wrong. I love Toronto, and there's no suggestion that it's a city from which one would want to flee. But when the weekend looms, the lure of a new adventure, a more rural experience, or an unfocused meander is irresistible. Add to that the fact that Toronto is set in the middle of one of the oldest and most historic parts of Canada—in its first iteration as York, it was the capital city of the country—and that it is surrounded by rich farmland, forests, and lakes, and you have an almost limitless landscape to explore.

Look to the north, and you find Ontario's famous cottage country, known simply as "Muskoka," where residents have summered for years. Granite rocks, pristine lakes, and thick forests make this a private and beautiful escape. Once the playground of the rich who moved their families and staff up to cottage country for the summer, the area today has grand resorts, championship golf courses, and campgrounds. Easily reachable from Toronto, yet far enough removed that the promise of a wilderness retreat is assured, Muskoka has become home to stars and millionaires. Kurt Russell, Goldie Hawn, Tom Hanks, Stephen Spielberg, and Martin Short are some of the recognizable names who have lived in private obscurity here during the summer months. Restored lake steamers are sailing these waters again and visitors can cruise past the waterside estates and historic cottages, many of which have been here since the late 1800s and are still owned by the same families. The cruises include lunch or candlelight dinners on the lake as well as visits to the little towns and elegant resorts of our Canadian version of The Hamptons.

Drive a bit further and you enter Algonquin Park, one of the world's most famous natural preserves, where crystal lakes, seemingly never disturbed by humans, offer canoeing, camping, and fishing in a challenging landscape that inspired Canada's Group of Seven painters.

To the west of Toronto lies Mennonite country with farms that seem to have been ripped from a turn of the 20th-century calendar. This is also Shakespeare country, with Stratford providing a home to the best Shakespearean Festival outside of Britain. Stars like Christopher Plummer, Peter Ustinov, Dame Maggie Smith, Alec Guinness, and William Shatner (known affectionately to local fans as "The Shat") have graced the stage here. It's also home to the Stratford Chefs School, which may explain the proliferation of excellent restaurants and the vibrant culinary scene.

You'll also find a London and a Paris, Ontario style. London is a bustling city, home to the University of Western Ontario, the storied Grand Theatre, and Banting House, the home and medical practice where Sir Fredrick Banting first made the theoretical associations that would lead to his discovery of insulin. Paris is a small southwestern town, named not for the French capital but for the local deposits of gypsum used to make plaster of paris. It is also called the "cobblestone capital of Canada" because of the many cobblestone houses in the town.

Then to the south a traveller finds the unexpected—miles of white sand beaches along the edge of Lake Erie. So many people think of Canada as cold and snowy, but the border of Ontario reaches as far south as the 43rd latitude. I once won a bet with the captain of a German river cruise boat when he refused to believe that Toronto was on the same latitude as Venice and Bordeaux. And while Erie is the 13th largest lake in the world, it is also the shallowest of the Great Lakes, which means it warms up beautifully in the summer. There's an active cottage and resort life all along its shores. Near Port Colbourne, a company called Horseplay Niagara runs horseback treks on the beach that include a romantic sunset ride along the shore.

But for me, day tripping is mostly about the serendipitous discovery of little hidden gems like the Inn the Pines farm market in Niagara. Don't be confused—there's no inn here, just one of the best fresh market farm stands around. Cheryl and Barney Barnes not only raise great fresh produce, like heirloom potatoes, tomatoes, and corn, but also chickens and roosters. The couple raises Chanticleer chickens which roam the property and are willing to pose regally for photos. She also sells their eggs, along with homemade preserves and freshly cut flowers. Everything on the stand is grown locally and offered only in season. A visit here is like a lesson in sustainable eating, and Cheryl will tell you how to cook every vegetable and fruit and is always ready to share recipes.

For the wine lover, Niagara is paradise. This is Canada's largest and most successful wine growing area, producing world class wines of depth and complexity—remember that latitudinal affinity with Bordeaux? There are close to 80 wineries in the area, each with a character of its own. One of my favourites is The Foreign Affair, a small boutique winery in Vineland Station where Len and Marisa Crispino turn their passion for Italian wine into a Niagara version of one of the world's best loved wines, amarone. If you drop in to their shop, try a taste of this exceptional wine, produced from grapes that have been dried according to the traditional *appassimento* method to produce a wine that is variously described as tasting of raspberry, chocolate, spiced plum, and black cherry. It is delicious, but dangerous, as all affairs seem to be. Some of the vintages are 17 percent alcohol.

I've suggested some of the large wineries to visit as well as some of the smaller and newer wineries that are pushing the envelope of winemaking. You can pick and choose the ones that suit your level of wine knowledge. Beginners would probably be happier at an established winery like Inniskillen where there will be lessons in wine tasting and guided samplings. Seasoned wine lovers might prefer a visit to the iconoclastic Daniel Lenko who hosts casual tastings in the dining room of his farmhouse but who is producing some of the best chardonnay in the peninsula.

Where good wine flourishes, great cuisine follows. Some of Canada's best chefs have moved to Niagara to be close to the vineyards and to benefit from the exceptional agricultural bounty that has been permitted here by the warming effect of the lake and the protective ridge of the Niagara escarpment. Tony DeLucca has two restaurants in the heart of wine country, and renowned Chef Marc Picone has opened a culinary studio with just one sought-after table, situated right in his kitchen.

Niagara-on-the-Lake, a perfectly preserved town on the shore of Lake Ontario, is home to the only festival devoted to the works of George Bernard Shaw and his contemporaries. The town's authentically restored Fort George celebrates the complicated history of this area, which has been fought over by the French, British, and Americans. Artists, actors, writers, and vintners have made their homes here, and it has been called the prettiest town in Canada. I love to walk the side streets to look at the gardens and steal ideas for my own flower beds.

The jewel in the Niagara Peninsula is the great Niagara Falls themselves which, though I have visited them many times both for work and just for pleasure, still give me shivers. Whenever I have guests, they always ask me to show them The Falls, and they are always thrilled. The Falls are one of the great geological wonders of the world and a must-see. Even the carnival fun of nearby Clifton Hill has its allure. Kids love the rides and fun houses. I discovered that one of the best places to photograph The Falls was from the top of the SkyWheel ride.

There is much to savour, much to learn and so many discoveries to make in every direction from Toronto. Whether you are exploring a destination for the first time, or revisiting a place you loved, I hope this guide encourages you to hit the road and experience the many pleasures that a day trip from Toronto can promise.

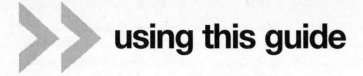

using this guide

Day Trips from Toronto is organized by general direction from Toronto: south, southeast, east, northeast, north, northwest, west, and southwest. Listings in the Where to Go, Where to Shop, Where to Eat, and Where to Stay sections are arranged in alphabetical order, unless otherwise specified. If several places in a given town offer similar opportunities, listing titles highlight broad categories (e.g., "wineries") rather than the names of specific businesses or locations. Each stop on every day trip includes a Where to Go listing, but Where to Shop, Where to Eat, and Where to Stay are only included when there are appropriate listings worth visiting.

scheduling your trip

The best day trips are often spontaneous, but a bit of good planning can make most trips that much better. Half the fun of day tripping is planning. Many a workday can be endured by imagining what fun you'll have come the weekend on an unencumbered day—just you and the open road, maybe a pal or two along for the ride, nowhere to go and all day to get there. As you fantasize about your next day trip, keep these things in mind: Friday night and Sunday night are always busy traffic times; it may be wiser to leave on a Saturday morning to avoid the rush hour. Sunday is a good day for day trips—in Ontario, most shops and attractions are open and the crowds are smaller. Winter changes things, though, so if your destination is one with a seasonal component, always check for opening hours which may be shortened in winter. If your heart is set on a certain destination, call in advance to check on hours and plan your trip accordingly. If you have the luxury of day tripping mid-week, doing so can be a fabulous option. The crowds are thinner during the week, yet most services are open. That said, be aware that many tourist-dependent businesses in smaller towns choose to close shop mid-week, often on Monday or Tuesday, in order to accommodate the majority of travellers and yet still have a break themselves. Also, most museums are closed on Monday. A little foresight can help you to choose the best day to hit the most of your selected destinations.

hours of operation

Many businesses change their hours frequently or seasonally. Hours of operation are often included in these pages, but be aware that this information may change without notice.

Phone numbers and, when possible, websites for each listing are included here so that you can access current information on your own. Also, small businesses can be known to change location or phone number at whim. Keep in mind, too, that many businesses close on major holidays, even though that information may not be indicated in these pages.

pricing key

The price codes for restaurants and accommodations are represented as a scale of one to three dollar signs ($). The prices in this book are quoted in Canadian dollars. The Canadian and American dollars are very close in value, but the exact exchange rate regularly varies, though seldom by much in the last year or so. At the time of this printing, $0.98 American equals $1 Canadian. For an up to date exchange rate, check out a universal currency conversion site like www.xe.com.

Most businesses take credit cards these days, but you can't always be guaranteed of this convenience. Should a business require cash only, in most cases they can direct you to a nearby ATM to access cash, which will sometimes assess a small banking fee. Be prepared to pay 13 percent HST (Harmonized Sales Tax) on all purchases in Ontario.

The Harmonized Sales Tax (HST) took effect in Ontario in July 2010 and is applied to most purchases and transactions. It is a 13 percent value added tax (VAT) that replaces the federal goods and services tax (GST) and the provincial sales tax (PST). With regard to retail purchases, non-residents who purchase retail goods in Canada and remove them from the country are not eligible for an HST rebate, but Canadian retailers are not required to charge HST when they ship goods directly to a non-resident traveller's residence.

where to eat

The price code used here is based on the average price of dinner entrees for two, excluding drinks, appetizers, dessert, tax (13 percent), and tip. You can typically expect to pay a little less for lunch and/or breakfast, where applicable. If the business only serves lunch and/or breakfast, the code has been applied to those meals.

$	Less than $20
$$	$20 to $35
$$$	More than $35

where to stay

This book is intended primarily for those who wish to venture out of the city for just a day or half-day. However, overnight accommodations are included in many sections for those who wish to explore an area further. Sometimes a day trip is so good that you don't want it to end—or you discover that you need more time to really explore. Accommodations included here are all local hotels and bed-and-breakfasts. Large national chains are not included, though many of the larger cities in this book do have chain hotels. Where there are no suitable lodgings, the Where to Stay section has been omitted. Each day trip does not include accommodation listings for every stop, though typically at least one stop per day trip includes a suggested overnight lodging. With few exceptions, most towns in each trip aren't more than 40 minutes apart, and many are much closer. The following price code is used for accommodations throughout this book. It is based on the average price of a one-night stay in a standard, double-occupancy room, before taxes. Keep in mind that lodging prices often change seasonally or between the week and mid-week. Summer pricing is almost always higher, and weekends are very frequently more expensive, as well.

$ Less than $100
$$ $100 to $200
$$$ More than $200

driving tips

In general, highways in Ontario are well signed and getting from one town to another is straightforward. But in the smaller and more rural areas, the roads are more winding and narrower, and while altogether very pretty to traverse, are sometimes more difficult to navigate. Drive cautiously and keep your eyes open for road changes and directional signage. In heavily forested areas, deer or moose can be a hazard.

In the winter, many of the destinations included in this book can be subject to stormy weather. Occasionally some of the roads are closed due to weather conditions. Always travel with caution in the winter, and plan ahead. For road closures and weather information, there are several sources that you can consult. The **Traveller's Road Information Portal (TRIP)** is a website that gives you easy 24/7/365 access to Ministry of Transportation (MTO) road information on provincially maintained highways; www.mto.gov.on.ca/english/traveller/trip/index.shtml.

Alternatively, for really instant information, check **Twitter MTO Road Conditions @_mto Southern Ontario.**

You can also check **www.highwayconditions.com/on.htm** or call for road conditions at (416) 235-4686, (800) 268-4686. It doesn't hurt to carry water, blankets, and food when travelling in Ontario in the winter. A cell phone is always handy—charge it up before you leave!

Speed limits and distances are in kilometres (1 km=0.62 miles). Unless otherwise posted, the speed limit in urban and residential areas is 50 km/h (30 mph); on the highway, 80 km/h (50 mph). Unless otherwise posted it is legal in Ontario to turn right on a red light, after making a full stop. Seat belts are compulsory. Driving under the influence of alcohol is against the law.

Keep in mind that speed limits can change abruptly from one town to the next or stretch of highway to the next. While it's important to heed speed limits at all times when driving, be particularly cautious when passing through construction zones, where speeding ticket fines can be double. Many smaller highways in these trips pass directly through small towns, necessitating a speed limit change on either end. Respect the residents of these towns, and avoid getting pulled over by a police officer, by slowing down appropriately.

Mileage is calculated from downtown Toronto. Depending on the specific part of Toronto from which you embark on your day trip, mileage and directions will vary. Use a good city or provincial map, or GPS to determine how to best merge onto major arterials out of town from your exact starting point.

Another thing to keep in mind is that car travel isn't your only option for many of these day trips. The train and bus systems in Ontario are excellent and often are the best way to visit some destinations. Another option is your bicycle. Many of the smaller, more rural roads and destinations in this book are simply perfect for road biking. **VIA Rail's Bike Train** (www.biketrain.ca) makes it easy for cyclists to travel to different parts of the province by train, transporting your bike, and to cycle the area. Be safe and wear a helmet, please.

highway designations

For consistency's sake, this book typically refers to highways by the highway number (e.g., Regional Road 29). In many cases, that number will be followed by a road name. In some situations, multiple highways run along the same path. In other cases, the same highway may have more than one name. A good map, GPS, or mapping service like Google Maps or MapQuest can help you sort things out.

where to get more information

Day Trips from Toronto attempts to cover a variety of interests and destinations, but those looking for additional travel information can contact the following agencies by phone, mail or the web. Keep in mind that online reviews can be contradictory, as everyone experiences places differently. Call directly or stick with advice from respected travel organizations.

For General Travel Information:

Ontario Tourism
www.ontariotravel.net

Tourism Burlington
(905) 634-5594, (877) 499-9989
www.tourismburlington.com

Tourism Hamilton
(905) 546-2666, (800) 263-8590
www.tourismhamilton.ca

Tourism London
(519) 661-5000, (800) 265-2602
www.londontourism.ca

Tourism Niagara
(905) 984-3626, (800) 263-2988
www.tourismniagara.com

Niagara Falls Tourism
(905) 356-1355
www.niagarafalls.ca

Norfolk Tourism
www.norfolktourism.ca

Stratford Tourism Alliance and Visitor Centre
(800) 561-7926 (SWAN)
www.welcometostratford.com

Canadian Automobile Association (CAA)
www.caa.ca

Camping & Recreation Information
www.ontarioparks.com
www.bikeontours.on.ca

National Parks of Canada
www.pc.gc.ca

For Information on Farms, Wineries & Culinary Tourism:

Farm Visit
www.ontario.farmvisit.com

Farmers' Markets Ontario
www.farmersmarketsontario.com

Harvest Ontario

www.harvestontario.com

Niagara Culinary Trail

www.niagaraculinarytrail.com

Ontario Culinary Tourism Alliance

www.ontarioculinary.com

Pick Your Own

www.pickyourown.org/canadaon.htm

VQA Ontario

www.vqaontario.com

Wine Country Ontario

www.winesofontario.org

south

day trip 01

south

grand living on the lake
mississauga, oakville, burlington

The area to the west of the city, stretching from Toronto to Burlington, is one of the most affluent in Canada. It is part of what is often called the Golden Horseshoe, in reference to the area that curves around the western end of Lake Ontario.

mississauga

Mississauga, Canada's sixth largest city, is also home to the largest cluster of ethnic groups in the country. This is a city that has attracted many Fortune 500 companies, is home to Canada's biggest and busiest international airport, and boasts some of the best upscale shopping. Yet there are tree-lined streets with elegant homes, and the waterfront area is alive with activity. There are also some important and well-preserved historical sites, as well as ample evidence of the rich diversity for which the city is famous. Name a cuisine and you can find a restaurant here that specializes in it. This is also a good place to access the Waterfront Trail. The trail is more than 650 km (400 miles) long and runs along the shores of Lake Ontario and the St. Lawrence River, stretching from Niagara-on-the-Lake all the way to the Quebec border. In Mississauga, 22 km (15 miles) of the trail stretch from Etobicoke Creek through to the Oakville border and meander past streams and parks and woodlands.

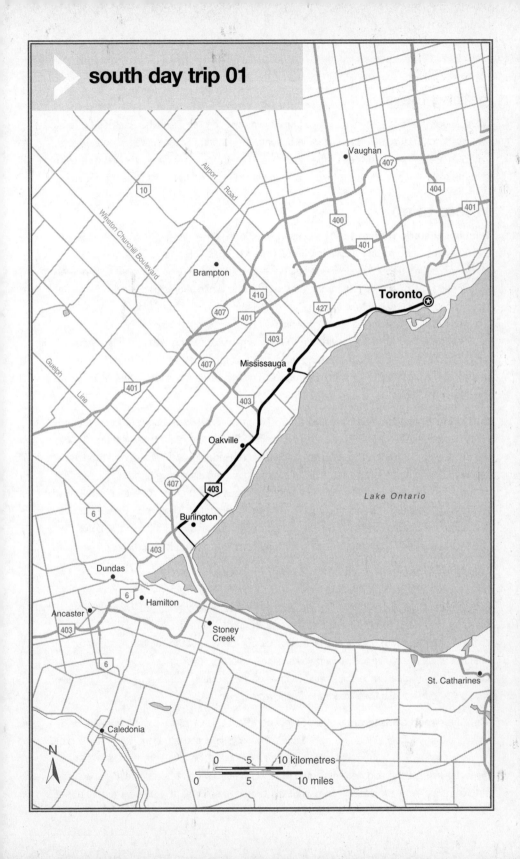

south day trip 01

getting there

Mississauga is about a 20-minute drive from downtown Toronto. Take the Gardner Expressway West for 15 km (9 miles) until it merges into the Queen Elizabeth Way. Continue for 8
km (5 miles) and exit at Mississauga Road. Head north for the bustling shopping districts
and the airport, while south will take you to the lakeshore and the quiet residential areas.

where to go

Benares Historic House. 15007 Clarkson Rd. North, Mississauga; (905) 615-4859, ext.
2110; www.museumsofmisssissauga.com. While Mazo de la Roche is seldom read today,
she was a hugely popular writer in the first half of the 20th century. She is best remembered
for her series of 16 books that chronicled the life of the Whiteoaks family who lived in a gracious manor house called "Jalna." The Benares Historic House of Mississauga, Ontario, was
the inspiration for *Jalna* and is now maintained by the Ontario Museum Association. The
author lived in Trail Cottage, located on the property, while writing *Jalna.* The Benares collection has a number of Mazo-related artifacts. When I toured the house, lovingly restored
to the 1918 time period, I felt I had entered the era of the Whiteoaks family that de la Roche
created in her series.

Fo Guang Shan Buddhist Temple. 6525 Millcreek Dr., Mississauga; (905) 814-0465;
www.fgs.ca. It's the last thing you would expect in the middle of a busy Western city, but
the Fo Guang Shan temple is an uplifting example of Buddhist architecture and thought. A
visit here gives you an insight into a different culture and an alternative approach to life. The
centre offers classes in stress reduction and meditation. If you come for a tour, remember
to dress moderately and that no meat is allowed in this totally vegetarian place. You can
purchase a vegetarian meal for $5, or you can enjoy tea and delicacies in the Lotus Tea
House. Free guided tours are offered in English every Sun from 1 to 3 p.m.

Lakefront Promenade Park. 800 Lakefront Promenade, Mississauga. Mississauga has
been careful to both celebrate and preserve its lakefront. The Promenade is one of the largest waterfront developments in Ontario with more than 40 hectares (104 acres) of public
parkland dedicated to outdoor recreation and the protection of wildlife habitat. There's a
protected harbour with two marina facilities, outdoor licensed eatery, a playground area that
features a water splash pad, boardwalks, picnic shelters, cycling paths, and concession
facilities. It's an ideal place for a fine-weather daylong outing with the family. This is also
where you can access the Waterfront Trail.

The Riverwood Conservancy. 4300 Riverwood Park Lane, Mississauga; (905) 279-5878;
www.theriverwoodconservancy.org. Riverwood is a public garden, park, and nature preserve, a green jewel in the middle of the urban expanse of Greater Toronto. On weekends
there are self-guided and naturalist-guided walks that are "heart-healthy" along the many
nature trails. The park also includes heritage buildings such as the 90-year-old Chappell

House, with its beautiful Arts and Crafts style garden. There are scheduled star-gazing nights which are run in partnership with members of the Earthshine Astronomy and Space Science Organization and the Mississauga Centre of the Royal Astronomical Society of Canada. Programs and guided walks are free, but pre-registration is necessary.

where to shop

Dixie Outlet Mall. 1250 South Service Rd., Mississauga; (905) 278-7492; www.dixieoutlet mall.shopping.ca. There's great shopping here for bargains on more than 150 brand names in this busy enclosed mall, the largest outlet mall in Canada.

Mississauga Chinese Centre. 888 Dundas St., East, Mississauga; (905) 566-5606; www .mississaugachinesecentre.com. Come here to find unique treasures in shops that feature an authentic selection of Chinese apparel, accessories, and giftware. The entranceway is a 43-foot-tall gateway and surrounding structures are modern replicas of ancient Chinese architecture, while the Nine Dragon Wall is the only one of its kind outside of Asia.

where to eat

Nirvana: The Flavours of India. 35 Brunel Rd., Mississauga; (905) 501-5500; www.nirvana theflavoursofindia.com. As you might expect in such an ethnically diverse city, there are many different cuisines to choose from. Indian is one of my favourites and you won't find much better than Nirvana. Don't be put off by the exterior. It may look like an ordinary res-taurant in a rather tacky strip mall, but this is the real deal. The interior is well appointed and the tandoori offerings are some of the best you will get in the GTA. There are many delicious Indian specialties from the tandoori oven, like the *murg kali mirch,* succulent ginger and black pepper marinated chicken breast, and the naan bread is freshly made and delicious, especially the kashmiri version with chopped dried apricots and raisins. $$

Rogues. 1900 Dundas St. West, Mississauga; (905) 822-2670; www.roguesrestaurant .com. I have been dining here for years and have yet to have a meal that wasn't special and wonderful. This is classic Italian cooking, done with care and style. There are white tablecloths, a great wine list, and a rambunctious open kitchen. Risottos are perfectly done, and veal and homemade pasta dishes are excellent. Great wine list. Tony is the owner and maitre d', and he has been front and centre from its first day. $$$

Snug Harbour Restaurant. 14 Stavebank Rd. South, Port Credit; (905) 274-5000; www .snugharbourrestaurant.com. Good fresh seafood, pizzas, and pasta in a heated and cov-ered outdoor patio with a view of all the action in the marina. This is a very family friendly place with lots of variety, where you can have a quick lunch or a leisurely dinner. $$

Tung Hing Bakery Co. 888 Dundas St. East, Unit 3A, Mississauga; (905) 270-1288; www .tunghingbakery.ca. This cosy Chinese/Vietnamese bakery in the Chinese Centre is a per-fect place for a quick snack or to pick up take-home dishes. One of the newest specialties is a Three Flavour Bun stuffed with red bean, green bean, and taro pastes. There's also delicious Vietnamese Banh Mi as well as the traditional barbecue pork buns. $

oakville

The next city along this curve of the Golden Horseshoe is Oakville, home to the Ford Motor Company and Appleby College, one of Canada's finest private schools. The lakeshore here is peopled with large estates and massive manor houses. It is a decidedly upscale town, but the main street in the old part of Oakville, with its riverside charm, is almost English in its quaintness. The shops are often small and personal, and there is a thriving arts community here. Take a walk through the maze of streets between downtown Oakville and the lake to see the perfect gardens and well-preserved historic homes that co-exist with elegant new ones. Oakville was an important stop on the Underground Railway, the path to freedom for many slaves who fled the United States in the mid-19th century. The Oakville Museum has a permanent exhibition that documents Black History in Ontario.

getting there

Oakville is about a 30-minute drive from Toronto, or around 38 km (24 miles). Take the Gardner Expressway West for 15 km (9 miles) until it merges into the Queen Elizabeth Way. Continue for 18 km (11 miles) and then take exit 118, Trafalgar Road South, a busy winding road which will take you to Lakeshore Road and into the centre of downtown Oakville.

where to go

Glen Abbey Golf Course. 1333 Dorval Dr., Oakville; (905) 849-9700; www.glenabbey.ca. Golf enthusiasts will love a visit to Glen Abbey, one of Canada's best known golf courses. Designed by Jack Nicklaus, it has hosted the Canadian Open multiple times and has been played by famous golfers like Tiger Woods, Vijay Singh, and Mike Weir. The Club House has an excellent Sunday brunch that is open to the public. A round of golf in prime season costs $235, so your swing better be in top form. Glen Abbey is also home to the Canadian Golf Museum and Hall of Fame. It is open 7 days a week and costs $4 for adults.

Merrick Thomas House. Lakeside Park, Navy Street, Oakville; (905) 844-2695 (Historical Society). Built in 1829 and moved to its present site in 1955, the Merrick Thomas House is a fine example of a settler's second house. The one-and-a-half-storey structure with a saltbox roofline is constructed of white pine logs on a fieldstone foundation. The Oakville Historical Society operates the house and provides guided tours and admission is free. They also conduct guided walks of historic downtown Oakville.

Oakville Galleries. 1306 Lakeshore Rd. East, Oakville; (905) 844-4402; www.oakville galleries.com. Oakville Galleries in Gairloch Gardens is a public contemporary art gallery located in a preserved lakeshore estate and gardens that date from the 1920s.

saved from oblivion

In 1829, one of Oakville's original settlers, Merrick Thomas, bought a farm in his new community and built a typical settler's house, sturdy but compact. In this 16' x 24' house, he and his wife raised seven children. In 1955, the Department of National Defense acquired the Thomas Farm and planned to demolish the farmhouse. Recognizing the value of this historic though humble little house, Hazel Matthews and the Oakville Historical Society raised the money to purchase it. It was dismantled, moved, and reassembled in the town where it now serves as an inspiring example of a period farm home of the early 1800s.

Oakville Museum. 8 Navy St., Oakville; (905) 338-4400; www.oakvillemuseum.ca. This 4-acre property includes the 1858 home of Oakville's founding family, the Chisholms, restored to its 1925 appearance. There's also a coach house and gardener's cottage. The property is now home to the Oakville Museum.

where to shop

Lakeshore Road in old Oakville is lined with many specialty shops, gourmet food emporiums, and galleries. Here are a couple of highlights:

Turner Chapel Antiques. 37 Lakeshore Rd. West, Oakville; (905) 338-3252; www.turner chapelantiques.com. One of the most beautiful historical structures in Oakville, this building is now the home of Turner Chapel Antiques. It was built in 1890 by the African Americans who escaped slavery in the United States. Owner Jed Gardner is somewhat of a local star, having his own cable television show called *The World of Antiques.* Stop by if you have an interest in top quality silver, china, glass, or bronzes.

Win Henstock Gallery. 334 Lakeshore Rd. East, Oakville; (905) 844-5711; http://win henstockgallery.com. Located on downtown Oakville's historic main street, the gallery features a diverse collection of artists and showcases a range of works—from impressionist to abstract, from oil to watercolour, from bronze sculptures to authentic Inuit carvings.

where to eat

Ristorante Julia. 312 Lakeshore Rd. East, Oakville; www.juliasristorante.com. This sexy bistro serves a fusion of Italian and Nuevo Latino cuisine in a warm atmosphere of frescoed walls and marble tabletops. Start with a Key Lime Martini and relax in this attractive yet comfortable restaurant. Try the Pollo di Mollo Poblano, crusted chicken with quinoa, infused with cashews, portobello mushrooms and spinach, finished with a classic mole poblano sauce. This is exciting food! $$

Stoneboats. 49 Bronte Rd., Oakville; (905) 825-2727; www.stoneboats.com. This casual restaurant, specializing in seafood, has one of the best venues in town, overlooking Bronte Harbour. There's an outdoor patio that gets pretty busy on summer nights, but the ambience is friendly. $$

Sweetsmoke Barbeque and Grill. 3420 Rebecca St., Oakville; (905) 465-0335; www .sweetsmoke.ca. Specializing in southwestern barbecue, this little place gets it right. Fabulous pulled pork sandwiches with sides like cowboy beans, baked three cheese mac and cheese, and jicama slaw are addictively good. They do takeout. $

burlington

This busy city, rated one of the best places in Canada to live, sits almost at the end of Lake Ontario and brags of being the home of actors Jim Carrey and Ryan Gosling. (My son went to the same high school as Carrey and once was issued a math book with the actor's name inside it.) It is also the home of Canada's largest Ribfest, hosts a highly popular Sound of Music Festival, and possesses one of the best botanical gardens in North America. In the past few years, Burlington has nurtured a vibrant dining scene.

getting there

It's a 45-minute drive in good traffic, but try to avoid the rush hours, from 7 to 9 a.m. and 4 to 6 p.m. Follow the Gardener West to the Queen Elizabeth Way then continue to the Brant Street exit. Turn right, toward the lake and follow Brant Street to Lakeshore Road.

where to go

Bronte Creek Provincial Park. 1219 Burloak Dr., Oakville; (905) 827-6911; www.ontario parks.com. This large park and conservation area has every attraction you could think of—a working farm with animals that the kids can visit, a play barn, an ice rink in winter, hiking and biking trails, swimming, and many programs that explore the environment and the wildlife of the area. Open year-round.

Burlington Art Centre. 1333 Lakeshore Rd., Burlington; (905) 632-7796; www.thebac.ca. Whenever I need a truly unique gift, the shop at the Burlington Art Gallery is the place I turn to. Local artists, potters, and painters have work for sale here and each piece is definitely one of a kind. The museum is home to the largest collection of contemporary Canadian ceramics in the country. There are continuous exhibitions as well as classes and workshops, and seven craft guilds maintain studio space here. There's also a nice little cafe for a light lunch. Open daily. Admission is free.

Halton Region Museum. 5181 Kelso Rd., Milton; (905) 875-2200; www.halton.ca. Housed on the grounds of Kelso Conservation Area, this important museum is centred on a historic farm and farmhouse. The collection of area memorabilia is better than you might expect, and is displayed on open shelves where visitors can get up close and personal with the likes of shadow box wreaths made from human hair, antique baby buggies, original farm implements, quilts, and the judge's chair from the old Milton courthouse. There is a large area for event rentals and weddings as well, and a library. Open Mon to Fri, year-round. Admission is free, but visitors must pay admission to Kelso Conservation Area from Apr to Oct.

Ireland House. 2168 Guelph Line, Burlington; (905) 332-9888; www.museumsofburlington .com/ireland-house. This lovingly restored historic home and farm was the family home for generations of one of the founding families of the area. The property consists of 4 acres of woodland, gardens, potting shed, cottage/drive shed, and picnic areas. Tours of the property, living historical demonstrations, special events, and educational programs are offered. There's always a family friendly activity going on, either baking in the wood burning oven or making an antique toy. Closed Monday.

Joseph Brant Museum. 1240 North Shore Blvd. East, Burlington; (905) 634-3556; www .museumsofburlington.com. A replica of Joseph Brant's original home from 1800, the museum celebrates one of the founding fathers of Burlington. The 2,200 square feet of exhibit space and more than 10,000 artifacts explore Burlington's heritage, including Iroquois life, the European settlement of the region, the importance of the waterfront, and the life of Joseph Brant.

Kelso Conservation Area. 5234 Kelso Rd., Milton; (905) 878-5011; www.conservation halton.on.ca. Tucked along the edge of the Niagara Escarpment, this lovely area offers lake swimming and canoeing, fishing, camping facilities, and exceptional walking and hiking trails. In the winter it is home to the Glen Eden Ski hill and offers cross country skiing trails and snowshoeing. Open daily, year-round.

Royal Botanical Gardens. 680 Plains Rd. West, Burlington; (905) 527-1158; www.rbg.ca. Artists come here to paint, gardeners come to steal ideas, nature lovers come to swoon, and hikers come to traverse the many paths through the gardens and along the bay. The RBG is Canada's largest botanical gardens and owns the world's largest collection of lilacs, and people come from all over to see them bloom in the spring. There are gardening and nature activities all year, including geocaching. There's an excellent gardening store that also features the work of local artists, a tea room, and a restaurant.

Spencer Smith Waterfront Park. Lakeshore Road, Burlington; www.cms.burlington.ca. I can't imagine a finer place to spend a summer afternoon. Spencer Smith Park is edged by a breakwater and walking promenade that looks out over the Burlington Bay and the Skyway Bridge. The Centennial Pond features ice skating in the winter months, and is used as a model sailboat pond in the summer. There's the Dofasco Waterjet plaza that is a water play area for children with jets spraying water in the air and a state-of-the-art children's playground. The promenade is perfect for walking, cycling, or rollerblading. There are performance areas, historic monuments, expansive lawns, and landscaped gardens. Spencer's at the Waterfront is here, and at the other end of the park, the Waterfront Hotel. The park plays host to the great Ribfest (www.burlingtonribfest.com) and the Sound of Music Festival (www.soundofmusic.on.ca).

where to eat

The Alex. 480 Brant St., Burlington; (905) 220-0520; www.thealexrestaurant.com. This new restaurant is small and cosy, but their plates, though small, are huge in flavour. The focus here is small plate dining, with popular specials like Bacon-Wrapped Bacon or Cashew Crusted Shrimp with Mango Slaw, designed to be shared by diners. It's highly sociable dining, with superb food, and one of my favourite places to go with friends. The outdoor patio is ideal on a summer evening. $$$

Crema di Gelato. 1477 Lakeshore Rd., Burlington; (905) 634-3694; www.cremadigelato .ca. The line-ups stretch out the door in summer, but even in the winter, there's still a demand for good gelato. Tubs of smooth, brightly coloured gelato fill the cases—cherry mania, Madagascar vanilla, Niagara grape, bubblegum, and candied chestnut—the variety is huge. Buy a quart of this heavenly ice cream to take home and serve as a dessert at your next dinner party, accompanied by a little biscotti and a few raspberries, and you'll have a simple and elegant ending to your meal. Open daily. $

JC's Hot Bagels. Roseland Plaza, New Street, and Guelph Line, Burlington; (905) 631-6258. I think of this little restaurant as the miracle store. How has it managed to survive, selling coffee and bagels, when it is situated next to Canadian icon Tim Hortons? But the bagels are outstanding and there is a devoted clientele that come regularly for these fresh bagels, served hot with great toppings. Try the bacon and egg bagel for breakfast. If you have weekend guests, load up on a range of bagels. They also keep really well in the freezer, but they are best fresh, right there. Buy them on Wed, which is Bagel Day when a dozen is $8. With a toasted bagel topped with strawberry cream cheese, and a cup of fair trade coffee, you can't start your day better than at JC's. Open daily. $

Kindfood. 399 John St., Burlington; (905) 637-2700; www.kindfood.com. For gluten-free products, chemical-free vegetables, hard to find vegan or vegetarian products, organic and environmentally friendly food, Kindfood is the place. The Organic Vegan Cafe serves soups, salads, sandwiches, and desserts. Try the Happy Buddha Bowl (steamed brown rice, roasted sweet potato, chopped onion, tomato, almonds, sunflower seeds, cilantro, basil, olive oil, sprouts, and tamari) or a Zen wrap (brown rice, scrambled tofu, spinach and tomato in a tortilla wrap). There's also a gluten-free vegan bakery. Open daily. $

Pane Fresco. 414 Locust St., Burlington; (905) 333-3388; www.panefresco.ca. This is my favourite place to eat for a casual meal, and I always buy my bread here. Mark Albanese is a gifted baker, and his breads are magical. There's also Roman-style pizza, homemade gelato, and delicious fresh soups, as well as chocolate croissants and brioche. Sit on the patio if the weather permits, but be prepared to wait in line. This place is popular, and the space is limited so there is almost always a line up to place your order. $$

Red Canoe Bistro. 398 John St., Burlington; (905) 637-6137; www.redcanoebistro.com. A small bistro on a quiet side street, the Red Canoe is the place to go if you want to experience real Canadian cuisine. Chef Tobias Pohl-Weary scours the farmers' markets for the best local ingredients and marries them with a great respect for flavour and freshness. $$$

Spencer's at the Waterfront. 1340 Lakeshore Rd., Burlington; (905) 633-7494; www.spencers.ca. There's a sophisticated vibe at Spencer's, maybe because the decor has a contemporary beauty, or because the view of the lake and the Skyway through the floor-to-ceiling windows is so cool. Food is excellent, always innovative and challenging. Chef Christopher Haworth studied with Marco Pierre White in London before falling in love with a Canadian girl and being lured to the colonies. Try your bison burger with a slice of grilled foie gras added on top. Burgers will never taste the same again. $$$

where to shop

Casteleyn Belgian Chocolatiers. 368 Brant St., Burlington; (905) 631-8074; www.can pages.ca. Handmade chocolates are presented in pretty boxes, and the hot chocolate is made from scratch and wickedly good.

A Different Drummer Books. 513 Locust St., Burlington; (905) 639-0925; www.web.mac .com/diffdrum/site/welcome.html. This spot is famous, and could be the poster child for the independent book store. The decor invites browsing and lingering, there's a resident cat, and the staff can always recommend a good read. The Drummer also runs authors' talks that sell out in hours.

Joelle's. 457 Brant St., Burlington; (905) 631-7918; www.joelles.com. Look for funky fashions, the latest and edgiest dresses, and, in the back section, cool stuff for the guys.

where to stay

Waterfront Hotel. 2020 Lakeshore Rd., Burlington; (905) 681-5400; www.thewaterfront downtown.com. The hotel sits beside the Waterfront Park and offers views of the lake and the park, and easy access to the shopping district on Brant Street. It's an American-style hotel with no surprises, but the view makes it special. $$

day trip 02

south

pioneer country
hamilton, dundas, ancaster,
stoney creek

The area at the tip of Lake Ontario was a natural place for early settlers to land, with its large and calm bay and fertile land protected by the gentle sweep of the escarpment. Visitors to the area are today surprised to find it so green and so rich with waterfalls and parkland. Many just know the area as the home of the large steel manufacturers whose processing plants are so visible from the highway. Here, in the bustling city of Hamilton, and the surrounding smaller cities of Ancaster, Dundas, and Stoney Creek, Ontario's early history thrives. You'll find several well preserved historic homes, pioneer villages, and important museums. As a reflection of the area's fertile farming land, there are famous farmers' markets and roadside vegetable stands that are always worth a stop. The area is also a mecca for artists, perhaps fleeing the high prices of Toronto, who have brought a vigorous arts vibe to this little corner of Ontario.

hamilton

This bustling city is home to McMaster University, one of Canada's most prestigious universities and the home of a highly reputed medical school. One of the charms of the city is the existing architecture that has been retained in the heart of downtown. Stand on the corner of James and Main Streets and you'll see what I mean. On the northeast corner is the discrete Hamilton Club, a private club that is home to one of the best private art collections in the province. The Hamilton Club itself is quite beautiful, one of the earliest brick buildings in

12

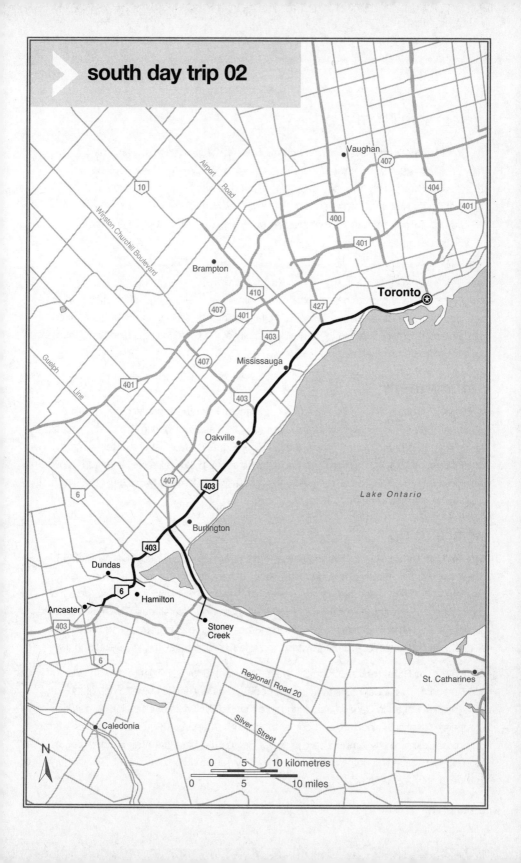

south day trip 02

> ## for more information
>
> **Tourism Hamilton Visitor Information Centre.** *2 King St. West, Unit 234
> (Jackson Square), Hamilton; (905) 546-2424 ext. 5771, (800) 263-8590; www
> .tourismhamilton.com. Need a map? Want suggestions for dinner? Need help
> planning activities or booking a tour? The Visitor Information Centre has a com-
> plete collection of current information on every aspect of Hamilton. Open Mon to
> Fri 8:30 a.m. to 4:30 p.m.*

the city, but the architecture on the three other corners is breathtaking—the Gothic Revival elegance of the Pigott building and the Sun Life building, the soaring pillars of the Landed Banking and Loan building and the refined solemnity of the Gowlings Law Firm premises in the old Bank of Montreal building.

getting there

Hamilton is about a 50-minute drive from downtown Toronto, approximately 75 km (47 miles), in good traffic. I have actually made the trip in less, but during high traffic times, the trip can take much longer. Follow the Gardiner Expressway West until it turns into the Queen Elizabeth Way. Continue along the QEW for about 16 km (10 miles) and then follow the signs for Highway 403 which veers to the right. Take the Hamilton Main Street exit which will lead you into the centre of the city.

where to go

African Lion Safari. R.R. 1 Cambridge, Hamilton; (519) 623-2620, (800) 461-WILD (9453). When you visit this game park, you are the ones who are caged—in your car. The animals, over 1,000 of them, roam free. Lions, zebras, giraffes, and baboons thrive here, and you can choose to drive through the park in your own car or on a safari bus. There are lots of activities including animal shows, a water park, boat rides, a playground, and parrot and elephant demonstrations. A great day trip for the family. Open May to Oct. Call for hours.

Art Gallery of Hamilton. 123 King St. West, Hamilton; (905) 527-6610; www.artgalleryof hamilton.com. This is Canada's third largest public art gallery and is home to one of the finest collections of art in Canada, featuring more than 9,000 works of art including historical European, historical Canadian, and contemporary art. After an $18 million renovation and expansion designed by Hamilton-born architect Bruce Kuwabara, the AGH is now a beautiful exhibition space and home to the Joey and Toby Tanenbaum collection of 19th-century European art. Closed Monday.

Canadian Warplane Heritage Museum. 9280 Airport Rd., Mount Hope at the Hamilton International Airport, Hamilton; (905) 679-4183; www.warplane.com. There's a royal connection here too, as Prince Charles is the patron of this museum dedicated to the aircraft used by Canadians or Canada's Military from the beginning of World War II up to the present. The museum's collection includes aircraft that really fly and several that remain on static display. There are interactive flight combat simulators, educational experiences, interactive video displays, movies, photographs, and memorabilia from Canadian History. Great place for an airplane buff or history lover. Open daily.

Dundurn Castle. 610 York Blvd., Hamilton; (905) 546-2872; www.hamilton.ca. Dundurn Castle is a classic Regency-style villa, restored to the style of 1855, that operates as a historic window to the past. Costumed guides give visitors a glimpse into the life of a prominent 1850s Victorian family and their servants. You get an insight into both above stairs and below. The gardens have been extensively restored, notably the kitchen garden that is a replica of the garden that fed the MacNab family, all its servants, and many of the neighbours. Open daily June 30 to Labour Day; Tues to Sun from Labour Day to June 29th. You can save 20 percent on your admission ticket by buying online.

History & Heritage. 165 James St. North, Hamilton; (905) 526-1405; www.historyand heritage.ca. This small and intimate museum is dedicated to the history of Hamilton and the people who built the city. There are revolving photographic and video shows and displays that explore the architecture, the stories, and the cultural influences. Open Thurs to Sat. Free.

HMCS *Haida*. 57 Discovery Dr., Hamilton; (905) 523-0682; www.hmcshaida.ca. The HMCS *Haida* is a national historic site. As the last of the Tribal Class destroyers built for the Canadian, British, and Australian navies, the ship is a living history of naval battles and life

the duchess & the castle

Dundurn Castle has recently earned royal notice by acquiring as their patron, Camilla Parker Bowles. Prince Charles and Camilla, the Duchess of Cornwall, visited Dundurn Castle in 2009. Built between 1832 and 1835, the distinctive Regency-style chateau was constructed for Sir Allan Napier MacNab, Bowles' great-great-great grandfather. In addition, during a visit to Hamilton in 1860, the then Prince of Wales (later King Edward VII) who was also the Great Great Grandfather of the current Prince of Wales dined at Dundurn Castle with MacNab. The castle now has its own princess!

aboard a destroyer. Tours of the ship are a special treat for those who love naval history. Open daily in summer. Call for hours.

McMaster Museum of Art. Alvin A. Lee Building, McMaster University, 1280 Main St. West, Hamilton; (905) 525-9140, ext. 2308; www.mcmaster.ca/museum. This is a museum for the true art lover. There are more than 6,000 works in the permanent collection, which is recognized internationally for its early 20th-century German prints, European paintings, drawings and prints, significant holdings of Cape Dorset prints, sculptures, and artifacts as well as historical and contemporary Canadian art. Closed Sunday and Monday. Pay by donation (suggested $2).

Whitehern Historic House and Gardens. 41 Jackson St. West, Hamilton; (905) 546-2018; www.whitehern.ca. Whitehern is a historic urban estate, part Georgian, part Edwardian, and part Victorian, where the McQuesten family lived from 1852 to 1968. The family was instrumental in establishing the Royal Botanical Gardens in Hamilton, McMaster University, and the Queen Elizabeth Way. The gardens are particularly notable, having been lovingly restored to the design created in the early 1930s by well-known landscape architect and founder of Sheridan Nurseries, Howard Dunnington-Grub. It is a green surprise in the centre of the city. Open daily June 30 to Labour Day; Tues to Sun from Labour Day to June 29. You can save 20 percent on your admission ticket by buying online.

where to shop

There's an ongoing and vibrant Farmers' Market every Tues, Thurs, and Sat next to the Hamilton Public Library on James Street. It has been in existence since 1837 and provides tantalizing browsing for the locavores among us. Several areas of the city have become real shopping destinations.

Ottawa Street has long been the place to go for bargains on fabric, buttons, and interior design materials, but it has been morphing of late into a more artsy and broadly based shopping area. **Locke Street** is the place to browse for antiques and gourmet fare. **James Street North** has grown to be the new Art shopping district, with eclectic galleries and unique ethnic dining.

Cheese Store on Locke. 190 Locke St. South, Hamilton; (905) 920-2633; www.cheese shoppeonlocke.com. This 2,500-square-foot shop is a place where it would be easy to lose an afternoon. Almost everything is local, from the cheeses to the pottery by Burlington potter Barbara Taylor. One of the most interesting items—frozen croissants—are flown in from France. You bake them yourself, then close your eyes and imagine you are in a Paris bistro. There are fresh soups, Wildly Delicious compotes and tapenades, bread boards, and hard-to-get artisanal Fifth Town Cheese. Open daily.

European Textiles. 263 & 277 Ottawa St. North, Hamilton; (905) 549-7714; www.european textiles.ca. Anything you might be searching for to create your design ideas, from drapery and upholstery fabrics to designer silks and Irish linen, you will find it here. This is one of the textile stores that has made Ottawa Street a destination for sewers and interior designers.

J. Taylor Antiques. 192 Locke St. South, Hamilton; (905) 521-6844; www.taylorsantiques .com. The shop specializes in high quality antiques and collectibles. Fine furniture, like a beautiful Louis XV fruitwood armoire or a George III mahogany chest of drawers, can be found here, as well as smaller treasures. Closed Monday and Tuesday.

The Millionaire's Daughter. 272 Ottawa St. North, Hamilton; (905) 543-8000; www.the millionairesdaughter.com. This is a casual and fun shopping place for used and consignment furniture. You may just find that special piece you have been searching for at a fantastic price. Open daily.

Mixed Media. 154 James St. North, Hamilton; (905) 529-2323; www.mixedmediahamilton .com. This is an independent art shop in the heart of the resurging James North art scene. It specializes in art and printmaking supplies, specialty paper, and stationery products. It also features locally made gift items, greeting cards, books, and magazines, and an art gallery with changing exhibitions. Closed Sunday.

where to eat

Earth to Table Bread Bar. 258 Locke St. South, Hamilton; (905) 522-2999; www.bread bar.ca. Just enter the Bread Bar on Locke Street and you're engulfed in the smell of freshly baked bread. And what bread it is, freshly made daily by the diva of dough Bettina Schormann. Fat brown loaves of rosemary focaccia and Red Fyfe sourdough line the counter. There's more than bread for the dinner table, though. The Bread Bar's pizza, sold whole or by the slice, is made from fresh house-made dough, a little thicker than you might be used to but so good. There are desserts too—like monkey bread, a unique version of timbits, scones, pies, and bread & butter pudding. There's also fair trade Reunion coffee. Open daily. $$

Mulberry Street Coffee House. 193 James St. North, Hamilton; (905) 963-1365. Created from the good bones of the old Hamilton Hotel, and once a laundry, the coffeehouse serves excellent vegetarian chili, panini, and soups. On the day I visited, the soup special was a heavenly sweet potato and pear. For take home, try the carrot cake muffins or the fresh baked brownies or blondies. Open daily. $$

Ola Bakery. 230 James St. North, Hamilton; (905) 296-6064. Come for the *natas*—Portuguese custard tarts—which are wonderful, and pick up some of the round soft Portuguese bread that looks like an oversized English muffin and makes great toasted sandwiches. On Fri they bake fresh sponge cakes. At $5.99, they sell out quickly, but they make a perfect and effortless dessert topped with fresh fruit and a little whipped cream. Good coffee and tea, too. Closed Monday. $

the hamilton cemetery

I don't think it's macabre to visit graveyards—it is there that you can read the history of a place and some of them are quite beautiful, like this one at 777 York St., just across the street from Dundurn Castle. This is Ontario's oldest municipal cemetery, and it is the final resting place of many notable figures. When it was first established, it would have had a fine view of the bay. Today the cemetery is a quiet and elegant tribute to the city personalities of the past, with intricate monuments and ornate family crypts.

Many of the city mayors are buried here as well as:

William Cooke (died 1876). A soldier who was killed with Custer at his last stand at the Battle of Little Big Horn.

Adelaide Hoodless (died 1910). Social reformer and founder of the Women's Institute.

Robert Land (died 1818). The founder of Hamilton and the first white settler in the area.

Isabella Whyte (died 1865). She was reputed to be the half sister of Queen Victoria, and visits by Royals to her during her lifetime seem to bear out the truth of the rumours.

where to stay

There are no boutique hotels in Hamilton, but there are several good dependable chain hotels and some excellent B&Bs.

Rutherford House Bed & Breakfast. 293 Park St. South, Hamilton; (905) 525-2422; www.rutherfordbb.com. Located in the Heritage District of the Durand Neighbourhood, this 19th-century home has 2 rooms each with en suite baths. It is centrally located so guests can walk to most of the city attractions. $$

Sheraton Hamilton Hotel. 116 King St. West, Hamilton; (905) 529-5515. This is a clean and newly renovated hotel in the heart of the city. There's a pool, fitness centre, and restaurants. No surprises. $$

dundas

Affectionately known as the Valley Town, Dundas is a charming and beloved historic town with a distinct character. It's a bit funky, very artsy, and home to many of the faculty and students from nearby McMaster University. Its well-preserved small town main street has served as the backdrop for several movies, as well as being used in a few episodes of *The West Wing*. One of the big attractions for movie shoots is the Deluxe Restaurant, an establishment that was closed up by the owner's widow and kept exactly as it was from the mid '50s. It has recently reopened as the Bangkok Spoon Deluxe, a Thai restaurant, but still retains elements of the old Deluxe, including vintage photographs on the walls. Dundas is also famous for The Collins Hotel, the longest running hotel in Ontario.

getting there

Take Main Street West out of the centre of Hamilton, drive past McMaster University, and turn right onto Cootes Drive, which becomes King Street and will take you right into the centre of Dundas.

where to go

Dundas Historical Museum. 139 Park St. West, Dundas; (905) 627-7412; www.dundas museum.ca. This museum is dedicated to preserving the history, artifacts, and archives of the town. The collection is particularly strong in the areas of decorative and fine arts, social history objects, and photography. Open daily. Admission by donation.

Dundas Valley School of Art. 21 Ogilvie St., Dundas; (905) 628-6357; www.dvsa.ca. This prestigious art school is small but carries a big reputation. Started in 1964, it is now housed in a designated heritage building, formerly known as "Canada Screw Works." The building also served as a munitions factory in World War I. Dating from the 1860s, it still features the neo-Georgian windows and, among its many studios, a small art gallery, the Dofasco Gallery, and a large space with beamed ceiling suitable for performances. If you drop in, there will usually be an excellent art show in the Dofasco Gallery featuring local artists or works by student and faculty. The annual art auction, held each April, attracts buyers from across the country who snap up works from the teachers and students at the school and from several highly respected artists, like Robert Bateman, who donate work for the sale. Closed Sunday, except for special programs.

Westfield Heritage Village. 1049 Kirkwall Rd. (Regional Road 552), Rockton; (519) 621-8851; www.westfieldheritage.ca. The village is comprised of a collection of more than 30 historical buildings which has made Westfield one of the most interesting historical destinations in Ontario. It is staffed with costumed interpreters who help to bring to life the true spirit of early Canadian culture. Visitors can see living history demonstrations and take part in guided tours of the 130-hectare (321-acre) site. Open Sun and holidays from Mar to Oct.

where to shop

Carnegie Gallery. 10 King St. West, Dundas; (905) 627-4265; www.carnegiegallery.org. Opened in 1910, the Carnegie was the site of the town's first library and was funded by a donation from American industrialist, Andrew Carnegie, and the citizens of Dundas. The Carnegie Gallery houses a gallery shop offering visual art, pottery, sculpture, jewellery, glass, woodworking, textiles, and photography from only the best Canadian artists. Closed Monday.

Mickey McGuire's Cheese Shop. 51 King St. West, Dundas; (905) 627-1004. The shop is small but the collection of cheeses is immense. Rich and creamy French cheeses, Cashel Blue from Ireland, cheese from Neal's Yard Dairy, the best of Canadian artisanal cheeses, and different kinds of cheese from all over the world—you will find them here—and he gives sample tastings. You should always travel with a cooler in the car for just such situations, so you can take home a few lovely cheeses for dinner. Closed Sunday and Monday.

Picone Fine Food. 34 King St. West, Dundas; (905) 628-8642; www.piconefinefood.ca. Picone's is an institution in Dundas. The store has been owned and operated by the Picone family for 95 years, and a visit here is like as step back in time. Olive oils, 25-year-old balsamics, foie gras, and vegetable rarities—you will find them here, including homemade soups, sandwiches, and desserts, as well as an espresso bar. Closed Sunday.

where to eat

Matsu Sushi. 29 King St. West, Dundas; (905) 628-0133. This restaurant features sushi, and there are those who swear it is the best in Southern Ontario. Sushi lovers from Buffalo to Toronto rave about it. The chef is a fanatic for freshness, and insists that you eat your sushi within 20 minutes of it being prepared. Closed Monday. $$

Quatrefoil Restaurant. 16 Sydenham St., Dundas; (905) 628-7800; www.quatrefoil restaurant.com. Possibly the prettiest dining room in the area, Quatrefoil was just named one of Canada's best 10 new restaurants by *enRoute* magazine. Chef Fraser Macfarlane makes classic French dishes with a modern twist. There's also a nice outdoor patio for fine weather dining. Closed Monday and Tuesday. $$$

where to stay

Osler House Bed & Breakfast. 30 South St. West, Dundas; (289) 238-9278; www.osler house.com. This Victorian home was built in 1848 and has been lovingly preserved. Three elegant bedrooms, decorated with antiques and personal treasures, allow you to sleep in great comfort in the middle of history. $$

ancaster

getting there

Continue up Highway 403 to the top of the escarpment and take exit 64, to Mohawk Road towards Rousseaux Street. Follow this street until it comes to a T intersection with Wilson Street. Turn left onto Wilson and you will be in the centre of Ancaster.

where to go

Fieldcote Memorial Park & Museum. 64 Sulphur Springs Rd., Ancaster; (905) 648-8144. Fieldcote is a lovely heritage home that was left to the city and has become an important cultural centre and historical museum. There are regular art shows held here, as well as workshops and musical events. The house also includes a beautifully landscaped garden and walking trails. Open year-round, Wed to Sat. The gardens are open any time.

Griffin House. 733 Mineral Springs Rd., Ancaster; (905) 546-2424 ext. 7220. This simple home was purchased by Enerals Griffin in 1834. He and his wife, Priscilla, crossed the border in 1829 to escape slavery in the United States. For the next 150 years, their descendents lived and farmed here. It is now a National Historic site and an important site for Black history. Open holiday Mondays May to Oct.

The Spa at Ancaster. 343 Wilson St. East, Ancaster; (905) 648-1443; www.ancasterspa .com. Fancy a day of pampering, with no outside distractions? This spa will provide a whole range of treatments, from massages to body scrubs, in the quiet surroundings of a heritage building from 1872. You could go for the Royal Treatment, a full day of total pampering that includes a spa lunch. Closed Sunday.

where to eat

The Ancaster Old Mill. 548 Old Dundas Rd., Ancaster; (905) 648-1828; www.ancastermill .com. If you are looking for a scenic place to dine, this is it. The main rooms of The Old Mill overlook a waterfall and garden. Food here is exceptional, under the sure hand of Chef Jeff Crump, a devotee of fresh and local ingredients, who has forged relationships with the best local suppliers. The Sunday brunch is famous. Closed Monday. $$$

Rousseau House Restaurant. 375 Wilson St. East, Ancaster; (905) 648-8863; www .rousseauhouse.ca. This charming casual restaurant is located in a historic home that was once the home of local artist Frank Panabaker. Rousseau House is best known for its tapas. Closed Monday. $$$

where to stay

Shaver's Bed & Breakfast. 1868 Shaver Rd., Ancaster; (905) 648-3326; www.theshavers bnb.com. There is just one elegant suite here, but it has every luxury you could ask for, including fluffy robes and free wireless Internet. $$

stoney creek

getting there

Return to Highway 403, Toronto bound, and follow that to the junction with the Queen Elizabeth Way. Take the QEW to Niagara, crossing the Skyway Bridge and continuing to the Highway 20/Centenial Parkway exit. Follow Highway 20 South to King Street, and turn left. King Street will lead you in to Stoney Creek.

where to go

Battlefield House Museum. 77 King St. West, Stoney Creek; (905) 662-8458; www.battle fieldhouse.ca. It was here, on June 6, 1813, that the Battle of Stoney Creek took place during the War of 1812. Nestled under the Niagara Escarpment, this historic site is located on 32 acres of park land linked to the Bruce Trail, Canada's oldest and longest footpath. Visitors can see costumed interpreters demonstrate the way of life of early Canadians. There is an important military reenactment of the Battle of Stoney Creek held here every June. The event was declared one of the top 100 events in Ontario by Festivals and Events Ontario in 2009. Closed Monday.

Erland Lee Museum. 552 Ridge Rd., Stoney Creek; (905) 662-2691; www.erlandlee.com. The museum is recognized as the birthplace of the first Women's Institute, an international organization formed in 1897 to promote the education of isolated rural women. The home was built in the Gothic Revival Architectural style and the earliest parts date from 1808. In addition to the carefully restored interiors, there are displays of antique quilts, model railroads, and local historical artifacts. Hours vary. Call for details.

where to eat

Edgewater Manor. 518 Fruitland Rd., Stoney Creek; (905) 643-9332; www.edgewater manor.com. One of the best things about this upscale restaurant is the view of the lake, especially at sunset. It's very romantic. The house itself has an interesting story and a long history. Most of what is visible on the exterior of the building today are pieces, and in some cases, entire sections of old buildings torn down in the City of Hamilton. The cuisine is classic and well executed. Closed Sunday. $$$

day trip 03

south

>>> **a grand river**
exploring the grand river,
caledonia, cayuga

The Grand River is one of Ontario's historic rivers. It flows through the heartland of southern Ontario, from the Grand Valley northwest of Toronto, past farms, towns, cities, through wetlands and forests, and empties into Lake Erie. It has been witness to much history. Today, a quiet drive along the river will take you through startlingly beautiful scenery and through little villages that have hardly been changed by time. And always there's the fresh sparkle of sun on the river and the twisting water that has a story all its own. It has been designated a Canadian Heritage River, and its fame has been immortalized in poet Pauline Johnson's "The Song My Paddle Sings."

One of the best places to enjoy the river and its beauty is along the section from Caledonia to Cayuga, where you can hike the Grand Valley Trail or canoe along the river. There are many small parks beside the river that are ideal for a quiet picnic.

exploring the grand river

getting there

The Grand River Area in Haldimand County is about a 1 hour and 15 minute drive, or 92 km (57 miles) from Toronto. Take the Gardner Expressway West for 15 km (9 miles) until it merges into the Queen Elizabeth Way. Continue for 16 km (10 miles) until the QEW merges with Highway 403. When the two highways divide just before Hamilton, follow Highway 403

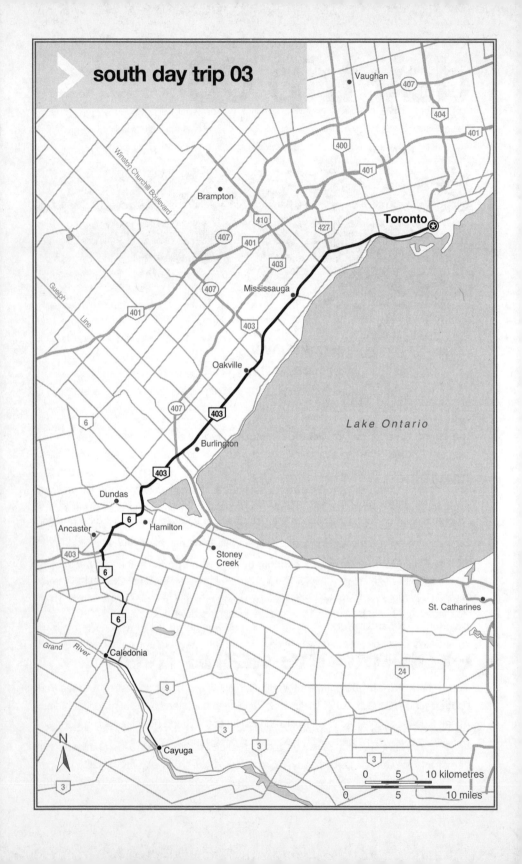

south day trip 03

Vaughan
407
404
401
400
401
Brampton
Winston Churchill Boulevard
410
427
Toronto
407
401
403
Guelph Line
407
Mississauga
401
403
Oakville
407
6
403
Lake Ontario
403
Burlington
Dundas
6
Ancaster
Hamilton
403
6
Stoney Creek
St. Catharines
6
24
Grand River
Caledonia
9
3
N
Cayuga
3
3
3

0   5   10 kilometres
0   5   10 miles

through Hamilton and towards Brantford. Exit at Highway 6 South, following the signs for Caledonia/Port Dover. Highway 6 turns left, but stay on what will now be the Hamilton Port Dover Plain Road, and that becomes Argyle Street. You can turn left or right at Highway 54, also called Caithness Street, as it parallels the river.

hiking

Grand Valley Trail. For information about trails and access points, contact The Grand Valley Trails Association, Waterloo; (519) 576-6156; www.gvta.on.ca. The Grand Valley Trail is 275 km (171 miles) long and runs from Rock Point Provincial Park on Lake Erie to Orangeville. Hikers are able to identify the main Grand Valley Trail by the white blazes approximately 5 cm wide by 15 cm high. The trail is well maintained and has good relationships with the nearby landowners.

Rotary Riverside Trail. www.grandrivercountry.com/trails. This 5.7-km linear trail runs parallel to the Grand River just downstream of Caledonia. Developed and managed by the Rotary Club of Caledonia, most of the trail is on land owned by Haldimand County, with the rest of the trail on private land. The trail is open all year. It begins at the Seneca Park parking lot, on the east side of the Grand immediately below Caledonia, and ends at the town of York. There are several opportunities to exit the trail onto roadways, including Highway 54 at River Road, Abbey Road, and Stoney Creek Road. The trail user may also opt to simply reverse to the beginning.

canoeing

If you are a boater with his own canoe or kayak, a trip on the Grand is perfect. There are several access points for boating on the Grand where you can launch a canoe or kayak easily.

North of Caledonia—Harrison's Landing or LaFortune Park. On the left or east bank, just off Highway 54, approximately 2 kilometres (1.2 miles) downstream of Big Creek. (Launching and/or parking fees may apply and parking is day use only.)

Caledonia—Kinsmen Park. Pull out on the left bank above the low head dam or weir, immediately upstream of the railway bridge. From Highway 54 re-enter just below the dam at Kinsmen Park.

York—York Park in the village of York. Off Highway 54, just downstream of the York bridge on the left or east bank. The channel running through the park is of historical interest. At one time the channel led to a lift lock, and a dam of the Grand River Navigation Company was situated where the present bridge crossing now stands.

Cayuga—Bob Baigent Park. Gain access in Cayuga downstream of the Highway 3 bridge on the east or left bank, at the Bob Baigent Memorial Park public boat ramp off Ouse Street. Ouse was an early English name for the Grand River.

Grand River Kayak. 2 Port Maitland Rd., Dunnville; (905) 701-6818; www.grandriverkayak .ca. If you don't own your own boat, or prefer to have a guided experience, this company can arrange tours of the Grand River. You can rent a kayak or bring your own on one of their many tours, from short jaunts on the Grand, to cold weather paddling. They give lessons and have an excellent store with kayaking equipment and clothing. Open Thurs to Sun.

caledonia

The only 9-span bridge of this kind in Canada is located here, and links the entire community. The bridge is also the first reinforced concrete bridge ever built. It is a historic river town, once prosperous because of the river, its transport, and its mills. Now it's a more bucolic town. The town, which is bordered by the Six Nation Indian Reserve, became notorious because of the Six Nations Land Dispute and the resulting confrontations that made headlines.

getting there

Follow the Hamilton Port Dover Plain Road, which becomes Argyle Street. After about 2 km (1.2 miles), it runs directly into the centre of Caledonia.

where to go

Caledonia Grand Trunk Railway Station. 1 Grand Trunk Lane, Caledonia; (905) 765-5072. The station has been restored to its Grand Trunk splendor, and is a busy place accommodating the office for the Caledonia Regional Chamber of Commerce, a year-round

for more information

Caledonia Train Station Information Centre. 1 Grand Trunk Lane, Caledonia; (905) 765-8322. This information office is open year-round, 10 a.m. to 4 p.m. daily.

Cayuga Tourist Information Centre. 1 Talbot St. West Corner of Highway 3 and Highway 54, Cayuga; (905) 772-5954.

Tourism Haldimand. 45 Munsee St., North Cayuga; (905) 318-5932 ext. 232, (800) 863-9607; www.tourismhaldimand.com. Open weekdays.

Tourist Information Centre and a popular museum of local railway artifacts, displays and an operating "G" scale model train. Daily. Free admission.

Caledonia Old Mill. 146 Forfar St. West, Caledonia; www.caledoniamill.org. It's the last mill of its type remaining in the Grand River Watershed. For more than 150 years it has survived, when other mills in the area disappeared. This huge frame building operated as a flour and grist mill right up to the late 1960s. The mill is located just downstream from the Caledonia dam, a favourite spot for sport fishermen. The interior is currently not open to the public, but it is well worth seeing from the exterior.

where to eat

Cafe Amore. 49 Argyle St., North Caledonia; (905) 765-3878. This is a small and personal family style restaurant, with good homemade soups, baked goods, and specialty teas. There is an all-you-can-eat buffet on Sun. Closed Monday. $$

Grand River Dinner Cruises. 36 Brant County Rd. 22, Caledonia; (905) 765-4107, (800) 847-3321 (Canada or US); www.grandrivercruises.ca. Enjoy a traditional roast beef dinner while you cruise the Grand River. This company runs 3 cruise boats for lunch and sunset cruises, with live entertainment and historic commentary accompanied by the idyllic scenery of the historic Grand. May 19 to Oct 4 (7 days a week) Reservations required. $$$

where to stay

Heron House on the Grand. 487 Caithness St. East, Caledonia; (905) 765-3975; www .linetap.com/heronhouse. This modest bed-and-breakfast has 2 rooms and looks out on the Grand River. This is a favourite nesting area for the Great Blue Heron, hence the name. Open all year. $

cayuga

Cayuga is located on the banks of the Grand River between Port Maitland and Caledonia. It is home to the Cayuga Speedway that draws thousands of visitors every year. It is a quiet town that straddles the river, with a small commercial centre, but a large farm community and networks of growers and producers who are known for excellent quality and careful husbandry.

getting there

Continue along Highway 54, also called Caithness Road and River Road, for about 16 kilometres (10 miles) until you reach Cayuga. This is a beautiful drive along the river, and it passes several historic markers, like the Nelles Tract and Sims Locke.

where to go

Cayuga Speedway. 901 Indian Line Rd., Cayuga; (905) 768-1177; www.cayugamotor speedway.ca. Stock car racing is a prime attraction at the Cayuga 2000 Speedway although there are also occasional concerts, and plenty of serviced campsites nearby. Open Apr to Oct. Admission varies.

Cottonwood Mansion. 740 Haldimand Rd. 53, Selkirk; (905) 776-2538; http://linetap .com/cottonwoodmansion. Built as a private farm home, Cottonwood has been lovingly restored by a relative and through the support of many local initiatives. It now serves as a living museum of Victorian life. It is located north of Selkirk near Lake Erie in open countryside, on land originally owned by the Hoover family, the first settlers to the area. The mansion is an Italianate style 3-story building with a belvedere (meaning beautiful view, sometimes known as a widow's walk). It is a large 6,000-square-foot, 15-room house, built around 1870, of variegated orange brick. Open July 1 to Labour Day, Fri to Sun and holiday Mondays.

Haldimand County Museum & Archives. 8 Echo St., Box 38, Cayuga; (905) 772-5880; www.haldimandmuseums.ca. This small museum can be found in the Courthouse Park, and includes an authentic log house used by one of the first families in the area. The archives are a valuable resource for researchers and hobbyists with an extensive collection of family histories, local histories, newspapers, church records, cemetery transcripts, census records, and some birth, marriage, and death records. Open year-round, closed Sun and statutory holidays. Free.

Ruthven Park National Historic Site. 243 Highway 54, Cayuga; (905) 772-0560; www .ruthven.ca. This elegant mansion sits at the end of a forested drive and comes as a complete and unexpected surprise. This 19th-century Greek Revival Mansion overlooks the Grand River. Here, visitors have the opportunity to see what life was like for the five generations of the Thompson family who lived there from 1845 to 1993. Today it is a National Historic Site. Tours of the mansion are available as well as a 1,500-acre park with nature trails and picnic areas. There's a birding centre as well as the spooky remains of a ghost town, Indiana, which is in the process of being excavated. You can access the Ruthven Riverside Trail here. Tours run in summer: from Victoria Day weekend until Thanksgiving Day on Wed through Sun and holiday Mondays from 10 a.m. until 5 p.m. Tours are on the hour with the last tour at 4 p.m. Tours are also available most weekends in Nov and Dec. Call for details.

Toronto Motorsport Park. 1040 Kohler Rd., Cayuga; (905) 772-0303; www.torontomotor sportspark.com. Funny car races and dragsters are just two of the motor attractions at Toronto Motorsports Park. Jet cars also make an appearance from time to time. The drag strip was originally a runway built for training British Commonwealth pilots during World War II. Open Apr to Oct. Admission varies.

where to eat

Twisted Lemon Restaurant. 3 Norton St. West, Cayuga; (905) 772-6636; www.twisted lemon.ca. You wouldn't expect to find a restaurant of this caliber in a tiny town like Cayuga, so it is a surprise to discover Chef Dan Megna's brilliant cuisine. There is always a foie gras dish on the menu, and the ingredients are fresh and local, including ale from Grand River Brewing Co. and Niagara Wines. With front-of-the-house partner Laurie Lilliman and sommelier Patrick Field, Megna has created a dining room that is definitely worth a drive. Closed Sun and Mon. $$$

where to stay

The Broecheler Inn. 4648 Highway 3, Cayuga; (905) 772-5362; www.broechelerinn.com. There are 3 bedrooms in this large and sparkling clean inn, only minutes from Cayuga. Rooms are air conditioned and there is free wireless. Best of all, Helga Broechler is a renowned baker, and turns out breads, cakes, strudels, and German specialties to die for. They also do dinner and catering. Open year-round. $

Gingerbread House Country Inn & Restaurant. 311 Haldimand Hwy. 54, Cayuga; (905) 772-1776; www.thegingerbreadinn.com. There are 4 country-style rooms in this B&B that sits beside the Grand River and is right next to Ruthven Park. Open all year. $$

day trip 04

south

norfolk county: the breadbasket of ontario & home of the famous lake erie beaches
port dover, turkey point, long point, point rowan

This is a unique area of Ontario. Apples, sour cherries, asparagus, pumpkins, green onions, Saskatoon berries, zucchini squash, and sweet corn—Norfolk, with its sandy soil and perfect growing conditions is the number one producer in Ontario of all of these crops. Chances are, most of the greens, vegetables, and berries you have on your plate were grown here. A visit to Norfolk will take you along roads that wind through prosperous farmland, past roadside markets and alongside fields of peanut and ginseng. And then you get to the beaches of Lake Erie. These shores continually surprise visitors with their long white sand beaches and the warm waters of Erie, the largest but shallowest of the Great Lakes.

port dover

Along the coastline you'll find the small towns, like Port Dover with its romantic pier (also Port Rowan, Long Point, and Turkey Point, below), which has lured visitors looking for a quiet and serene lakeside holiday . . . unless it's Friday the 13th! Port Dover is famous for the festivities that break out on this date, having become the party destination for thousands of bikers who come to celebrate the auspicious 13th.

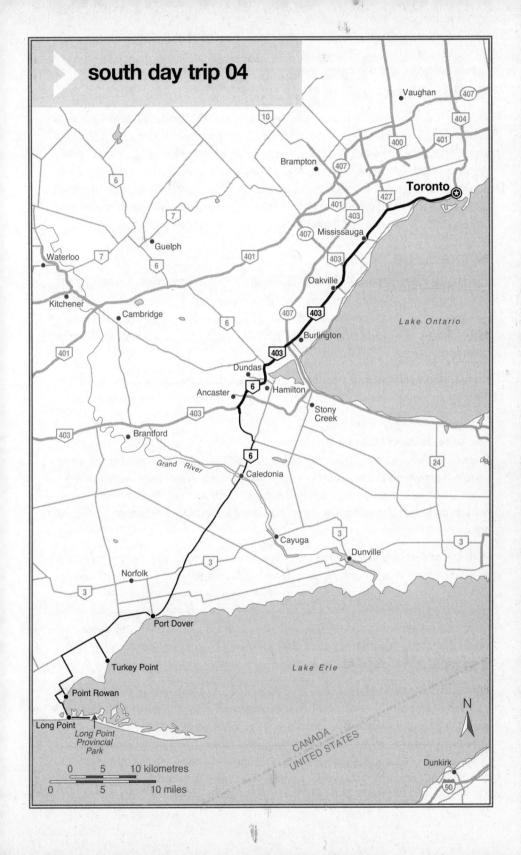

getting there

Port Dover is about a 2-hour drive from Toronto, about 133 kilometres (83 miles). Take the Gardner Expressway West for 15 km (9 miles) until it merges into the Queen Elizabeth Way. Continue for 16 km (10 miles) until the QEW merges with Highway 403. When the two highways divide just before Hamilton, follow Highway 403 through Hamilton and towards Brantford. Exit at Highway 6 South, following the signs for Caledonia/Port Dover. The highway winds through small Southern Ontario towns like Hagersville and Jarvis and through farmland to Lake Erie and Port Dover.

where to go

Lighthouse Festival Theatre. 247 Main St., Port Dover; (519) 583-2221, (888) 779-7703; www.lighthousetheatre.com. This regional theatre celebrated its 31st season in 2010. It presents live theatre, all homegrown Canadian plays, and makes its home in the hundred-year-old town hall building. There are also revolving displays of art works by local artists. Open May to Sept.

Norfolk County Tourism & Economic Development. 30 Peel St., Simcoe; (519) 426-9689; www.norfolktourims.ca. In summer drop by one of the visitor information centres in Port Dover, Port Rowan, and Simcoe, or look for the South Coast van.

Port Dover Harbour Museum. 44 Harbour St., Port Dover; (519) 583-2660; www.norfolk county.ca/harbourmuseum. This small maritime museum has been named one of the best small museums in the province, and for good reason. Housed in two buildings, one of which is part of an actual 1934 fishing boat, the museum chronicles the Lake Erie fishing history, and tells the stories of the steamers, shipwrecks, and Rum-Runners of the past. Open daily. Admission by donation.

Port Dover's Friday the 13th. Port Dover; www.pd13.com. Bikers and motorcycle enthusiasts from all over North America gather for this one-day event on every Friday the 13th. The town closes the main streets to all vehicle traffic except motorcycles. There is entertainment at several indoor and outdoor locations provided by local organizations. The restaurants have specials, and the bars are full. It's a wild, colourful, and happy celebration, though it's mostly grown-up fun. Best of all is the people-watching. Viewers enjoy seeing amazing get-ups and some incredible bikes.

Silver Lake Farmers' Market. 320 St. Patrick St., Port Dover; www.portdoverlions.org. As you would expect in a county that is the breadbasket of the province, the farmers' market is great. It is located in a spacious area of 22,000 square feet inside a large green community complex on the banks of Silver Lake. Products include exotic foods, local cheeses, baked goods, fresh produce, meats, honey, in-season plants and flowers, deli items, special coffees, and spices. Breakfast and lunch available (free coffee and tea) from 8 a.m. to 11:30 a.m. Open every Sat 8 a.m. to 1 p.m. year round.

where to eat

The Arbor. 101 Main St., Port Dover; (519) 583-0611. The Arbor is a local institution that has been feeding locals and tourists since 1919. Try their famous fresh fruit drinks or the fresh cut fries and foot-long hot dogs. Open daily mid-Mar to Thanksgiving. $

David's Fine Dining. 168 New Lakeshore Rd., Port Dover; (519) 583-0706; www.davids portdover.com. This is the most elegant restaurant in town, located just 5 minutes from the centre of Port Dover, on the north shore of Lake Erie. With great lake views and sophisticated white linen service, this is the place to dine, particularly at sunset. Seafood dishes and steaks are excellent. Closed Monday. $$$

Erie Beach Hotel. Walker Street, Port Dover; (519) 583-1391; www.eriebeachhotel .com. The Erie Beach Hotel is a classic. Dining here is a trip back in time, and depending on how you think about the past, you will either love it, or be unimpressed. The specialty—and the only thing to order—is the fresh local perch and pickerel dinner. It is fresh and delicious, and comes with accompaniments like marshmallow salad, horseradish salad, mandarin orange salad, jellied salad, a pickle and celery plate, and homemade bread and fries. Open daily. $$

Imaginations Fine Foods. 301 Main St., Port Dover; (519) 583-9195; www.imaginations finefoods.com. This specialty deli in the heart of downtown Port Dover specializes in gourmet condiments, pastas, breads, meats, cheeses, and organic fair trade coffees and teas. Everything you might need for a gourmet picnic on the beach. Open daily. $$

Willie's. 6 St. George St., Port Dover; (519) 583-3687. This beach stand offers a great view of the beach along with fish, burgers, BBQ chicken and ribs, foot longs, and ice cream. Open daily. $

where to stay

Cherrington Manor Bed & Breakfast and Cottage Rental. 18 Chapman St. East, Port Dover; (519) 583-1450, (519) 427-3587; www.bbcanada.com/aa7175. This designated Ontario Heritage home features 3 bedrooms with fridge, microwave, and free wireless. Open all year. $

Clonmel Estate B&B. 150 Prospect St., Port Dover; (519) 583-0519; www.kwic.com /~clonmel. Clonmel is a ca. 1929 Georgian Revival Estate that is perched on a hill surrounded by a stone wall fence, hand-built by Irish stone masons. It is modeled after an Irish country house with a music room, library, billiards room, and large bed rooms. Open year-round. $$

turkey point

Although named after the wild turkeys that used to populate the area, today Turkey Point is best known for its sandy beaches, parks, and summer cottages. Turkey Point was the capital of Norfolk County until the courthouse burned down in 1815, when the capital was moved to Vittoria. Turkey Point's 2 miles of groomed sandy beach offers safe swimming for all ages, with ample beach parking available. Fishing, hiking, water sports, and golfing are all readily available

getting there

Turkey Point is about a 25-minute drive from Port Dover or 25 kilometres (15 miles). Drive along Main Street for about 7 km (4 miles). Turn right on Highway 6 South and continue for 7 km (4 miles). Turn left at County Road 24 and proceed for 10 km (6 miles). Turn left at Turkey Point Road/Regional Road 10, and continue a few kilometres into Turkey Point.

where to go

Turkey Point Provincial Park. Turkey Point; (519) 426-3239; www.ontarioparks.com/english /turk.html. The only provincial park with a golf course, Turkey Point is also a naturalist's paradise. Hiking trails cover marshes, bluffs, and oak savannah, and lead to a fish culture station, a hatchery pond, and panoramic views of Lake Erie. Camp on the bluffs, swim and sail at the beach, fish for perch, or play 9 holes of golf. Open May to Oct.

long point

The hamlet of Long Point, near the mouth of Big Creek, is home to seasonal cottagers and some year-round residents. Long Point Bay boasts world-class small and large mouth bass fishing. In winter, cross country skiing, hunting, and ice fishing attract many visitors. But it is the beaches, the wildlife, and the outdoor adventure in summer that is the trademark of this area.

getting there

Long Point is about 40 minutes, or about 40 kilometres (25 miles) from Port Dover. Drive along Main Street for about 7 km (4 miles). Turn right onto Highway 6 South and continue for 10 km (6 miles). Turn left on County Road 24 and drive for 14 km (9 miles). Then turn left at Highway 59 and drive for 12 km (7 miles), which will take you onto Erie Boulevard and into the centre of Long Point.

where to go

Long Point Provincial Park. Box 99, Rowan; (519) 586-2133; www.ontarioparks.com. This park is part of a 40-kilometre-long sand spit in Lake Erie which is recognized as a biosphere reserve by the United Nations. Its delicate dunes and marshes also teem with songbirds, spawning fish, turtles, and frogs. The area has a temperate climate making it an ideal destination for spring and fall, as well as the summer months. The temperate climate allows plants and animals to thrive which aren't seen anywhere else in Canada, like North America's only marsupial, the Virginia Opossum. The park is one of the first landfalls on the northern shore of Lake Erie, and as such, is one of the best birding areas in the country during spring and fall migration. Over 350 species have been identified on the peninsula. There are camping facilities and excellent beaches for swimming, scuba diving, and kayaking. Open May to Oct.

Long Point Zip Line & Eco-Adventures. 1730 Front Rd., St. Williams; (519) 586-9300; www.lpfun.ca. This new attraction boasts zip-lines and suspension bridges as well as kayaking. A unique experience offered here is the Full Moon zip-line, where you get to zip by moon and star light. There is an observatory for evening stargazing. Open Apr to Oct.

port rowan

This is a small lakefront town that has been here since the late 1700s and still survives as a fishing and boating harbour and a summer activities destination. Campers and visitors can shop and dine here and load up on supplies.

getting there

Port Rowan is about 30 minutes, or about 35 kilometres (22 miles) from Port Dover. Drive along Main Street for about 7 km (4 miles). Turn right onto Highway 6 South and continue for 10 km (6 miles). Turn left on County Road 24 and drive for 14 km (9 miles). Turn left at Forestry Farm Road/Regional Road 16 (signs for Forestry Farm Road/Saint Williams/Port Rowan) and drive for 4 km (2,5 miles), then turn right at Queen Street West/Regional Road 42. This will bring you into Port Rowan.

where to go

Backus Heritage Conservation Area. R.R. 1, Port Rowan; (519) 586-2201; www.lprca .on.ca. This conservation area is a blend of nature and history, with an old 1798 grist mill and a heritage village, as well as a conservation education area, wooded trails, and wildlife observation. Open May to Oct.

Bayview Harbour Marina. 156 Wolven St., Port Rowan; (519) 586-2083; www.bayview harbour.com. This family style marina is a good place for boaters, a relaxing place to hang out by the water, and a nice place to picnic. Open May to Oct.

where to eat

Causeway Restaurant and Marketplace. 3 Erie Blvd., Port Rowan; (519) 586-7900; www.atplay.ca. This is a place with a view and with aspirations to be fresh and local. There's the usual (burgers and foot longs), but also fresh Lake Erie perch and pickerel. Daily in summer. Closed Mon to Wed in winter. $$

where to shop

Cashmere & Cobwebs. 6 Erie St., Port Rowan; (519) 586-8577; www.cashmereand cobwebs.com. Stop in here for gifts, home decor items, creative accessories, and upscale clothing.

Cranberrie Lane. 1016 Bay St., Port Rowan; (519) 586-3566; www.cranberrielane.com. Specialty items for home decor and for the garden, including Crabtree & Evelyn, Burt's Bees, baby gifts, linens and quilts, and jewellery. Open daily.

where to stay

At Play Adventures Vacation Resort. 50 Erie Blvd., Long Point; (519) 586-2301; www .atplayadventures.com. Clean and relatively basic rooms and large and cheerful cottages for rent, each of which comes with a boat dock. This is the only hotel within the Long Point world biosphere area. Open year-round. $$

southeast

day trip 01

southeast

niagara wine country
grimsby, beamsville, vineland

We are blessed to live beside the best and largest wine producing area in Canada. Niagara is creating some of the finest vintages in the world right now, and its vintners have matured into skilled craftsmen and women who are designing the ambrosial whites and reds which are solidifying Niagara's international wine reputation. It's no longer just about our ice wine—which is still the best in the world—but it is now a story of the distinct wines produced from grapes grown in the often limestone soil in a climate that is marginal—the ideal for robust flavour—at the same latitude as Bordeaux.

With wine comes food, and Niagara has become a foodie heaven, with some of the best chefs in the country coming to the peninsula. They are attracted by the wine, and by the generous supplies of excellent local produce and by an increasingly knowledgeable body of visitors who come for the total Niagara experience.

The Niagara Peninsula is a very lucky geographical accident. Cradled by the temperate waters of Lake Ontario on one side, and protected by the rock face of the escarpment on the other, the land here has a longer growing season than anywhere else in Canada. Because of that, and the warmer temperatures and milder winters, we can grow soft fruits like peaches, apricots, and nectarines, as well as pears, plums, and apples.

It's a palate-pleasing paradise!

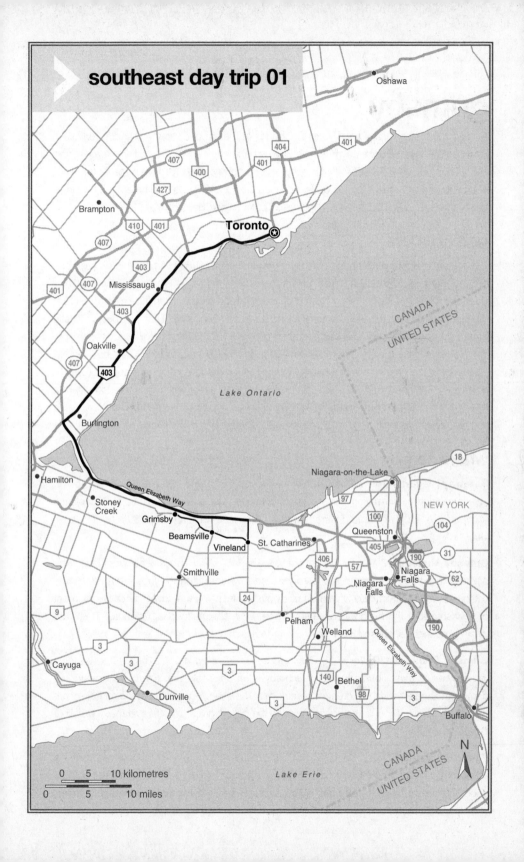

southeast day trip 01

grimsby

A small and history-heavy town, Grimsby stands at the entrance to the Niagara Peninsula. Founded by United Empire Loyalists, the town is predominantly connected with farming and fruit growing. Tree-lined streets with early historic homes make a drive through the town enjoyable and the main street is a classic, lined with small shops and cafes. It is home to two marinas, and is a convenient hopping-on point for the Bruce Trail.

getting there

This should be just over an hour's drive in good traffic, about 89 kilometres (55 miles). Follow the Gardiner Expressway West until it turns into the Queen Elizabeth Way. Continue along the QEW for about 16 km (10 miles) until the road divides. Continue along the QEW Niagara bound, over the Skyway Bridge and down the Peninsula. Take exit 66 to Christie Street. Continue to Main Street and turn left on Main Street to head into downtown Grimsby.

You can drive quickly down the peninsula on the Queen Elizabeth Way, but you will miss a lot of the charm of wine country. I would recommend continuing along Highway 8, now called Regional Road 81, also Main Street and King Street as it winds through different towns, but it is all the same road. While it will take you longer, this is part of the Wine Route and will reward you with a good old-fashioned country drive experience.

where to go

Gateway Niagara Information Centre. 424 South Service Rd., Grimsby; (905) 945-5444. This large tourist information office is an easy access just off the QEW at the Casablanca exit, and is open year-round. Hours: 9 a.m. to 6 p.m. (Sept to June), 8:30 a.m. to 7 p.m. (July to Aug).

Grimsby Museum. 6 Murray St., Grimsby; (905) 945-5292. This museum includes exhibition galleries which interpret the history of the town including the area's prehistory, the settlement of "The Forty" by United Empire Loyalists in 1787, the growth and development of Grimsby, and the history of Grimsby Park—"The Chautauqua of Canada." There are rotating exhibitions. Closed Monday.

Grimsby Public Art Gallery. 18 Carnegie Lane, Grimsby; (905) 945-3246; www.town .grimsby.on.ca/exhibitions/art-gallery. Grimsby is an artistically rich town, with many resident artists and a flourishing creative community. The changing exhibits at the art gallery are well worth a visit. Though the space is small, the gallery gives exposure to many excellent Canadian artists. Open daily.

Peninsula Ridge Winery. 5600 King St. West, Grimsby; (905) 563-0900; www.peninsula ridge.com. One of the first wineries on the winery trail, this very pretty establishment is a good place for a "newbie" wine taster to get some tips and to learn about Niagara wines.

Their vineyards are located on the Beamsville Bench, considered one of the best wine growing spots in the peninsula. Wine writer Tony Aspler has this to say about their chardonnay: "The 2008 Inox Chardonnay is straw coloured with a nose of minerals and apples; it's medium-bodied and round on the palate with dry, apple and pineapple flavours and a warm alcoholic finish. It costs $12.75 a bottle." The tasting rooms are located in a large renovated barn, and there are regular tours and tasting seminars. The Kitchen House Restaurant has a lovely patio for lunch. Open daily.

where to eat

The Kitchen House Restaurant. 5600 King St. West; Grimsby; (905) 563-0900; www.the kitchenhouse.ca. This 65-seat restaurant is part of Peninsula Ridge Winery and offers an excellent chance to dine after your wine tasting. The patio is a great place to eat in good weather, with nice views of the vineyards and the lake. The food is sophisticated—like the Braised Ontario lamb shank on saffron risotto with fresh Parmesan, confit tomatoes, and spiced date sauce. Try the 5-course tasting menu for a perfect meal, and match it with the wines from Peninsula Ridge. Service is smooth and the surroundings are attractive. Seasonal hours; call for details. $$$

13 Mountain Street Bistro. 13 Mountain St., Grimsby; (905) 945-1997; www.13mountain st.com. The cuisine is labeled Pan Global, with an emphasis on fresh and local ingredients. Enjoy moules with pernod, or chipotle and goat cheese stuffed chicken, along with a good selection of vegetarian dishes. Closed Sun and Mon. $$$

where to shop

The Dutch Shop. 52 Main St. West, Grimsby; (905) 945-3688; www.dutchshoponline .com. The Dutch Shop has been supplying Canadians with Dutch specialties since 1968 and continues to expand, with a large in-house bakery and a lunch counter. Look for some *Chocoladehagel Puur,* chocolate sprinkles to top warm buttered toast, Senseo Coffee, *honig* soup mixes, Indonesian *nasi goreng,* and my current addiction, *stroopwafels,* the round syrup waffles that taste so good with a hot cup of tea. Closed Sunday.

Monks Chocolates. 134 Main St. East, Grimsby; (905) 309-6161. Stop in for an ice cream and coffee when you are down the peninsula and make sure to pick up some handmade chocolates, especially the unique pieces like the little chocolate hazelnut hedgehogs and raspberry Turkish delight. The house-made gelatos are delicious, there's good espresso and gourmet hot chocolate, as well as chocolate covered apples. Lovely. Open daily.

Vik's Meats. 257 Main St. East, Grimsby; (905) 309-4552. Vik is a star in the sausage world. Kielbasa and sausages are laid out like artwork in the cases in his store in Grimsby. His big claim to fame was originally built on his kielbasa, but the range expanded to include a large variety of sausages, bacon, and specialty cuts of meat. Currently, the family-owned business is run by Rick Laciok, Viktor's son, and family. Look for house-smoked bacon and Angus The Pieman meat pies, either steak and mushroom, chicken, or vegetarian. They freeze well and make a great quick lunch. Closed Sunday.

where to stay

Beamer Falls Manor at Falconridge Farm. 140 Ridge Rd. West, Grimsby; (905) 945-1864. Sleep in a Gothic Revival farmhouse on top of the Niagara Escarpment. It borders the Hawk Watch Conservation Area of Beamer Falls and the Bruce Trail, and is ideal for hiking and cycling and exploring the Niagara peninsula. It is also within a few miles of many of Niagara's top Bench wineries. There are 4 large bedrooms, walkways, a shaded verandah, and a salt water pool. $$

Vinifera Inn. 245 Main St. East, Grimsby; (905) 309-8873; www.viniferainn.ca. This Italianate inn has 4 rooms decorated in elegant Victorian style, with a library and in-ground pool. $$

beamsville

The town is home to numerous Dutch and United Empire Loyalist families. Beamsville was named after Jacob Beam who founded the town in 1788. Both of his homes—the original one located on the Thirty Mile Creek, as well as the one near downtown Beamsville—are still intact today. The town is surrounded by vineyards, wineries, and fruit orchards.

getting there

Beamsville is about a 1 hour and 10 minute drive from Toronto (93 kilometres or 58 miles). If you are coming along the QEW, take exit 54, Ontario Street. Follow Ontario Street south to King Street (Regional Road 81). You will now be in the centre of Beamsville. If you are following the scenic route along Regional Road 81, the road runs right into the centre of town.

where to go

You're in wine country! Head for the best!

Angel's Gate Winery. 4260 Mountainview Rd., Beamsville; (905) 563-3942; www.angels gatewinery.com. This elegant mission-style winery has a great gift shop selling all kinds of wine paraphernalia, as well as aprons, cookbooks, condiments, and, of course, wine. The patio looks out over the escarpment and Lake Ontario and is one of my favourite places to take guests for a real Niagara lunch. Winery open daily, patio open for summer season.

Daniel Lenko Estate Winery. 5246 King St., Beamsville; (905) 563-7756; www.daniel lenko.com. This is guerilla wine tasting. Don't be put off by the casual nature of the surroundings here, or by the fact that the tasting room is actually Lenko's dining room. There are those who claim he is making the best chardonnays in the peninsula. His white caber-net—"Strawberry, red currant, and pear combine with hints of confectioner's sugar to unveil a fresh and lively nose. Cassis and raspberry bring together good acidity with a wonderfully balanced palate"—is my favourite summer wine. Lenko's a character, and if you catch him on a good day, he can be delightful. Tastings are Sat and Sun (noon to 5 p.m.), otherwise by appointment.

EastDell Estates. 4041 Locust Lane, Beamsville; (905) 563-9463; www.eastdell.com. Tucked away on the Beamsville Bench, this rustic-style winery also has walking trails and entrance paths to the Bruce Trail. There is also the Heron's Nest Cabin on EastDell Pond that is available for rent. There are wine samplings in the tasting room available, as well as "tutored tastings" by appointment. Open daily.

Hidden Bench Vineyards and Winery. 4152 Locust Lane, Beamsville; (905) 563-8700; www.hiddenbench.com. It is all about the wine at Hidden Bench. Quite probably the best in the area, this winery makes small lot wines with exacting care and their wines sell out almost immediately. This is a connoisseur's winery, and an experienced wine lover will note the fine quality and expert vintnering. If you like a good Riesling, try the Hidden Bench "Roman's Block—Rosomel Vineyard" Riesling 2008 VQA Beamsville Bench. Spectacular.

Legends Estates Winery. 4888 Ontario St. North, Beamsville; (905) 563-6500; www .legendsestates.com. Do a tasting at this lakeside winery, which has recently won seven awards at the world's largest wine competition—or call ahead and book a tour of the facili-ties as well as a tasting. Open daily.

Organized Crime. 4043 Mountainview Rd., Beamsville; (905) 563-9802; www.organized crimewine.com. Named after an incident involving a Mennonite church and a purloined pipe organ, this small winery makes limited production, hand-crafted wines. Try their 2006 Pinot Noir with notes of dried cherry, silky and delicious. Open during the season Wed to Mon; in winter Fri, Sat, and Sun.

Thirty Bench Wine Makers. 4281 Mountainview Rd., Beamsville; (905) 563-1698; www .thirtybench.com. Thirty Bench is a producer of premium wines grown exclusively on estate vineyards in the Beamsville Bench appellation. They specialize in Rieslings and red varietals in small lots. Weekends there is often a special tasting experience, with one of the winemak-ers, where guests can sample some of the small lot wines and tour the facilities. Open daily.

where to eat

The Good Earth Food and Wine Co. 4556 Lincoln Ave., Beamsville; (905) 563-6333; www.thegoodearthfoodandwine.com. The dining room and patio are small, but the food is fresh and delicious, particularly the pizzas from the outdoor wood burning pizza oven. This is a perfect place for a vineyard lunch or to pick up supplies for a picnic. You can order a custom picnic in a picnic basket to go. There are popular cooking classes in the on-site school and the new winery is producing some very drinkable wines. Winery open daily. Lunch is seasonal. Call for hours. $$

View Restaurant at EastDell Estate Winery. 4041 Locust Lane, Beamsville; (905) 563-9463; www.eastdell.com. The restaurant, in a spacious and comfortable room with access to a patio for good weather, serves a range of dishes, from game to Niagara grown lamb. Their Sunday brunch is popular, and you can combine it with a tasting and a hike on their nature trails. Open Fri to Sun. $$$

where to shop

The Good Earth Food and Wine Co. 4556 Lincoln Ave., Beamsville; (905) 563-6333; www.thegoodearthfoodandwine.com. Recently expanded and branched out as a winery and a food emporium, this cooking school is the only place I know of to buy duck fat. And if you have ever had potatoes fried in duck fat, you know how valuable this ingredient is. Veal jus, vanilla beans, and homemade chicken stock, as well as herbed butters are made in the school by the resident chefs. The stock will change according to what is being made and of course the season, but these are quality food stuffs that take time to make. There's also jams, jellies, crisps, flavoured vinegars, and, of course, wine. Their chardonnay is good. Seasonal. Call for hours.

vineland

This little town is the epicentre for the Bench vineyards. It's a bustling and busy town for its size and sees a big influx of tourists and winery visitors in the summer months. The area is recognized as Canada's premier tender fruit region particularly because of the research on growing tender fruits in Canada that is centred at the Vineland Research Station.

getting there

Vineland is about a 1 hour and 20 minute drive from Toronto (101 kilometres or 63 miles). If you are coming along the QEW, take exit 57, Victoria Street. Follow Victoria Street south to King Street (Regional Road 81). You will now be in the centre of Vineland. If you are following the scenic route along Regional Road 81, the road runs right into the centre of town.

where to go

Foreign Affair. 4890 Victoria Ave. North, Vineland Station; (905) 562-9898 or (877) AMA-RON1 (262-7661); www.foreignaffairwine.com. Len and Marisa Crispino fell in love with the amarone style wines of Italy during a diplomatic posting in Milan. When they returned to Canada, the love affair continued, and the couple opened a winery that would be devoted to developing Niagara wines produced using the *appassimento* process the method of manually harvesting only perfect bunches of fruit which have been left on the vine longer than usual to concentrate sugars. The harvested grape bunches are laid out on straw or bamboo mats in controlled atmosphere rooms to allow air to freely flow around the grapes. The grapes are left to dry for several months, until they have lost from 35 to 40 percent of their weight, and have developed high concentrations of sugar and flavour. It is an expensive and labour-intensive method of wine production, but the wines are considered to be some of the world's most delicious, with rich raisin aromas, and powerful full bodied flavours. Housed in what used to be the Vineland Experimental Station, Foreign Affair has succeeded in turning Niagara grapes into the Canadian interpretation of the Italian amarone. A bottle of their Cabernet Franc 2006 with its hints of dried raisin, licorice, and sweet cherry, is a special and memorable treat.

John Howard Cellars of Distinction: Megalomaniac. 3930 Cherry Ave., Vineland; (905) 562-5155, (888) MEGALO1; www.megalomaniacwine.com. Howard is one of the founders of Niagara wines, having created the blockbuster success of Vineland Estates. His retirement project, Megalomaniac Wines, is audacious and innovative. Housed in a winery that is mostly buried in the limestone of the Niagara escarpment, the wines have achieved overnight success. His winemaker, Sue-Ann Staff, comes from a long established Niagara farming family. Certainly the stylish labels and provocative names—Sonofabitch Pinot Noir, Narcissist Riesling, Big Mouth Merlot, Cold Hearted Cabernet Franc Icewine—are garnering lots of attention. But the wines are also winning prizes and praise. You can taste the wines at the winery on Cherry Avenue at a long oak bar set up right in the winery so visitors can watch the winemaking process while they sip. Open weekends.

No. 99 Estates Winery. 3751 King St., Vineland; (905) 562-4945; www.gretzky.com. Wayne Gretsky is a Canadian ice hockey icon, having made the top 10 list of the CBC's *The Greatest Canadian*. So when he turned his interest to Niagara Wine, there was much attendant publicity. While he is participating from a distance—he still lives in Arizona—he has played a significant part in the development of the wines. The winery, on King Street just outside of Vineland, has a small casual restaurant and welcomes visitors for tastings. Open daily.

Old Mennonite Cemetery. Corner of King Street and Martin Road, Vineland. For history buffs, this is an interesting site. Here you will find a centuries-old Mennonite cemetery. The Vineland Mennonite Cemetery is in an area sectioned off by a stone wall. This area contains many old Mennonite stones dating back to 1841. Vineland is the site of the oldest existing settlement of Mennonites in Ontario.

Tawse Winery. 3955 Cherry Ave., Vineland; (905) 562-9500; www.tawsewinery.ca. The modern architecture of the Tawse winery building features clean, simple lines, making its presence in the landscape unobtrusive. The 2007 Laundry Vineyard Cabernet Franc 004 Robyn's Block Estate Chardonnay is buttery and smooth, rich with aromas of damson plum, tobacco, and black raspberry. Open daily.

Vineland Estates Vineland Estates Winery. 3620 Moyer Rd., Vineland; (905) 562-7088, (888) 846-3526; www.vineland.com. This winery is reached by a drive down a tree-lined country road, and it is easily one of the most attractive wineries in the peninsula. Set on a reconstructed 1845 Mennonite village, Vineland Estate's stone-clad coach house and adjacent buildings nestle comfortably into the landscape. It's one of the largest wineries in Niagara. The 2007 Chardonnay, Non-Oaked, won gold at the 2009 Ontario Wine Awards. It is fresh and balanced, with apple and citrus flavours. Open daily.

where to shop

Granny's Boot Antiques and Country Pine. 3389 King St., Vineland; (905) 562-7055, (877) 211-0735; www.grannysbootantiques.com. Handcrafted country pine pieces are a specialty here. You'll also find folk art, unique antiques, rustic furniture, and primitives. Open Tues to Fri, weekends by chance.

Vineland Antiques. 4227 Victoria Ave., Vineland; (905) 562-9145; www.vinelandantiques .ca. This is a multi-dealer antiques shop, housed in the original general store in the village of Vineland. It has retained its original high tin ceiling, pine floors, and cash desk, and offers a large selection of antiques and collectibles. Opening days vary. Call for details.

where to eat

About Thyme Bistro. 3457 King St., Vineland; (905) 562-3457; www.aboutthymebistro .com. You could easily miss this little boite of a place. It looks quite unassuming from the outside. Inside you will find a very professional French style bistro that serves the best steak and frites in the area, complete with house-made ketchup. Chef Ryan Shapiro's bistro char-cuterie plate has his own smoked bacon and sausages, there's foie gras and duck confit and a great wine list. With a "Bring Your Own Wine" license, customers are encouraged to buy local wines and bring these bottles to the restaurant to be uncorked and enjoyed with their meals. The patio has become the place where local winemakers come for lunch or dinner, bringing their wines with them, and often still in their muddy boots. It's a place with real authentic locality. Open Wed to Sun. $$$

De la Terre Cafe and Bakery. 3451 King St., Vineland; (905) 562-1513; www.delaterre .ca. Chef Jans hand shapes the lovely organic loaves and prepares them for proofing. All the breads here are artisanal and organic and the cafe serves fair trade coffee and tea, pastries, and breads. Call for hours. $

Mark Picone's Culinary Studio. 4075 Moyer Rd., Vineland; www.chefmarkpicone.com. It was Chef Mark Picone who raised the dining room at Vineland estates to iconic levels. Now, he's still creating inventive and heavenly dishes but for a much more select audience. Mark Picone's Culinary Studio is the intimate and personal dining venue that he has created in his farmhouse in Vineland. In a beautifully appointed room with views of the vineyard and the lake, he cooks for one table—and he cooks amazing meals. Guests are by reservation only, and if they like, they can join in with the preparation. His menus are seasonally driven, and the ingredients come, as much as possible, from local farmers. Dinner with Mark is about savouring the best the region can produce, about intimacy, about paying attention to detail, about learning, and, ultimately, about sharing. There is music, usually classical, there is conversation, and there is slow and careful appreciation for what is being consumed, where it came from, and how it was prepared. To be a guest at Mark Picone's table is one of the ultimate dining experiences. By appointment only. $$$

The Restaurant at Vineland Estates Winery. 3620 Moyer Rd., Vineland; (888) 846-3526. The bucolic surroundings—a vineyard amidst rolling hills set in an old Mennonite village—make a visit here an event. The menu, which changes seasonally and makes good use of local ingredients, is traditional fine dining fare but it's accented with subtle changes and fresh additions. Open summer daily, winter Wed to Sun. $$$

where to stay

Black Walnut Manor Bed & Breakfast. 4255 Victoria Ave., Vineland; (905) 562-8675, (800) 859-4786; www.blackwalnutmanor.com. There are 3 lovely well-appointed suites, a large pool, and a great location in the middle of wine country, close to Niagara-on-the-Lake and its restaurants and theatres, and a short drive from Niagara Falls. Year-round. $$

day trip 02

southeast

jordan & the twenty valley
jordan (including jordan village
& jordan station)

The Twenty Valley is a lovely green swath that embraces the Twenty Mile Creek, a small tributary that winds through forests and farmland to empty into Jordan Harbour and Lake Ontario. This is one of my favourite destinations in Niagara. Jordan Village is always busy and full of life, yet historic and engaging. The stores are irresistible, and the little town is home to some of the best dining and accommodations in the area. The green areas around, along the river and through the valley to Lake Ontario, offer great biking and hiking opportunities. And there are delightful wineries here, as well as a first rate spa, good harbour fishing and the small but charming Jordan Historical Museum.

jordan (including jordan village & jordan station)

getting there

The drive from Toronto will take you about 1 hour and 30 minutes (110 kilometres or 68 miles) in good traffic. If you are coming along the QEW, take exit 55 to Jordan Road. Follow Jordan Road for about 3 km (2 miles) to Fourth Avenue, and then turn left at Nineteenth Street and then a quick right onto Wismer Street which turns into Main Street, where you will find yourself in the centre of the shopping district. If you are following the scenic route

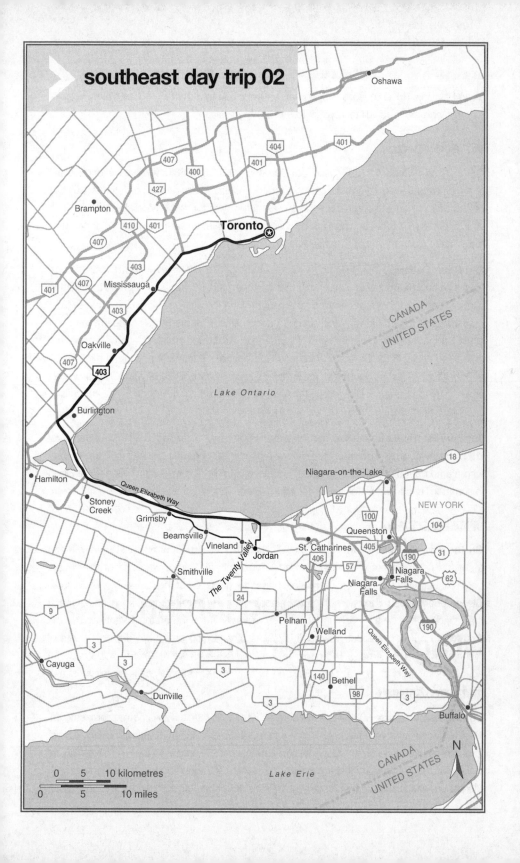

southeast day trip 02

along Regional Road 81, follow along until you reach Main Street in Jordan, where you will turn left, and the road will take you into the centre of town.

where to go

Cave Spring Cellars. 3638 Main St., Jordan; (905) 562-3581; www.cavespringcellars .com. Cave Spring's tasting room, wine shop, and cellars are located in a historical building on the main street which means you can saunter in here for some wine after you've done your shopping. Tutored tastings are held on weekends in the winter and daily in the summer. Their Cabernet/Merlot is heavenly. Open daily.

Flat Rock Cellars. 2727 Seventh Ave., Jordan; (905) 562-8994; www.flatrockcellars.com. This is an environmentally aware winery that has been winning prizes for its wine and getting a lot of attention. What really excites me, though, is the food truck! This is one of the coolest new things to happen in the food scene in a long time. The food truck concept has been big in California and has now spread to Niagara. El Gastronomo's compact foodmobile will be parked at Flat Rock Cellars on weekends for most of the summer and into the fall. Enjoy gourmet tacos, tapas, Southeast-Asian dishes, salads, and desserts without fuss or ceremony. Try the Bangkok Dangerous taco, with coconut red curry beef short rib, cucumber, coriander, fried shallots, and lime juice. Winery is open daily.

Jordan Historical Museum of the Twenty. 3800 Main St., Jordan; (905) 562-5242; www .1812history.com. The museum has several old restored buildings and artifacts, a cemetery where a number of pioneers are buried, and access to the Twenty Valley hiking trails. Open in summer Tues to Sun. Call for winter hours. Free.

where to eat

On the Twenty Restaurant. 3836 Main St., Jordan Village; (905) 562-7313; www.innon thetwenty.com. Situated in quaint Jordan Village, this restaurant was one of the first to begin Niagara's reputation for fine cuisine, under the guidance of the founding chef, Michael Olson. It continues to be one of the best places to dine in the area, with an inventive menu that concentrates on the fresh and local. You can stay at the Inn on the Twenty across the street, and not worry about how many glasses of wine you drink with dinner. Guests of the inn have breakfast here. The decor is very pleasing, with warm Tuscan colours, and a spectacular view over the Jordan Valley and Twenty Mile Creek. Service is professional and courteous. Open daily. $$$

Zooma Zooma Cafe. 3839 Main St., Jordan; (905) 562-6280; www.zoomazoomacafe.ca. This "funky, retro" cafe is the perfect place for a light, casual lunch or afternoon coffee stop. Their grilled vegetable pizza—with sweet peppers, zucchini, and eggplant—is a highlight as is the warm brie with apricot Riesling jelly on flatbread. A regular concert series of music on the patio makes for a great summer night. Open daily. $$

where to shop

The Copper Leaf. 3845 Main St., Jordan; (905) 562-0244; www.thecopperleaf.com. Gardeners will happily browse here for ages, wandering among the statuary, garden tools, furniture, garden decor items, and a small selection of live plants. Open daily.

Heritage Gift Shop. 3836 Main St., Jordan; (905) 562-4849. Proceeds from sales at this shop support the Jordan Historical Museum. In the shop, which is fully staffed by volunteers, you will find an assortment of gift items and pieces for the home—china, pottery, glassware, candles, linens, and decorative seasonal florals.

Jordan Antiques Centre. 3836 Main St., Jordan Village; (905) 562-7723; www.jordanantiques.com. This is a cooperative kind of marketplace for antiques, featuring inventory from 25 dealers. Items include antique toys, Christmas decorations, jewellery, and silver. Open daily.

shopping in the wine boutiques

While all of the wineries sell wine at the cellar door, some of them have gone further and extended their offering to almost anything you can think of that has to do with wine and good food. There are many desirable objects that would make an excellent memento of a day in wine country.

All of the following wine boutiques have a range of wines and ice wines, food items, and wine-related gifts, including wine glasses, limited edition prints, unique bottle openers and bottle stoppers, aprons, cookbooks, sauces, flavoured oils and vinegars, and much more:

Angel's Gate Winery. *4260 Mountainview Rd., Beamsville; (905) 563-3942; www.angelsgatewinery.com*

Hillebrand Estates Winery. *1249 Niagara Stone Rd., Niagara-on-the-Lake; (800) 582-8412; www.hillebrand.com*

Inniskillin Niagara Winery. *1499 Line 3 at the Niagara Parkway, Niagara-on-the-Lake; (905) 468-3554; www.inniskillin.com*

Peller Estates Winery. *290 John St. East, Niagara-on-the-Lake; (905) 468-4678, (888) 673-5537; www.peller.com*

Peninsula Ridge Estates Winery. *5600 King St., Beamsville; (905) 563-0900; www.peninsularidge.com*

Jordan Art Gallery. 3845 Main St., Jordan Village; (905) 562-6680; www.jordanartgallery .com. This gallery is owned by a group of local contemporary artists who also staff the store, so there is always a knowledgeable and enthusiastic person on hand to chat about the art. In addition to showcasing the work of the gallery owners, other selected artists' works are exhibited. There's jewellery, wearable art, paintings, dishes, sculptures, and more. Seasonal hours.

Mosaika Gallery. 3769 Mai St., Jordan; (905) 562-1136; www.mosaikagallery.com. This small store specializes in handmade Canadian jewellery, one of a kind pieces that are easy to pack and make a perfect gift. By appointment only.

Nantucket. 3836 Main St., Jordan; (905) 562-9281. This is a high-end fashion store that also carries home and garden accessories. Open daily.

Ninavik Native Arts. 3845 Main St., Jordan; (905) 562-8888, (800) 646-2848; www .ninavik.com. Visit this store for an impressive collection of Native art and sculpture. Stunning pieces by established Native sculptors as well as works from younger, up-and-coming indigenous artists are also featured. Open daily.

S&B Antique Gallery. 3845 Main St., Jordan Village; (905) 562-5415, (877) 337-4577. This store specializes in fine furniture, decorative arts, and collectibles, including furniture, china and glass, estate jewellery, and art works. Call for hours.

Tintern on Main. 3836 Main St., Jordan Village; (905) 562-5547; www.tinternonmain.ca. House designed high-end fashion, as well as a number of other fine designer labels are available that include Franco Mirabelli, Michael Kors, and Virani. Open daily.

Toute Sweet Ice Cream & Chocolate. 3771 Nineteenth St., Jordan; (905) 562-9666. You can customize your ice cream by choosing fresh fruit, brownies, cookies, chocolate, or nuts, and they will blend it with their premium ice cream on a frozen granite stone while you wait. Chocoholics should stop by, too, for hand-molded Belgian chocolates. Icewine truffles are also on the premises. Seasonal hours.

Upper Canada Cheese. 159 Jordon Rd., Jordan Station; (905) 562-9730; http://upper canadacheese.com. It is worth the drive to Jordan Station to get these artisanal cheeses. Comfort Cream may be the best soft cheese I have ever had, and Guernsey Gold is a firmer but delicious cheese to serve with crackers and fruit. UCC has just introduced a new cheese that will be perfect for winter meals. Guernsey Girl is a halloumi-style grilling cheese, perfect fried up to a brown crispness. It tops a grilled cheese or finishes a poutine and makes a creative topping, cubed and browned, for a warm salad. The store also features many local products, like Pingue's prosciutto, jams, jellies, and flatbreads. Open daily.

where to stay

Inn on the Twenty. 3845 Main St., Jordan; (905) 562-5336, (800) 701-8074; www.innon thetwenty.com. This is one of my favourite bolt-holes in the Niagara Peninsula. The rooms are large and sumptuously furnished, the bathrooms are elegant and, maybe best of all, guests have breakfast across the street of the inn at On the Twenty Restaurant. There is an in-house spa, gas fireplaces, and Jacuzzi tubs. Some suites have private gardens. Open year-round. $$$

Jordan House Tavern & Lodging. 3751 Main St., Jordan; (905) 562-9591; (800) 701-8074; www.jordanhouse.ca. This very affordable inn is a bargain. All of the rooms have queen beds and a flat screen TV, and there's live music in the downstairs tavern every Fri night. Open year-round. $$

day trip 03

southeast

history & drama
niagara-on-the-lake, st. davids

The British, the French, the Americans—they all wanted this lovely part of Ontario. They fought bitterly for it, and no wonder. It occupies the fertile land beside the Niagara River as it winds its way from Lake Erie and the Falls through to Lake Ontario, an abundant and beautiful part of the province, and one with a long history. Today it is home to the world famous Shaw Festival, to numerous wineries, well-preserved historic sites, an active artistic community, and some of the finest places to dine in the country. The area is Toronto's favourite day trip destination.

niagara-on-the-lake

Many have labelled this the "prettiest town in Canada" and it's hard to disagree. The tree-lined streets, historic buildings, and flower-filled gardens make this the perfect destination for a warm weather getaway. The added attraction of great theatre, a unique shopping area, and fine dining mean there is always a reason to come back for another visit. But NOTL is always busy from June to the end of Sept, with the theatre crowd and day trippers. The main street can become quite hectic. Best time to visit, in my opinion, is in the shoulder season, when the flowers in the window boxes and street gardens are still blooming but the big crowds have gone. And in winter, the town looks like a Currier & Ives engraving, and a hot cup of tea by the fire in the Charles Inn is a warming experience.

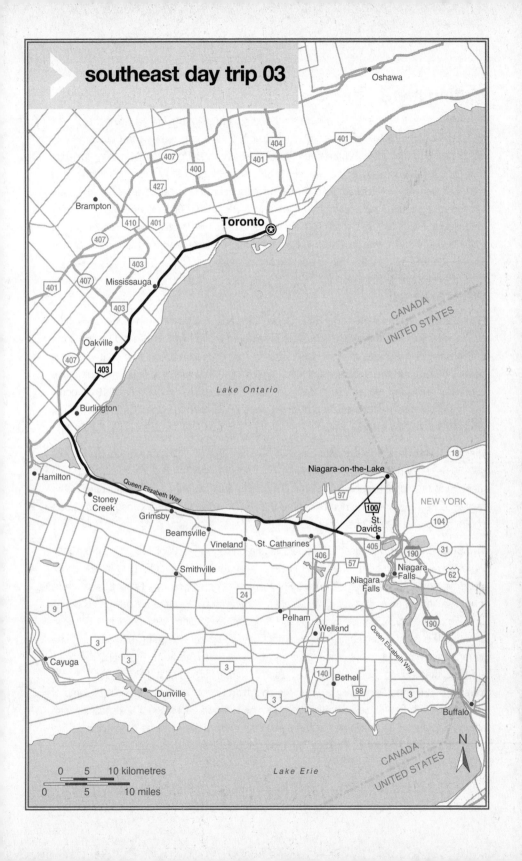

getting there

This should be 1 hour and 45 minute's drive in good traffic (about 134 kilometres or 83 miles). Follow the Gardiner Expressway West until it turns into the Queen Elizabeth Way. Continue along the QEW Niagara bound, over the Skyway Bridge and down the Peninsula. Once you have crossed over the Garden City Skyway Bridge, just past St. Catharines, take the Glendale Avenue North exit (exit 38B) and turn right onto Glendale Avenue North. Follow this for about 500 metres and then turn left onto York Road. Follow York Road (2.3 km or 1.5 miles) to Niagara Stone Road. Turn left here and drive for 12 km (7 miles). Niagara Stone Road becomes Mississauga Road. Follow it to Queen Street, and then turn right. Queen Street will take you right through the centre of the town.

where to go

Fort George National Historic Site. Queen's Parade, Niagara-on-the-Lake; (905) 468-4257; www.pc.gc.ca/fortgeorge. The lovingly restored old fort was the headquarters of the British Army during the War of 1812. Visitors can enjoy a re-creation of life as it was lived by the soldiers and their families stationed here nearly 200 years ago. There are numerous activities, tours, and reenactments. With the 200th anniversary of the War of 1812 looming, many special events are being planned. Very family friendly. Open daily May to Oct, weekends from Nov to Apr.

Niagara Historical Society Museum. 43 Castlereagh St., Niagara-on-the-Lake; (905) 468-3912; www.niagarahistorical.museum. This small museum contains one of Ontario's most important local history collections. Containing artifacts from native settlement to the present day, the museum is home to more than 8,000 artifacts, 40,000 documents, 2,500 photographs and 600 books. Open daily.

The Shaw Festival. 10 Queen's Parade, Niagara-on-the-Lake; (905) 468-2172, (800) 511-7429; www.shawfest.com. The Shaw Festival is the only festival of its kind in the world, presenting the plays of George Bernard Shaw and his contemporaries. Great Shavian treasures like *My Fair Lady*, *Arms and the Man*, and *Caesar and Cleopatra* are presented alongside contemporary works like *Summer and Smoke*, *Gypsy,* and *The Importance of Being Ernest.* It is a prestigious theatre company that has won great popularity, perhaps because its repertoire has such great range, from serious "idea" plays to frothy musicals. The plays are presented during the season in four different venues. The Festival Playhouse is home to most of the larger productions, while the charming Royal George plays host to some of the musicals and comedies. The theatre also runs tours of backstage, Q&A sessions with actors, and snack and beverage services in its theatres. Tickets can be purchased on line or at the Festival Theatre box office. Open May to Oct. Ticket prices vary.

wineries of niagara-on-the-lake

You will find another group of wineries here, all of them in the Niagara-on-the-Lake appellation, and most of them excellent. They not only produce award-winning wines, they are home to some superlative dining rooms and unique shopping boutiques. They are a day trip all by themselves. Try to visit at least a few of these:

- **Hillebrand Estates Winery.** 1249 Niagara Stone Rd., Niagara-on-the-Lake; (800) 582-8412; www.hillebrand.com

- **Jackson-Triggs Vintners.** 2145 Regional Rd. 55, Niagara-on-the-Lake; (905) 468-4637, (866) 589-4637; www.jacksontriggswinery.com

- **Peller Estates Winery.** 290 John St. East, Niagara-on-the-Lake; (905) 468-4678, (888) 673-5537; www.peller.com

- **Southbrook Vineyards.** 581 Niagara Stone Rd., Niagara-on-the-Lake; (905) 641-2548, (888) 581-1581; www.southbrook.com

- **Stratus Vineyards.** 2059 Niagara Stone Rd., Niagara-on-the-Lake; (905) 468-1806; www.stratuswines.com

where to eat

Charles Inn. 209 Queen St., Niagara-on-the-Lake; (905) 468-4588, (866) 556-8883; www.charlesinn.ca. Set in a 1832 Georgian-style house, this restaurant is a throwback to gracious service and an elegant romantic dining experience; expect to linger for a few hours. If the weather is fine, ask for table 64 on the veranda and enjoy views of the river and the golf course, and perhaps a perfect sunset. Chef William Brunyansky is consistently brilliant. His commitment to seasonality and to local ingredients means that every dish is authentic and fresh. Open daily in summer; Wed to Sun in winter. $$$

DeLuca's Wine Country Bistro. 111C Garrison Village Dr., Niagara-on-the-Lake; (905) 468-7900; www.tonydeluca.ca. Tony de Luca is one of the architects of Niagara wine country cuisine. He ruled the kitchens of Hillebrand Winery and the Oban Inn, and now has two restaurants of his own. This one, his intimate bistro, is dear to his heart. The bistro is small but perfectly designed to make guests feel comfortable. The walls are a shade of olive that almost looks blue in some lights, and seems to change with the time of day and the angle of the sun. The food is superb. The chef has suggested wine pairings on the menu to match each course. He only serves VQA wines, many available by the glass. Despite the high quality of the ingredients and cuisine, the bistro is still affordable. There's also a cosy patio with views of the nearby wineries and vineyards. Opening times vary with the season. Call to verify. $$$

Niagara-on-the-Lake Golf Club Dining Room. 143 Front St., Niagara-on-the-Lake. This is one of the best bargains, and best kept secrets in town. It's right opposite the Oban Inn, perched along the river with wonderful views of the sailing boats and Fort Niagara. The patio is one of the most scenic places to dine. Food is definitely affordable, and while not gourmet by any means, it is substantial, with comfort food favourites like braised lamb shanks, back ribs, and spaghetti with meatballs. Members of the public are welcome. Open daily. $$

Peller Estates Winery Restaurant. 290 John St. East, Niagara-on-the-Lake; (905) 468-4678; www.peller.com. Chef Jason Parsons has made this dining room a culinary destination. I have sat with friends on the sunny patio, with the vineyards beginning just a few steps away, and enjoyed some of the most authentically local and delicious food in the area. He's a brilliant chef, with a total commitment to using the bounty of the area. The restaurant is very pretty, too, with excellent service. $$$

Zee's Patio & Grill. 92 Picton St., Niagara-on-the-Lake; (905) 468-5715; www.zees.ca. This is one of the busiest restaurants in town, primarily because the Festival Theatre is just a few steps away and so it is the perfect choice for theatregoers. It's upscale casual, with a convivial and light hearted approach to food. The lobster poutine is fabulous. Open daily. $$$

where to shop

Angie Strauss Gallery. 129 Queen St., Niagara-on-the-Lake; (905) 468-2255; www.angie strauss.com. Local artist Angie Strauss creates oil and watercolor paintings in the impressionist style and has a line of women's fashions. Strauss paints popular local scenes and landmarks, florals, landscapes, and country collages. Open daily.

BeauChapeau Hat Shop. 126 Queen St., Niagara-on-the-Lake; (905) 468-8011; www .beauchapeau.com. There is no such thing as a bad hair day, just a good hat day. There are thousands of hats in the store—fedora, homburg, bowler, or safari, and those elegant, hard to find Eric Javits beauties. They're all here. The shop often supplies the male actors with their hats for productions at the Shaw Festival. Open daily.

Cows. 44 Queen St., Niagara-on-the-Lake; (905) 468-2100; www.cows.ca. They advertise that they make the best ice cream in the world and it well may be. It's made fresh with the best of ingredients. Try a scoop of the Gooey Mooie or the Turtle Cow. Also carries clothing, cups, toys, and souvenirs, all with cows on them. Open daily.

Edward Spera Gallery. 135 Queen St., Niagara-on-the-Lake; (905) 468-7447; www.spera art.ca. Spera paints predominantly wildlife, in carefully realistic detail. His original acrylics as well as prints are for sale in this attractive gallery. All reproductions have been personally signed, titled and numbered by the artist and are printed on 100 percent acid-free paper. Open daily.

From Japan. 187 Victoria St., Niagara-on-the-Lake; (905) 468-3151; www.fromjapaninc .com. This may be my favourite shop, even if I just hang out there for a while. Compared to the noise and bustle of NOTL, this is an oasis of calm. The shop specializes in fine Japanese handicrafts. It is a spare and well-designed space, with lovely bowls, plates, kimonos, wood block prints, furniture, papers, incense, and even a stone fountain. Open daily.

Irish Design. 75 Queen St., Niagara-on-the-Lake; (905) 468-7233. For Irish books and music, Shetland wool sweaters, and Celtic jewellery, this is the place. The Irish tearoom in the back has Irish favorites such as Barry's imported teas, homemade scones, salmon dill fish cakes, and Bushmill's Irish coffee with a cinnamon shamrock served in your foam. Open daily.

Just Christmas. 34 Queen St., Niagara-on-the-Lake; (905) 468-4500. This is the perfect store for those who plan ahead. Every Christmas decoration and theme can be found in one of the many rooms of this festive store. Open daily.

Old Niagara Bookshop. 233 King St., Niagara-on-the-Lake; (905) 468-2602. This independent bookstore carries literary works, specializing in Canadiana and children's books. Open daily.

where to stay

Harbour House Hotel. 85 Melville St., Niagara-on-the-Lake; (905) 468-4683, (866) 277-6677; www.harbourhousehotel.ca. The 31-room Harbour House is a perfect home base for exploring the pleasures of Niagara, from the wineries, to the theatres, to the biking and walking trails along the Niagara parkway. Fort George is a short walk away. This is an inn that instantly makes you feel welcomed. Decorated in warm shades of Tuscan yellow, the lobby has a cosy fireplace, overstuffed sofas and chairs, and wireless Internet. Rates include a full breakfast. $$$

Oban Inn. 160 Front St., Niagara-on-the-Lake; (905) 468-2165, (866) 359-6226; www .obaninn.ca. This is one of the oldest hotels in town, and it has undergone a complete renovation. It's now a sleek inn and spa with rooms that are smartly modern, with spare clean lines and all the most modern comforts. O Spa is an in-hotel wellness retreat with a state-of-the-art exercise facility, a lap pool, outdoor hot spring, and steam room. The dining room, Kir, serves classic dishes, and the gardens are lovely, as is the view of the lake and Fort Niagara. $$$

Old Bank House. 10 Front St., Niagara-on-the-Lake; (905) 468-7136, (877) 468-7136; www.oldbankhouse.com. The 2-story Georgian home, built around 1817, has a direct view of old Fort Niagara across the river and was originally the first branch of the Bank of Canada. In 1902, the Prince and Princess of Wales stayed here. There are 9 bedrooms and the rates include breakfast. $$$

Prince of Wales. 6 Picton St., Niagara-on-the-Lake; (905) 468-3246, (888) 669-5566; www.vintageinns.com. This is a lovely hotel, the Grand Dame of hotels in town, situated on the main corner and central to everything. One of the best things to do on a visit to NOTL is to enjoy high tea in the Drawing Room here. Rooms are individually decorated, drawing their inspiration from days gone by, with an abundance of floral fabrics and antiques, but accompanied by 21st-century amenities. Traditional and deluxe guest rooms are a bit cramped; the premium rooms and suites have a separate living area. Bathrooms are also small but are bright and clean, and nightly turndown service includes a fresh rose on your pillow. $$$

Queen's Landing. 155 Byron St., Niagara-on-the-Lake; (905) 468-2195, (888) 669-5566; www.vintageinns.com.This is a sophisticated hotel with a high ceilinged lobby and beautifully designed public rooms. A short walk from all of the NOTL attractions, this Georgian-style hotel has an excellent restaurant, Tiara, whose sous chef has recently won a double gold at an international culinary competition. $$$

Three Forty Gate Bed-and-Breakfast. 340 Gate St., Niagara-on-the-Lake; (905) 468-9043; www.threefortygate.com. This striking B&B is located within easy walking distance of the theatre and shopping district. Unlike the usual folksy style that many B&Bs adopt, Three Forty Gate is sleek and classic in design. It has the feel of a fine inn, and even if you don't normally like to go the B&B route, this one will delight you. All 3 rooms (there is one more small bedroom that can be rented if a group needs an extra bedroom) are on the top floor and have excellent views of the creek and gardens. All the small details have been taken care of, including iPod docks in each room and premium quality coffee and teas. Pre-breakfast coffee and the daily newspaper arrive each morning, with a full hot breakfast to follow at 9 a.m. Trigger, the resident yellow Labrador, will greet you on arrival, and Spike the Cat may make your acquaintance before you leave. $$

st. davids

A tiny farming town at a crossroads, this is a microcosm of Niagara's past. Here you will find one of the oldest building in Ontario which is now a unique B&B, a new winery on an old property and one of the prettiest winery estates in the peninsula. And as a bonus, during growing season, there are excellent fruit and vegetable stands along the roads for food purchases to take home.

getting there

From Niagara-on-the-Lake, follow Niagara Stone Road (Mississauga Street) to Virgil and turn left at Four Mile Creek Road. Drive for about 7 km (4 miles) until you come to York Road. You will be in the centre of tiny St. Davids.

where to go

Chateau des Charmes. 1025 York Rd., Niagara-on-the-Lake; (905) 262-4219; www .chateaudescharmes.com. Built in the style of a French Chateau, this elegant winery produces some fine wines and conducts tours in several languages. The gift shop is well stocked with wine and wine-related gifts. Open daily.

Ravine Vineyard. 1366 York Rd., St. David's; (905) 262-8463; www.ravinevineyard.com. This is more than a winery. It is a family saga of conservation and preservation. The farm was purchased by Norma Jane's great-grandfather in 1867 and now she and her husband have restored the land and lovingly planted grapes that are producing excellent results. A must-do when visiting the winery is visit the Loyalist Georgian home, Woodruff House, a 200-year-old house that is one of Canada's top 50 most architecturally significant ancestral homes. Open daily.

where to eat

Ravine Vineyard Bakery & Deli. 1366 York Rd., St. David's; (905) 262-8463; www.ravine vineyard.com. A charmingly rustic location for a casual lunch, this deli and bakery has a small outdoor veranda for dining as well as space indoors. Breads are made daily in an outdoor wood-burning oven, and the ingredients in everything are fresh and usually local. Fresh soups, sandwiches, salads, and decadent desserts are on the menu. $

where to stay

Historic Secord House. 215 Four Mile Creek Rd., St. Davids; (905) 262-1030; www .petersecordinn.ca. This elegant stone house was built in 1782 and is lovingly restored. There are 2 bedrooms (both are upstairs so the rooms are not wheelchair accessible) which are charmingly tucked under slopped ceilings and immaculately kept. $$

day trip 04

southeast

a walk through history
queenston
(including queenston heights)

Steeped in history, Queenston remains a sleepy village nestled between the escarpment and the Niagara River, but it is a town that has seen a lot of action. It was here that Major General Sir Isaac Brock was killed in the Battle of Queenston Heights, one of the decisive battles of the War of 1812 that lead to the British Victory. Queenston was also home to another Canadian hero, Laura Secord, whose brave actions saved many lives.

queenston (including queenston heights)

getting there

From Niagara-on-the-Lake, head east on Queen Street, which becomes Queen's Parade and then merges into the Niagara Parkway. Drive about 5 km (3 miles) to the village of Queenston.

where to go

Laura Secord Homestead. 29 Queenston St., Niagara-on-the-Lake; (905) 371-0254. The homestead presents guided tours with costumed interpreters who tell the story of Laura

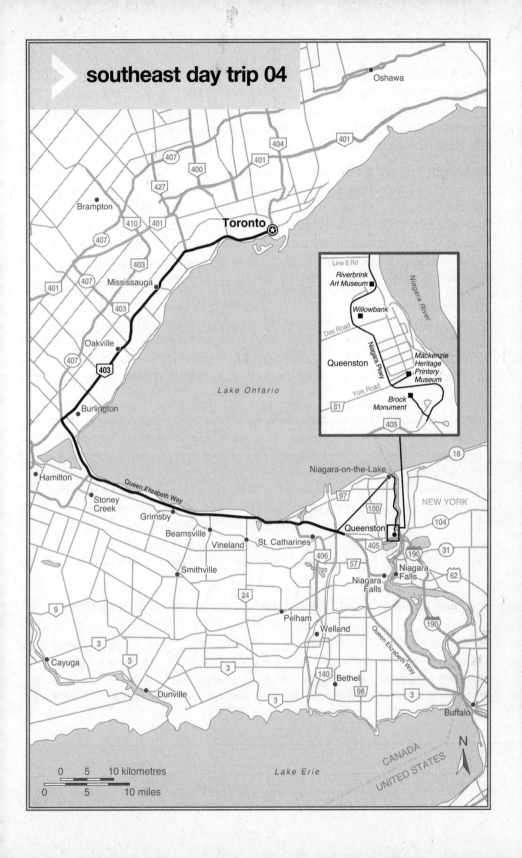

southeast day trip 04

Oshawa

Brampton

407
400
427
404
401

410 401
407

Toronto

403

407
Mississauga

403

Oakville

407

403

Burlington

401

Hamilton

Lake Ontario

Stoney
Creek

Queen Elizabeth Way

Grimsby

Beamsville

Vineland

St. Catharines

Smithville

406

57

24

Pelham

Welland

140
98

Bethel

Cayuga

3

3

3

Dunville

9

3

Lake Erie

Line 8 Rd

Riverbrink
Art Museum

Willowbank

Niagara River

Dee Road

Queenston

Niagara Pkwy

Mackenzie
Heritage
Printery
Museum

York Road

81

Brock
Monument

405

Niagara-on-the-Lake

97

100

Queenston

405

Niagara
Falls

Niagara
Falls

190

NEW YORK

104

31

62

190

18

Buffalo

Queen Elizabeth Way

CANADA
UNITED STATES

N

0   5   10 kilometres
0   5   10 miles

Secord and her times. She was responsible for saving the lives of British troops when she overheard American soldiers plotting an attack. She walked 20 miles to deliver the warning and saved many lives with her bravery. The home is faithfully recreated. Open daily in summer. Seasonal hours. Call for details.

Mackenzie Printery & Newspaper Museum. 1 Queenston St., Queenston; (905) 262-5676. The Mackenzie Printery is Canada's largest operating printing museum devoted to displaying historic presses covering more than 500 years of the letterpress printing era. It is housed in the restored home of publisher William Lyon Mackenzie. The museum displays the Louis Roy Press, oldest in Canada and one of the few original wooden presses remaining in the world. There are hands-on experiences for visitors. Open May to Sept.

MacFarlane House. 15927 Niagara Pkwy., Niagara-on-the-Lake; (905) 468-3322. This elegant Georgian styled home was built in 1800 by John McFarland and his sons, on land granted to him by King George III. It is one of the few buildings in Niagara-on-the-Lake which pre-dates the War of 1812. A visit here reveals the grace and manners of life in this time period. There is an excellent tea room, parkland, and places to picnic. Open May to Sept.

Queenston Heights Brock's Monument. Highway 405, Queenston Heights Park, Queenston; (905) 468-6621. Major General Sir Isaac Brock is one of our famous military heroes. He died defending Queenston Heights from American troops in the Battle of Queenston Heights in 1812. He was shot through the heart by an American sharpshooter. Some said he was an easy target as he insisted on being in the forefront of the fight, and he was one of the tallest men on the field at 6 feet 2 inches. He is buried at Queenston Heights and commemorated by a column. There is a self-guided walk along the heights that is marked by plaques which tell the story of Brock and the battle. The Queenston Heights Park is an excellent full-facility place for picnics. No admission fee. Open daily.

Riverbrink Art Museum. 116 Queenston St., Niagara-on-the-Lake; (905) 262-4510; www .riverbrink.org. The Riverbrink is an understated and delightful find on the banks of the Niagara River. It is the former home of lawyer and art collector Samuel Weir who donated the home and his collection to the public. The museum is operated by the Weir Foundation. In the collection of this fine little museum you will find important historical paintings and prints, works by prominent Canadian and British painters, rare books, old silver, and antique furniture. Open daily May to Oct.

where to eat

Queenston Heights Restaurant. 14184 Niagara Pkwy., Queenston; (905) 262-4274; www.niagaraparks.com/dining/queenston-heights-restaurant.html. Perched above the Niagara River, the dining room of this restaurant is in the heart of Queenston Heights Park. Try the tasting menu, which begins with 3 starters, and includes lamb and chicken entrees. Service is efficient, and the decor is attractive. The spectacular thing about this restaurant is the view. Get a window table, dine at sunset, and watch the colours on the river. Very nice. Closed Jan and Feb. $$$

where to stay

Queenston is minutes from Niagara-on-the-Lake where there are many types of accommodations available. Check the Lodging section for Niagara-on-the-Lake for some suggestions.

day trip 05

southeast

the mighty voice of thunder
niagara falls

Niagara Falls is one of the biggest tourist draws in North America. Last year more than 7 million visitors came to see the Falls. And no wonder. It is one of the most awesome natural geographical formations in the world, and you can walk right up to its edge. Even after many visits, I still catch my breath when I see it. There is something for every visitor here, from the natural beauty of the Falls and the parkway to the excitement of Clifton Hill.

niagara falls

The Canadian Falls have long been acknowledged to be the most spectacular, and Niagara Falls, Ontario, has not only developed sophisticated and multi-faceted tourism activities, it is also the best place to view all of the Falls. There are three of them—the American Falls and the Bridal Veil Falls across the river in New York State, and the magnificent Horseshoe Falls on the Canadian side.

You can walk behind the Falls, sail up to them on a boat, or peer down at them from a helicopter. However you do it, see this great natural wonder. It's on the must-see list of travellers from around the world. (When I was travelling in South Africa recently, every time I mentioned I was from Canada, people would say—"Oh, yes, Niagara Falls!".)

And after you've seen the Falls, enjoy great dining, nightlife, scenery, and history.

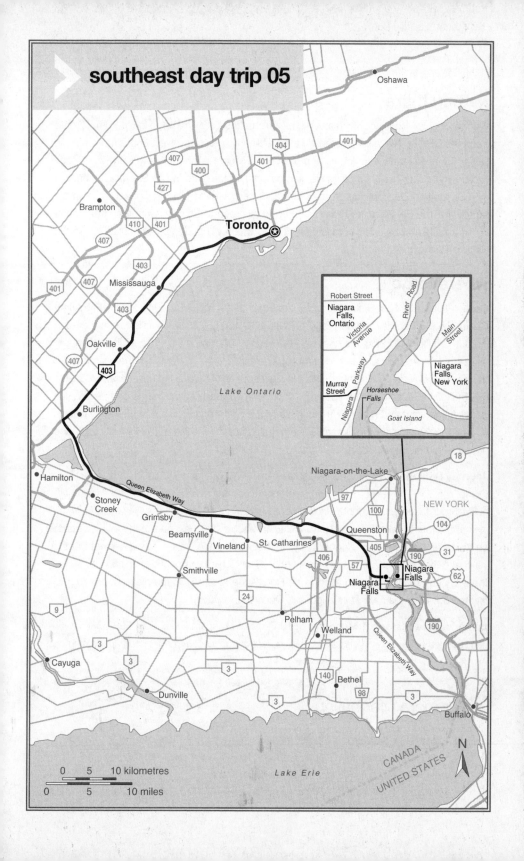

southeast day trip 05

Oshawa

Brampton

407
400
427

410 401

407

403

Mississauga

401

407

Oakville

407

403

Burlington

Lake Ontario

Hamilton

Stoney Creek

Queen Elizabeth Way

Grimsby

Beamsville

Vineland

St. Catharines

Smithville

406

57

24

9

Pelham

3

Welland

140

Bethel

98

3

Cayuga

3

Dunville

3

Niagara-on-the-Lake

97

100

Queenston

405

Niagara Falls

Niagara Falls

18

NEW YORK

104

31

190

Niagara Falls

62

Queen Elizabeth Way

3

190

Buffalo

Inset map

Robert Street

Niagara Falls, Ontario

Victoria Avenue

River Road

Main Street

Murray Street

Niagara Parkway

Horseshoe Falls

Niagara Falls, New York

Goat Island

CANADA

UNITED STATES

Lake Erie

N

0   5   10 kilometres

0   5   10 miles

getting there

It takes about 1 hour and 35 minutes (130 kilometres or 81 miles) to drive from Toronto along the QEW to Niagara Falls. Follow the Gardiner Expressway West until it turns into the Queen Elizabeth Way. Continue along the QEW Niagara bound, over the Skyway Bridge and down the Peninsula. Once you have crossed over the Garden City Skyway Bridge, just past St. Catharines, continue on the QEW and then take the exit for Highway 420 on the left toward The Falls/Niagara Falls USA. Follow this road to Stanley Avenue and turn right. In 1.4 km (1 mile), turn left onto Murray Street, which will bring you to right down to the Niagara Parkway and the Falls.

where to go

Casino Niagara. 5705 Falls Ave., Niagara Falls; (888) WIN-FALL (946-3255). **Fallsview Casino.** 6380 Fallsview Blvd., Niagara Falls; (888) FALLS-VU; www.fallsviewcasinoresort .com. It is difficult to ignore the casinos—the Fallsview Casino is a soaring edifice that dominates the Niagara Falls skyline and gambling brings in a large proportion of the visitors to the city. Even if you are not a gambler, there is a glamour and allure to the new Fallsview Casino that makes for an entertaining spectator sport. The original Niagara Casino on Falls Avenue is less flamboyant and more for the serious regular gambling crowd. The Fallsview Casino on Falls Boulevard is for the high rollers and the gamblers who like a little sophistication and drama with their game. Daily.

Journey Behind the Falls. 6650 Niagara River Pkwy., Niagara Falls (inside the Table Rock Complex); (877) 642-7275; www.niagaraparks.com/nfgg/behindthefalls.php. This self-guided tour takes you through tunnels bored into the rock behind the Canadian Falls, so it's not the tour to take if you suffer from claustrophobia. The best part of the tour is outside on the lower balcony at the northern edge of the base of the Falls. You will get wet but the view, and the closeness to the Falls is worth it. Recyclable rain ponchos are provided. Of all the ways and means you can access the Horseshoe Falls, this is the place where you will feel the power of the Falls at its mightiest. Open year-round.

Lundy's Lane Historical Museum. 5810 Ferry St., Niagara Falls; (905) 358-5082; www .lundyslanemuseum.com. Visit to see a collection of folklore and history pertaining to

for more information

Niagara Falls Tourism. 5400 Robinson St., Niagara Falls; (905) 356-6061, (800) 563-2557; www.niagarafallstourism.com. A helpful place to get information and maps. Open daily.

clifton hill

Clifton Hill is home to a concentrated group of entertainment attractions, fast food outlets, and night clubs. It is a rocking, raucous part of the Niagara Falls experience, and while you may have to be young to really enjoy it, it's a lot of fun. The contrast between the party mood of the Clifton Hill district and the breathtaking natural beauty of the Falls could hardly be more extreme. The area is sensory overload both day and night. You'll either hate it or love it. But the kids will definitely love it. **Clifton Hill Resorts,** *4960 Clifton Hill, Niagara Falls; (905) 358-3676 (attractions), (800) 263-2557 (hotel); www.cliftonhill.com.*

Niagara Falls. The limestone building dating back to 1874 includes everything from historical prints of the Falls to War of 1812 artifacts. Seasonal hours. Call for details.

Maid of the Mist. 5920 River Rd., Niagara Falls; (905) 358-0311; www.maidofthemist .com. If there is one adventure that you need to take in Niagara Falls, this is it. Even President Obama's daughters took a ride on the *Maid* when they were here, as did Brad Pitt and his kids, and Princess Diana and her two princes. Before climbing aboard, you will be handed a large blue rain poncho and you will need it. She's not called the *Maid of the Mist* for nothing. Get a spot on the upper deck of the starboard side of the boat for a close-up of the Horseshoe Falls, followed by a panoramic sweep past the American Falls as the boat returns to the dock. If you are visiting during July or Aug, schedule your boat ride for early- to mid-morning (the first sailing is at 9 a.m. during peak season), before the lines begin to form. Open daily from Apr to late Oct, depending on the weather.

Niagara Botanical Gardens Butterfly Conservatory. 2405 Niagara River Pkwy., Niagara Falls; (877) 642-7275; www.niagaraparks.com/nature/butterfly.php. A visit to the Butterfly Conservatory can be combined with a leisurely stroll around the Niagara Parks Botanical Gardens, as the building is located right on the grounds. The conservatory is a bright and airy rainforestlike environment that is carefully climate-controlled. Two thousand tropical butterflies, representing 50 different species, live freely in the conservatory. This is an absolutely delightful place to spend an hour or so. There is an abundance of natural light, and since the butterflies spend a considerable amount of time resting (you might almost believe they are posing for photos), it is a great place to bring your camera. The conservatory doubles as the display greenhouse for the Niagara Parks Botanical Gardens. With more than 100 exotic plants in its tropical plant collection, the Conservatory also provides a rare opportunity to come into close contact with plants rarely seen in the Northern Hemisphere, and another reason for photographers to indulge in their passion. Open daily.

Niagara Falls and Great Gorge Adventure Pass. www.niagaraparks.com. This money-saving pass is available between May and Oct, and grants you entry to the *Maid of the Mist,* Journey Behind the Falls, Whitewater Walk, and the Niagara Fury. Or you can customize your pass by selecting the venues you want to see. Included with the pass is all-day transportation on the People Mover bus and Incline Railway that connects the Fallsview area on top of the hill with the complex in front of the Horseshoe Falls at the bottom. You can book and print your ticket online from their website. Also, for a small fee (or free with a purchased pass) you can download an MP3 audio tour. You can also arrange for an MP3 player already loaded with the audio tour. Another advantage is the ability to pre-book your entry time to the attractions at peak tourist periods. There is a Winter Pass that covers many of the same attractions and is also a bargain. Order online.

Niagara Helicopters Canada. 3731 Victoria Ave., Niagara Falls; (905) 357-5672; www.niagarahelicopters.com. The only way to truly appreciate the awesome entirety of the Falls is from the air. Niagara Helicopter Tours takes you over the Falls and lets you see the perspective of the area. The trips are extremely safe, and there are commentaries provided through earphones in several different languages. An expensive adventure, but memorable. Daily flights, weather permitting.

Niagara's Fury: The Creation of the Falls. In the Table Rock Complex, 6450 Niagara Pkwy., Niagara Falls. This new installation at Table Rock is an experience that adds layers of significance to viewing the Falls. It starts with an 8-minute animated pre-show, where woodland characters explain how the Ice Age formed Niagara Falls. Then, in a specially designed, 360-degree theatre, the formation of the Falls is recreated in a 6-minute, multi-sensory show. The temperature drops 20 degrees, water bubbles, snow falls, and the floor tilts and trembles. The 360-degree screen is one of a kind, and a special 9-camera, digital rig was developed specifically for this theatre. Open daily.

Whitewater Walk. 4330 Niagara Pkwy., Niagara Falls; (877) 642-7275; www.niagaraparks.com/nfgg/whitewater.php. As you make your way down the boardwalk at the base of the

honeymoon haven: niagara falls

Niagara Falls received its reputation as the "Honeymoon Capital of the World" when Aaron Burr's daughter Theodosia chose a Niagara Falls honeymoon in 1801. She was followed up by Jerome Bonaparte, Napoleon's brother, in 1804 and, thus, a tradition was born. John Lennon and Yoko Ono spent their honeymoon here, as did Superman and Lois Lane, at least in the movie. Now more than 50,000 Niagara honeymoons are arranged each year.

Niagara Gorge (an elevator takes you down to the river level), you can hear the thunder of water all around you. Stand next to the Class V and VI Niagara River rapids, one of the world's wildest stretches of whitewater. The ever-changing display of waves, swell, foam, and spray is mesmerizing. Visit any time between Apr and Nov to see the rapids, but if you are in Niagara in the autumn, you absolutely must take this walk, as the wooden walkway is constructed under a canopy of deciduous trees. Warm autumn sunlight; orange, red, and gold leaves; the raging torrents of the rapids: it's a spectacular sight. And photographers take note—there are great nature shots here. Open Apr to Nov daily.

where to eat

Because this is a tourist town, the fast food outlets are numerous. But there are still some excellent places to dine, and, since you came to see the Falls, why not grab a table with a view of the main attraction?

AG at the Sterling Inn. 5195 Magdalen St., Niagara Falls; (289) 292-0000, (877) 783-7772; www.sterlingniagara.com. There's little doubt that this is the best restaurant in Niagara Falls, and possibly in the peninsula. On the menu you will find Fifth Town artisanal cheeses, Cro Farm Quail, Pinque prosciutto, Lakeland Farm duck, Simcoe asparagus, and Effingham greens. Dining here is a hedonistic pleasure, and the young but gifted chef Cory Linkson never makes a wrong move. Open Tues to Sun, dinner only. $$$

Antica Pizzeria. 5785 Victoria Ave., Niagara Falls; (905) 356-3844; www.anticapizzeria .ca. The Antica serves good Italian food in a casual atmosphere with a great view of the action and crowds on nearby Clifton Hill. The busy and cheerful pizza place has a genuine Napoletana brick oven and the pizzas are great and affordable. Get a table outside if the weather is good. Open daily. $$

Casa Mia. 3518 Portage Rd., Niagara Falls; (905) 356-5410; www.casamiaristorante.com. A family owned, sophisticated yet affordable restaurant just far enough away from the tourist fray to be relaxing. Pasta, veal, chicken, and seafood dishes, as well as fresh salads and pizzas are good bets. Open daily. $$$

Elements on the Falls. 6650 Niagara Pkwy., Niagara Falls; (905) 354-3631; www.niagara parks.com. Elements is located on the upper level of Table Rock, next to the Horseshoe Falls and the viewing gallery. Nowhere else can you get a good meal this close to the Falls. The main courses are heavy on protein like steaks, pork, and salmon, but there is usually a pasta dish available. Great place for a sundown cocktail. Open daily. $$$

Krieghoff Gallery-Cafe. 5470 Victoria Ave., Niagara Falls; (905) 358-9700; www.krieghoff .ca. Crisp white tablecloths, art on the walls, and platters for sharing make this a nice place for a quiet lunch away from the crowds fallside. After lunch you can tour the gallery. Open daily. $$$

Mide Bistro and Oxygen Bar. 4337 Queen St., Niagara Falls; (289) 296-5632; www .midebistro.com. Quirky and full of character, this bistro tucked in at one end of the newly re-invigorated Queen Street area of Niagara Falls serves several vegetarian and vegan offerings, and much of the ingredients are organic. There's a small tapas menu, and mains include several pastas, and meat and chicken dishes. If you need to clear your head, try the oxygen bar. There's live entertainment on weekends. Open daily. $$$

where to shop

This is tourist country so there are lots of souvenir shops and doodad stores. But there's good shopping here, if you look.

Galleria Fallsview Casino. 6380 Fallsview Blvd., Niagara Falls; (905) 371-3268; www .fallsviewcasinoresort.com. Whether you're a shopper or a gambler, or neither, it's worth a wander around the Galleria. Retailers lean toward the high end, including Swarovski Austrian crystal, Linda Lundström designer women's fashions, Linea di Mano for elegant accessories, and Philippe Artois imported Italian menswear. For more affordable fashion, there's Cotton Ginny, La Vie en Rose, and Tabi. For souvenirs, check out Canada's Finest, the official supplier of souvenir RCMP clothing and accessories, or First Hand Canadian Craft & Design, which stocks arts and crafts by Canadian artists. Enjoy treats from Swiss Fudge, or indulge in specialty teas from Teaopia. Shops open daily.

Mounted Police Trading Post. 5685 Falls Ave., Niagara Falls; (800) 372-0472; www .mountedpolicetradepost.com. You can find almost anything that has a connection to the Royal Canadian Mounted Police in this shop. How Canadian is that? Open daily.

Niagara Falls Factory Outlet Mall. 7500 Lundy's Lane, Niagara Falls; www.fallsdirect .com. This discount outlet mall offers over 40 brand name stores, Canada's first brand name factory outlet mall. Stores like Roots, Club Monaco, Guess, and Escada offer up to 75 percent off regular prices. It's a bargain hunter's paradise. Open daily year round.

Ochre Art Gallery. 6039 Fallsview Blvd. (inside the Doubletree Resort Hotel), Niagara Falls. Original paintings by Canadian artists are available for sale in this gallery within the Doubletree Resort. Paintings have been selected to reflect the beauty of nature and the great Canadian outdoors.

Reg's Candy Kitchen. Rainbow Bridge Plaza, Niagara Falls; (905) 356-4229. Reg's is a kind of local celebrity who has been making fudge at this location for more than 36 years. You can watch him at work in his candy kitchen, turning out fudge in flavours of chocolate mint, butterscotch, maple walnut, and vanilla. Open daily.

Shops at Table Rock. 6650 Niagara Pkwy., Niagara Falls. It's almost too easy to shop here, with all these stores right next to the Falls. The shopping area is called Canadian Treasures and features one of Canada's iconic shops, Roots (our Olympic athletes were

the old scow

If you look upriver from the Horseshoe Falls and scan the surface of the turbulent water, you will see an old scow that became stuck on the shoals way back in 1918. The scow, a flat-bottomed boat used for transporting cargo to and from ships, broke loose from its tugboat. Two men were stranded onboard as the scow made its way with increasing speed toward the Horseshoe Falls. In a desperate attempt to save themselves, the men opened the bottom doors of the scow and flooded it. Fortunately, the scow became wedged against a rocky ledge, but due to the complicated nature of the rescue operation it was 19 hours later when the men finally were brought on shore. Rumour has it, although it remains an urban legend, that both men's hair turned pure white after spending a night snagged on the edge of the Falls.

outfitted in Roots fashions for years, as were the American athletes in 2002–06) that carries high-quality clothing, bags, shoes, and outdoor wear. There is also Traditions, featuring Canadian glassware and jewellery; Canadian Diamonds; First Nations Arts & Crafts; and the Royal Canadian Mounted Police Boutique. When you are done, the incline railway is just outside the door to take you effortlessly up to your hotel. Open daily.

Swarovski. Galleria Mall, Niagara Fallsview Casino Resort, Niagara Falls; (905) 354-0118; www.swarovski.com. Glitter everywhere in this store that features the world-famous fine Austrian lead crystal. There are figurines and fine jewellery. Open daily.

where to stay

Chestnut Inn. 4983 River Rd., Niagara Falls; (905) 374-4616; www.chestnutinnbb.com. No frills and plain decor but good value with some good add-ons. Parents will appreciate the Grey Room—no one above or underneath to hear the pitter-patter of little feet. Every room except the loft has a single bed built into the curved windows—perfect for wee ones. Likewise, a large front lawn with gazebo and a pool in the back allow kids to be kids, or adults to linger. There are private patios for every room; all rooms are also equipped with electric fireplaces. A communal room has tea and coffee, as well as a hair dryer and iron. There's plenty of common space in the living and sun room, full of wicker chairs, with decks of cards and books. $$

Great Wolf Lodge. 3950 Victoria Ave., Niagara Falls; (905) 354-4888, (800) 605-WOLF; www.greatwolflodge.com. Unique in that the entire hotel is designed around children, this is a paradise for a family. The main attraction is more than 9,300 square metres (100,000 sq. ft.) of waterslides and pools. Wristbands, which act as room keys, can be loaded up with money for kids to spend at will. Could be dangerous. Rates include water-park passes and parking. $$$

Hilton Niagara Falls Fallsview. 6361 Fallsview Blvd., Niagara Falls; (905) 354-7887, (888) 370-0325; www.niagarafallshilton.com. In June 2009, this hotel officially became the tallest hotel in Canada with the completion of its new 53-storey tower addition. It is a big, busy American hotel, with all the amenities, pools, spa, restaurants, and services that you could want. The best part of staying here is the view. Don't skimp. If you stay, get a Fallsview room. $$$

Sterling Inn & Spa. 5195 Magdalen St., Niagara Falls; (289) 292-0000, (877) 783-7772; www.sterlingniagara.com. If you don't want a chain hotel and are not inclined to a B&B, the Sterling is the perfect fit. This is Niagara Falls's only boutique hotel. While the surrounding neighbourhood is a bit run down, the Falls are only a short walk away, and the Greg Frewin Dinner Theatre is just across the parking lot. The rooms are large and contemporary in style, with large glassed-in rainforest showers, fireplaces, and 4-poster beds. A great reason to stay here is the dining room. AG (clever—the symbol for Silver) is the best restaurant in Niagara Falls. There's free Wi-Fi in all the rooms and, best of all, complimentary breakfast is delivered to your room in the morning. $$$

Tower Hotel Ramada Plaza Fallsview. 6732 Fallsview Blvd., Niagara Falls; (905) 356-1501; www.niagaratower.com. The newly remodelled and renamed Tower Hotel features a mere 42 guest rooms, all in a pod at the top of the Konica Minolta Tower Centre. This gives the property a distinctive boutique hotel feel. The rooms have been updated to a funky almost art deco style, with upholstered headboards, flat screen TVs, and mirrored side tables, and the views of the Falls are fabulous. The hotel feels young and edgy. It's a great place for a quiet weekend getaway—just try not to think about the fact that all the rooms are suspended hundreds of feet above the lobby, with only a concrete elevator shaft linking them to the ground. And sometimes it sways in the wind. $$–$$$

day trip 06

southeast

the bike train

Trains have always been important for Canada. It was the railroad that brought the 10 provinces together, and the railroad that allowed Canadians to get around this huge country. While it still serves as a priceless service for conveying cargo and passengers, it has today become one of the important stimulators of recreational biking. The Bike Train has made it possible for Torontonians to tour their province on their bikes. The Niagara community has also made huge strides in organizing well-maintained, paved, multiuse paths that pass by various historical sites and waterways of the region. And if you're so inclined, put a basket on the front of a rented bike, visit some wineries, and take home some goodies.

VIA Rail Canada (800-VIA-RAIL [842-7245]; www.viarail.ca) has made biking Niagara even easier. The award-winning **Bike Train Initiative** announced ticket sales and new routes that will help visitors get active, travel local, and cycle Niagara in the summer. Originally developed by Toronto cyclist Justin Lafontaine and launched in partnership with VIA Rail between Toronto and Niagara in 2007, the Bike Train has proven to be a fun, economic, and environmentally friendly way to enjoy a cycling getaway. Getting to the destination is made easy as passengers travel in comfort while their bicycles are safely secured in a baggage car with bike racks. Knowledgeable Bike Train staff are available onboard to provide cycling maps and useful information. The Toronto-Niagara Greenbelt Express provides service between Toronto's Union Station and Niagara Falls Station, with a number of stops in St. Catharines.

Niagara Falls Station is ideally situated one block from the Niagara River Recreation Trail, a primarily off-road 56-km paved path. Cycle north on a beautiful 20-km ride to see

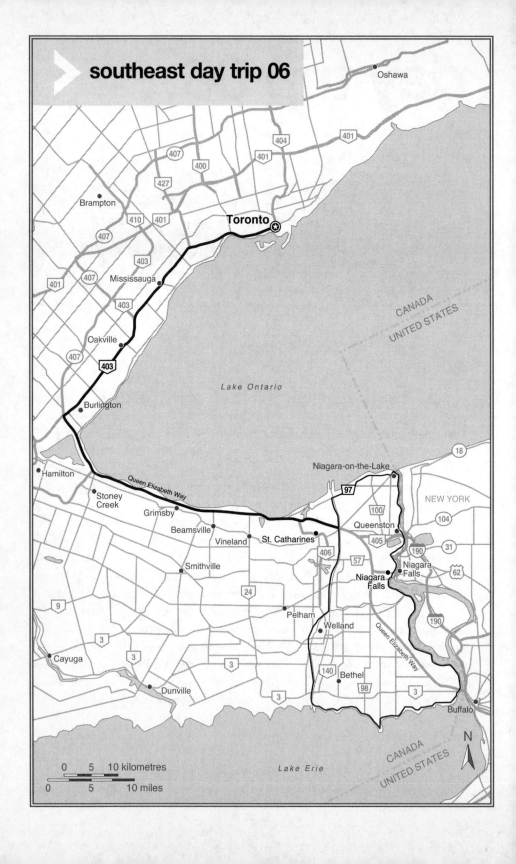

southeast day trip 06

the Niagara Gorge, abundant wineries, and historic Niagara-on-the-Lake. Cycle south on the path to see the magnificent Niagara Falls, and beyond to Fort Erie. St. Catharines station is located a short ride from the city's compact downtown. It is also a great starting point to explore Port Dalhousie, the historic Welland Canal, 20 Valley wine routes, and mountain biking trails around the Niagara Escarpment. There are a number of trails and routes to enjoy wherever you stop. The Toronto-Niagara Greenbelt Express will run 8 weekends from June to Oct with stops in Toronto, Niagara Falls, and St. Catharines. Cost: Adults $62 (US $54) return $31 (US $27) one-way; children 11 and under free.

bike rentals

If you want to pick a path and go it alone, rent a bike from **Steve's Place Bicycle & Repair** (181 Niagara Blvd., Fort Erie; 888-649-BIKE). Steve rents hybrid bikes (cross between a road and a mountain bike). Rentals include a lock, but you must provide your own helmet. The store is just off the Niagara River Trail—great location.

Another spot to pick up a bike is **Zoom Leisure** (2017 Niagara Stone Rd., Highway 55, Niagara-on-the-Lake; 866-811-6993). Choose from Trek hybrid bikes, tandems, kids', or mountain bikes for off-road riding. Every bike comes with map, helmet, and bike lock.

The **Greater Niagara Circle Route** is a trail system of more than 140 km (87 miles) of off-road, paved trails perfect for walking, cycling, or rollerblading.

getting there

Trains leave from Toronto's Union Station on Front Street. There are several places that you can access the trails and there is an excellent downloadable map from the website at **www .niagararegion.ca.** If you are using the Bike Train, you can get off in either St. Catharines or Niagara Falls.

where to bike

Here's some places that make perfect destinations to explore by bike. Consult the downloadable map at the Greater Niagara Circle Route website, www.niagararegion.ca/government /initiatives/gncr/default.aspx, for directions.

"Working on the Canal"—the **Feeder Canal Comprehensive Centre** in Welland.

The **Flight Locks in Thorold** where "the ships climb the mountain," and "Kissing Rock" beside the Visitors Centre at **Lock VII.**

Fort Erie—a historic fort at the junction of the Niagara River and Lake Erie.

Fort George in Niagara-on-the-Lake, the first Capital of Upper Canada and a historic community that is also home to the Shaw Festival.

Parts of the previous **historic canals** at various places.

Mud Lake Conservation Area and **Lock VIII,** the longest lock in the system, in Port Colborne.

Murals in Thorold and downtown Welland.

Numerous **Niagara Parks Commission attractions** and the world famous **Niagara Falls,** the reason for the Welland Canal.

The **St. Catharines Museum/Lock III Observation Area** where visitors may view a canals exhibit and perhaps see a ship pass through the lock.

The **South Niagara Rowing Club** in Welland, an internationally famous rowing course.

Vineyards, wineries, and orchards alongside Lakeshore Road between Niagara-on-the-Lake and St. Catharines.

east

day trip 01

east

>>> **the town that cars built
(and, ironically, the home of
canada's most famous horse)**
oshawa

Oshawa lies about 60 km (37 miles) from Toronto and is considered the eastern anchor of The Golden Triangle. The city remains an independent entity from Toronto, and continues to be populated largely by people of British or Northern European heritage. The downtown area has some interesting and well-preserved buildings that have found a new life. The once regal Genosha Hotel, for example, a 1920s building in the Chicago-style of architecture, which had fallen into disrepair during the post-industrial period of the city, has been renovated to create university student housing in the downtown. Besides the historic downtown, Oshawa is still a car town, home to General Motors, and the proud location of Parkwood, the baronial home of auto magnate R. Samuel McLaughlin, the founder of General Motors Canada. Oshawa was also home to Windfields Farm, a thoroughbred horse breeding operation and birthplace of Canada's most famous racehorse, Northern Dancer. While the farms have been divided up and are in the process of being turned into housing developments or commercial sites, some of the farm's historic barns, the grave of Northern Dancer, plus a trillium forest where 15 horses are interred, has been preserved as a commemorative park.

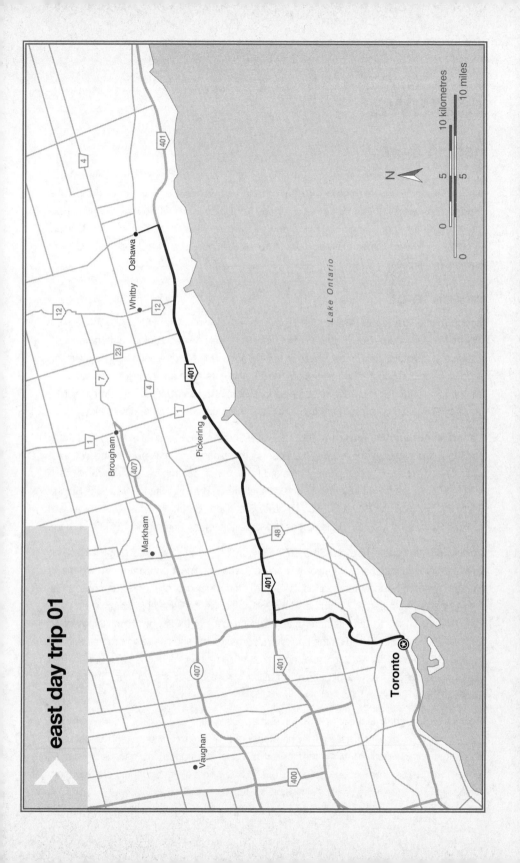
east day trip 01

oshawa

getting there

Oshawa is 60 km (37 miles), about a 45-minute drive in good traffic, from Toronto. Avoid the rush hours, 7 to 9 a.m. and 4 to 6 p.m. and you will have an easy drive. Follow the Gardner Expressway to the Don Valley Parkway North. Take the DVP to Highway 401. Take the 401 East for about 42 km (26 miles) and you will see signs for Oshawa. Take Regional Road 2 exit toward Simcoe Street. Turn left onto Simcoe Street, which will lead you into downtown Oshawa.

where to go

Bowmanville Zoological Park. 340 King St. East, Bowmanville; (905) 623-5655; www .bowmanvillezoo.com. Bowmanville is the oldest privately owned zoological park in North America. It maintains the largest stable of trained animals in North America and is a leading supplier of animal talent to the television, movie, and entertainment industry. The zoo concentrates on large feline predators and elephants, but also has a wide array of mammalian, reptilian, and avian species. There is a Zoo Cafe and a gift shop. Open May to Oct.

Canadian Automotive Museum. 99 Simcoe St. South, Oshawa; (905) 576-1222. Notable cars, tricycles, bicycles, trucks, pianos, washing machines, etc., make up the collection at this Oshawa museum, appropriately devoted to all things automotive. There are approximately 65 vehicles dating from 1898 to 1981 that are on display—made by Brooks Steam, Redpath, Tudhope, McKay, Galt Gas-Electric, Gray-Dort, Brockville Atlas, C.C.M., as well as Rolls Royce and Morris. This is a perfect destination for the automotive buff. Open daily.

Parkwood National Historic Site. 270 Simcoe St. North, Oshawa; (905) 433-4311; www.parkwoodestate.com. Parkwood is one of Canada's finest and last remaining grand estates, featuring architectural, landscape, and interior designs of the 1920s and 1930s. Once home to auto baron R. Samuel McLaughlin, founder of General Motors Canada, the site showcases the art, architecture, gardens, landscaping, and original furnishings of an auto baron. It has been used as the backdrop for many films and television programs, most notably *Studio 54, Billy Madison, Chicago,* and *X-Men.* The Greenhouse Tearoom serves light lunches, and there is a gift shop and either guided or self-guided tours. Open daily. Guided tours.

Robert McLaughlin Gallery. 72 Queen Street, Oshawa; (905) 576-3000; www.rmg.on .ca. This is a large public gallery that has furthered the Canadian art scene by focusing on contemporary visual art within the context of Canadian modern art, especially Painters Eleven. The Gallery's collections consist of over 6,800 works of art, and there are frequently changing exhibitions. Open daily. Admission by donation.

where to eat

Beanz Cafe. 82 King St. West, Oshawa; (905) 245-0581. Excellent coffee and light snacks. Great place for a coffee break. Open daily. $$

where to stay

White House Bed & Breakfast. 494 King St. East, Oshawa; (905) 579-0062; www .bbcanada.com/10408.html. This very pretty B&B has 5 bedrooms and offers a full breakfast that can be vegetarian or gluten free on request. Close to most attractions, this is a superbly decorated elegant home. $$

where to shop

Oshawa Jewellery. 419 King St., Unit 2432, Oshawa; (905) 728-5757; www.oshawa jewellery.com. While fine jewellery may not be the first thing you think of to buy when on a day trip, this little family-run jewellery store has magnificent pieces, as well as the ability to design one-of-a-kind diamond, precious stone, and gold and silver jewellery. Hint—their specialty is diamond engagement rings. Now that is an excuse for a day trip! Open daily.

day trip 02

east

historic small towns of the eastern shore
port hope, cobourg, grafton

This area along the edge of Lake Ontario occupies some of the earliest settled land in the province. While the busy Highway 401 travels along this way, a short step off the highway brings you to small towns that are still quiet, well treed and historically fascinating. Because of its long history, it's a perfect place for antique shopping, and the beaches and cottage areas are popular summer getaways for Torontonians.

port hope

Originally home to aboriginal groups, and then populated mainly by United Empire Loyalists, many areas of the old town of Port Hope, including the downtown commercial core, remain little changed from the days of Queen Victoria. Fortunately much of the town's original architecture has been saved from demolition in the name of progress. Port Hope's downtown is celebrated now as the best-preserved 19th-century streetscape in Ontario. With more than 270 heritage-designated buildings throughout the municipality, Port Hope has a higher per capita rate of preservation than any other town or city in Canada. It is a gorgeous time-capsule, with unique architecture, great shopping, and a charming harbour with safe, sandy beaches.

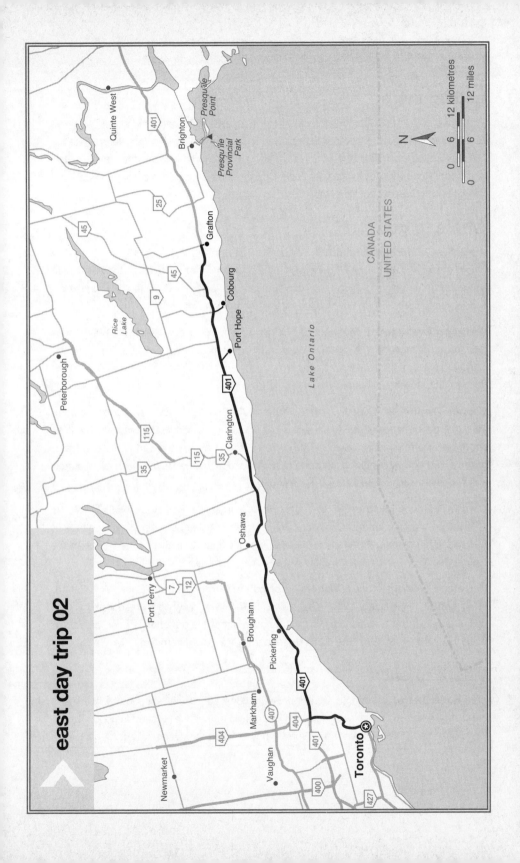

east day trip 02

getting there

Port Hope is just 100 kilometres (62 miles) or 1 hour east of Toronto (and about 200 years back in time). Follow the Gardner Expressway to the Don Valley Parkway North. Take the DVP to Highway 401. Take the 401 East for about 85 km (53 miles) and then take exit 461 for County Road 2 East toward Port Hope. County Road 2 merges into Toronto Road and takes you into the town of Port Hope.

where to go

Art Gallery of Northumberland. 60 Walton St., Port Hope; (905) 885-2115; www.artgallery ofnorthumberland.com. The Port Hope "Upstairs Gallery" displays part of the permanent collection of the works of prominent artists, mostly Canadian, and hosts changing exhibitions and programs. Open Wed to Sun. Admission by donation.

Canadian Fire Fighters Museum. 95 Mill St. South, Port Hope; (905) 885-8985; www .firemuseumcanada.com. A museum depicting the historical development of fire fighting in Canada, it collects, preserves, and exhibits a collection of fire fighting apparatus. Open daily, June to Oct. Admission by donation.

Capitol Theatre. 20 Queen St., Port Hope; (905) 885-1071; www.capitoltheatre.com. Take in a performance at one of Canada's last operating "atmospheric" theatres. The interior of the theatre gives the audience the illusion of sitting in an outdoor medieval courtyard, under a blue sky with twinkling stars and moving clouds. The theatre has been fully restored to its original 1930s grandeur. Open year-round.

Dorothy's House Museum. 3632 County Rd. 9, Garden Hill, Port Hope; (905) 342-2657. This frame cottage from the 1800s has been restored to resemble a workman's cottage of that period. It contains artifacts from the area, and includes an authentic barn and a Victorian garden. Open weekends through July and Aug. Admission by donation.

Port Hope Tourism Office & Visitors' Information Centre. Cameco Capitol Arts Centre, 20 Queen St., Port Hope; (888) PORT-HOPE (767-8467); www.porthopetourism.ca. The centre provides maps, brochures, and information about the area and is open daily June through Sept from 8:30 a.m. to 4:30 p.m. and from Mon to Fri from Oct to May.

where to eat

Zest Bar & Bistro. 64 John St., Port Hope; (905) 885-7200; www.zestfoods.ca. This modern bistro serves excellent fusion food. Sit out on the patio if the weather is good. Try the white bean cassoulet or the poutine. Sunday brunch is a treat. Open daily. $$$

where to shop

Port Hope has a reputation of being the antiques capitol of Ontario, with nearly 60 vendors within walking distance in the historic old town. These are just a few that are uniquely interesting, but there are many more.

Hinchcliff & Lee Distinguished Decor. 37 Walton St., Port Hope; (905) 885-5905; www .hinchcliffandlee.ca. The shop specializes in Oriental antique furniture, porcelain, artifacts, paintings, and stone statuary. Open daily.

Lord Russborough's Annex. 82 Walton St., Port Hope; (905) 885-9853; www.russ borough.com. The specialty here is old prints, paintings, and antique maps. Open Thurs to Sun.

Smith's Creek Antiques. 27 Walton St., Port Hope; (905) 885-7840; www.smithscreek antiques.com. You'll find this store in one of the historic buildings on the main street. It occupies 5,000 square feet on 2 floors offering a variety of antiques with a strong focus on early original painted and refinished Canadiana. Browse through a large selection of 19th-century furniture, pottery, art, folk art, and early Canadiana.

where to stay

Hillcrest Inn & Spa. 175 Dorset St., Port Hope; (905) 885-7367, (888) 253-0065; www .thehillcrest.ca. When I stayed in this grand estate-turned-inn-and-spa, I felt an immediate sense of comfort and retreat. It is a sophisticated inn with large rooms and an excellent spa. However, it has recently changed hands and is hopefully as well run under this new ownership. $$$

Waddell Hotel. 1 Walton St., Port Hope; (905) 885-2449; www.thewaddell.ca. Housed in a 165-year-old historic building, this boutique hotel has 12 guest rooms and is situated right in the heart of the historic district. $$$

cobourg

Some consider this one of the undiscovered gems of the eastern shores. The heart of the town is well preserved and historic, especially Victoria Hall, a building that now serves as the town hall and home of the Art Gallery of Northumberland, the Cobourg Concert Hall, and an Old Bailey-style courtroom that is now used as the Council chambers. The waterfront has been extensively beautified, with white sand beaches, a boardwalk, and boating facilities, with pathways that stretch through Victoria Park through to the downtown area. In the 1800s, the town was known for its pure air and health-promoting environment. Visitors came to breathe in the good air to cure their ailments or enjoy good living at the summer estates that sprang up in town. That continues today with more than 100 wellness

> ## for more information
>
> ***Town of Cobourg Business & Tourism Centre.*** *Marie Dressler House, 212 King St. West, Cobourg; (905) 372-5481, (800) 262-6874; www.cobourgtourism .ca. Call for hours.*
>
> ***Northumberland Tourism.*** *555 Courthouse Rd., Cobourg; (866) 401-3278; www.northumberlandtourism.com. Open daily in summer, Mon to Fri otherwise.*

practitioners, offering massage, acupuncture, reflexology, yoga, and other holistic therapies at spas and wellness clinics.

getting there

Cobourg is a 1 hour and 20 minute drive from Toronto, or 115 km (71 miles). It is 15 km (9 miles) from Port Hope. From Port Hope, continue along Highway 401 to exit 472, Regional Road 18/Burnham Street, which becomes William Street. Turn left at King Street and this will take you into Cobourg.

where to go

Cobourg Jail. 77 Albert St., Cobourg; (905) 373-4610; www.cobourgjail.com. Cobourg Jail was one of the biggest of its time, holding up to 100 inmates. The jail was finally closed to inmates in 1998 and now is a 20+ room country inn and hotel, complete with a restaurant and museum. Guests can actually sleep in a jail cell and view cells in the museum that once housed inmates. Open daily. Free.

Cobourg Marina. 55 King St. West, Cobourg; (905) 372-2397; www.cobourg.ca/marina .html. The Cobourg Marina, just steps from downtown is widely regarded by boaters as one of the best on the Great Lakes. Victoria Park, bordering the shoreline, has clean sand beaches and family friendly attractions. This is a perfect place to spend a sunny day, with picnic facilities, excellent swimming, and good nearby shopping and dining.

Primrose Donkey Sanctuary. 1296 Bowmanton Rd., R.R. 4, Roseneath; (905) 352-2772; http://primrosedonkeysanctuary.webs.com. This is an ideal day trip destination for a family, both to enjoy the animals and to learn a lesson about caring for abused or neglected animals. Sheila Burns gives sanctuary to abused, neglected, and unwanted donkeys, as well as other large farm animals such as mules, hinnies, miniature horses, pigs, and sheep. Here you will learn that donkeys are not stubborn or dumb, but are kind, patient, and loyal. The stories of the animals she has rehabilitated are inspiring. Open Thurs and Sun, 1 to 4 p.m. Free.

where to stay

Essex House Bed and Breakfast. 351 George St., Cobourg; (905) 377-3922; www .essexbb.net. This elegant home has 4 large bedrooms, and is situated within easy walking distance of the historic downtown. Open all year. $$–$$$

King George Inn & Spa. 77 Albert St., Cobourg; (905) 373-4610; www.thekinggeorgeinn .com. Try room number 9, The Trustee's Room, or number 18, The Penitentiary. Sleep behind bars in these jail cell–like (but still comfortable) rooms, and you can tell your friends you've been in jail for the night. Other rooms have a ship's theme, and the rest are large and comfortable rooms with a Victorian style that reflects the history of the area. There is also a full-service spa. Jail was never like this. Open all year. $$

where to shop

Zap Records. 4 King St. East, Cobourg; (905) 372-8231, (877) 562-2222; www.zap records.com. For the collector of vintage music or vinyl devotee, this record shop is a trea-sure trove. There's a large collection of rare and collectable music, records, and LPs. There are some real gems here. Open daily.

grafton

A small town with a big history, this little village was once a prosperous crossroads. Now it is a sleepy village but you can still smell the history. There are some fine antiques stores, a venerable inn, a restaurant, and an important house museum. But the real reason to go to Grafton is Ste. Anne's, the best destination spa in Canada.

getting there

From Port Hope, continue along Highway 401 to exit 487 at Grafton. Head south until you reach County Road 2 and then turn west into the village. It's difficult to miss.

where to go

Barnum House Museum. Highway 2, Grafton; (905) 349-2656. Barnum House was the first house museum to open in Ontario, restored and operated by the Architectural Conservancy of Ontario. It is home to a large collection of artifacts from the Georgian and Victorian periods, including furniture, china, books and newspapers, cookware, children's toys, photographs, scrapbooks, and more. Among these pieces is a Clementi piano from the early 19th century, believed to be the only one of its kind to survive. Open summer of 2011. Call for hours and fees.

Nawautin Nature Sanctuary and Wetlands Trail. Accessible from the Estate of Nawau-tin Shores, Lakeshore Road, south of Grafton. This 5.31-hectare (13-acre) sanctuary shelters a wide variety of wildlife including deer, fox, beaver, rabbits, and birds. Within the sanctuary you can discover a small covered bridge, several ponds, waterfront parks, and a pebbly beach that slopes gradually to Lake Ontario. Contact **Northumberland Tourism,** (866) 401-3278; www.northumberlandtourism.com for trail details.

where to stay

Grafton Village Inn. 10830 County Rd. 2, Grafton; (905) 349-3024; www.graftonvillageinn .ca. The historic inn has 6 lovely bedrooms, all different. There's also a good restaurant with a patio that is very nice for lunch in summer. The pecan pie is famous. Open year-round. $$$

Ste. Anne's Country Inn & Spa. R.R. 1, Grafton; (888) 346-6772; www.steannes.com. I have visited spas around the world, but none have made me feel more relaxed and healthy than Ste. Anne's. It's my perfect getaway place. This luxury destination spa is a true retreat, situated out in the country on more than 400 idyllic acres in the Northumberland Hills, away from everything. It's a hotel and dining destination as well as a wellness spa. The eucalyptus steam room is addictive. While you can easily drive here in just over an hour, you can take a VIA Rail train to Port Hope and someone from the inn will pick you up. It's great for a day trip, but even better if you stay over. Open all year. $$$

day trip 03

east

apples & lighthouses
brighton, presqu'ile point & lighthouse,
presqu'ile provincial park

This southern area of Northumberland County and Quinte West, tucked between the Great Pine Ridge and Lake Ontario has, for 200 years, enjoyed a rich agricultural history and is today part of the popular "Apple Route" (www.appleroute.com), a tourism trail that meanders through the orchards, towns, and villages between Port Hope and Trenton. Presqu'ile Provincial Park is, as its French name suggests, "almost an island" and is home to a historic lighthouse as well as excellent swimming, boating, and fishing. It is, in addition, an important birding area. A pristine and almost untouched natural area, this part of the eastern shores is a beautiful destination for a camping holiday or for exploring nature at its best. Brighton is also a great place for antiques shopping.

brighton

With its 19th-century architecture, the town retains the spirit of the early founders who established some of the finest apple orchards in Canada. In summer, the town is full of activity, with tourists, campers, and cottagers. There is a restored railroad station, a historical estate museum, and many antiques shops.

getting there

Brighton is about a 2-hour drive (160 kilometres or 99 miles) from Toronto and 30 minutes (42 kilometres or 26 miles) from Cobourg. From Cobourg, continue on Highway 401 to exit

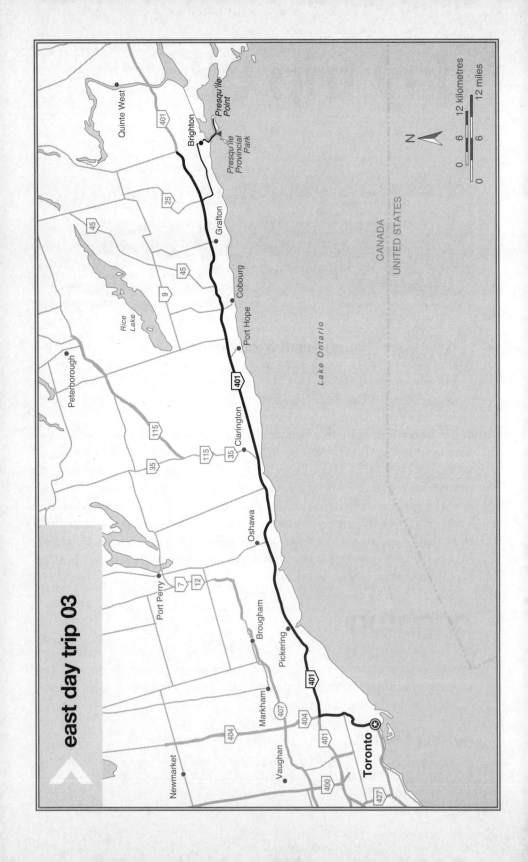

497 for County Road 25 toward Percy Street/Big Apple Drive and turn right. In 2.4 km (1.5 miles), turn left at County Road 2/King Street East. Continue to follow County Road 2 for 12 km (7 miles). Then turn right at Division Street North and take the first left onto Park Street. Take the first right onto Prince Edward Street which will take you into the centre of Brighton.

where to go

Brighton and District Chamber of Commerce. 74 Main St., Brighton; (613) 475-2775, (877) 475-2775; www.brightonchamber.ca. The chamber is open year-round and provides tourism information, maps, and brochures.

Memory Junction Railway Museum. 60 Maplewood Ave., Brighton; (613) 475-0379; www.memoryjunction.netfirms.com. Memory Junction Museum station is one of nine left of 32 stations built for the Grand Trunk Railway. The station was built in 1857 and has a restored agents room, waiting room, and express office that display hundreds of artifacts. The women's waiting room is a gift shop. Open June to Sept. Closed Tues and Fri. Admission by donation.

Proctor House Museum. 96 Young St., Brighton; (613) 475-2144; www.proctorhouse museum.ca. This 19th-century mansion was once the home of a wealthy shipping magnate and has been fully restored. Guided tours are given during the summer. There may be ghosts! There is a heritage garden and pathways that lead to the Lower Trent Conservation Authority, a perfect afternoon walk. Open July and Aug, Tues to Sun.

where to eat

The Gables. 14 Division St. North, Brighton; (613) 475-5565; www.thegablesrestaurant .net. Classic European dishes are served in this historic renovated 1872 era home. Try the deep fried camembert with lingonberry sauce as a refreshing starter, or the Wiener Schnitzel for a substantial main course. The Gables is listed in the *National Restaurant Guide* "Where to Eat in Canada." Open for lunch on Tues to Fri, for dinner on Tues to Sat. $$$

where to stay

Brighton Inn. 40 Young St., Brighton; (613) 475-9706, (888) 895-5807; www.brightoninn .com. This Victorian inn, located near the centre of town, has 4 bedrooms with pillow top mattresses, quality linens, and ensuite bathrooms. Breakfast is served in the airy sunroom— try the lemon crepes. Open year-round. $$

Timber House Country Inn. 116 Cedardale Rd., Brighton; (613) 475-3304; www.timber house.net. There are 9 guest rooms, a heated pool, and a sandy beach as part of the charm of this post and beam pine inn, and it borders on a nature preserve. It's quiet and peaceful, and there is a restaurant onsite. Open all year. $$

where to shop

Coach House Curiosity Shop. 199 Main St., Brighton. This antique market occupies a 2-storey coach house that is part of the historic White House Mansion. Shopping finds include a large selection of antiques, collectibles, jewellery, and vintage clothing. You may just find a treasure if you search. Open Tues to Sat in season.

Country Fixin's. 39 Richardson St., Brighton; (613) 475-2455; www.countryfixins.ca. Browse through this old fashioned general store with 3 floors of country design accents, antiques, and home decor. Closed Tues and Wed.

Main Street Furniture Outlet. 360 Main St., Brighton; (613) 475-0003; www.mainstreet antiquemarket.com. This is a shopping experience, an indoor/outdoor market, featuring antiques, furniture, dressers, architectural items, canoes, buggies—a good place for bargain sleuthing. Open daily.

presqu'ile point & lighthouse

getting there

The Point and Lighthouse are about 15 minutes, or 11 kilometres (7 miles) from Brighton. If coming along the 401, take exit 509 (Highway 30). Travel south for about 5 km (3 miles) to Highway 2 (Main Street) in the town of Brighton. Turn right at King Edward Street, and follow this to Harbour Street. Turn right and drive less than a kilometer (about 0.6 miles) to the Presqu'ile Park entrance. There are signs along the way to guide you to the park and the lighthouse.

A small day use fee is charged at the gate. Pick up a map at the gate. The main road is Bayshore Drive. You will reach a fork in the road that actually is part of a loop, Paxton Drive to the left, Lighthouse Lane on the right. Either road will take you to the lighthouse, which is at the opposite end of the loop, at the easternmost tip of the point.

where to go

Lighthouse Interpretive Centre. Park Office; (613) 475-4324. At the centre, you can find out about the influence of Lake Ontario on Presqu'ile's history through a talking mannequin called Jack Atkins, watch a video presentation on the sinking of the H.M.S. *Speedy,* and enjoy numerous interactive displays. There are also guided walks and cultural and nature presentations. A gift shop is located in the centre. The centre is adjacent to the lighthouse and is open 10 a.m. to 5 p.m. daily in July and Aug, and on weekends May to June and Sept to Oct.

presqu'ile provincial park

Presqu'ile Provincial Park. 328 Presqu'ile Pkwy., Brighton; (613) 475-4324; www.ontario parks.com/english/pres.html. A mecca for bird watchers every spring and fall, this peninsula south of Brighton is a major flyway for migrating birds, home to waterfowl and shorebirds, and a staging point for Mexico-bound monarch butterflies. A long boardwalk crosses wetlands where marsh birds live and fish spawn. The boardwalk is perfect for walks, biking, or rollerblading. On islands to the west, colonies of gulls, cormorants, terns, and herons nest. The campgrounds have 394 camping sites that are open for the shoulder season and through the summer, and cross country skiing is available in winter.

northeast

day trip 01

northeast

>>> **native culture, theatre & the lakeshore**
jacksons point, georgina, georgina island

This lakeside tourist area borders Lake Simcoe, the fourth largest fresh water lake in Canada, and is famous for water sports, cottage life, and leisure activities like golf and fishing. It is within easy reach of the GTA, just an hour's drive, yet far enough away that the pressures of city life are put aside. Spend a day hiking on Georgina Island, biking along the shore, or shopping in the small towns along the lake. It is the ice fishing capital of Canada and home to Sibbald Point Provincial Park. Cook's Bay and Lake Simcoe offer some of the best fishing in the province. The lake is fished year-round and is famous for its winter Lake Trout and Whitefish and is the site for the Canadian Ice Fishing championships.

jacksons point

This small town had its origins in its naval importance and its position on the lake. The marina is a busy hub for boaters and fishermen. The active outdoor life is well appreciated by the many cottagers who have bought vacation properties here.

getting there

Jacksons Point is an easy 1-hour (60-kilometre or 37-mile) drive from Toronto. Take the Don Valley Parkway North. Continue onto Highway 404 North. Take exit 51 for Regional Road 31/Davis Drive, and turn right. Drive for about 9 km (6 miles) and then turn left on Highway 48. Proceed for 23 km (14 miles), following the signs for Sutton. Turn left at High Street/

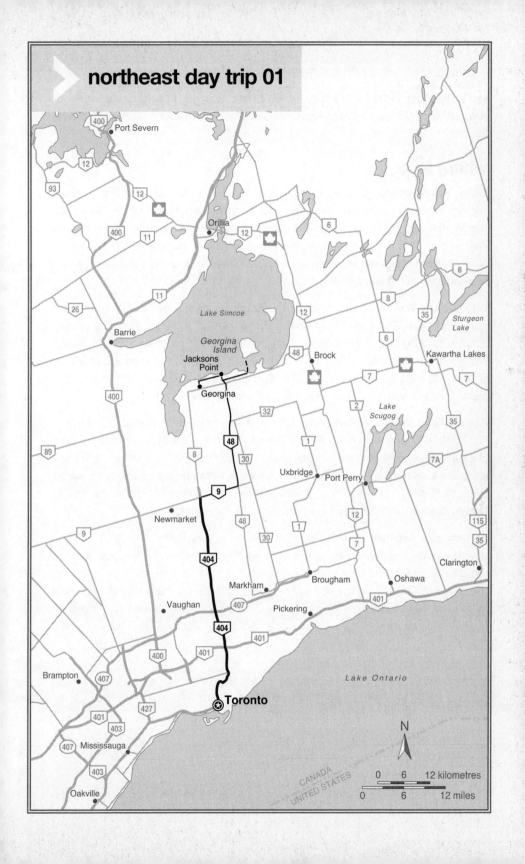

Regional Road 9 and drive for just over 1 km (.5 mile) and then turn right at Dalton Road/ Regional Road 9 (signs for Dalton Road/Jacksons Point) which will take you into Jacksons Point.

where to go

Eildon Hall Museum. 26465 Park Rd., Sutton West; (905) 722-8061. The Sibbald family home, purchased in 1835, was transformed from a small cottage into a rural estate named **Eildon Hall** after the family estate in Scotland. Today the building serves as a museum dedicated to life in rural Ontario during the mid-19th century. The museum is also known as the **Sibbald Memorial Museum** and displays 19th-century artifacts and furniture. The house is open during July and Aug. Free.

Lake Simcoe Trail. Town of Georgina; (905) 722-6516; www.ontariotrails.on.ca/trails-a-z /lake-simcoe-trail. This 50-km trail follows a former railroad and skirts the shore of Lake Simcoe, travelling past beaches, small towns, parks, and natural areas, including several viewpoints overlooking Lake Simcoe. Parking lots are located at each end and at several points along the trail. The western end of the trail is just south of Ravenshoe Road. The eastern end is in Virginia, Ontario. You can walk, bike, or rollerblade this trail.

Sibbald Point Provincial Park. Lake Simcoe, 26465 York Rd. 18, R.R. 2, Sutton; (905) 722-8061; www.ontarioparks.co. Sibbald Provincial Park is located on the southern shore of Lake Simcoe and east of the vacation town of Jacksons Point. The park has 604 camp-sites, long sand beaches, large grassy picnic areas, and a forested hiking trail. Once owned by the Sibbald family, the park opened in 1957. The park has camping facilities that can be booked through the Ontario Parks website. Open May through Oct.

St. George's Anglican Church. 408 Hedge Rd., Jacksons Point; (905) 722-3726. The church was built by Susan Sibbald's sons to replace an existing small wooden church, and was dedicated as a memorial to her. Completed in 1877, it still functions as a local church today. The east window above the Communion Table was hand-painted in England by some of the daughters of Governor Simcoe. The cast iron work at the end of the pews represents an art form of the period in which the church was built. Pew 19 was where

for more information

York Region Tourism. 17250 Yonge St., Newmarket; (905) 883-3442, (888) 448-0000; www.yorktourism.com. Inquire for up-to-date information of events that are happening in the region.

Stephen Leacock, as a boy, worshipped with his family. Attached to the church is a small cemetery which contains the graves of many prominent citizens of the Lake Simcoe area including writers Stephen Leacock and Mazo de la Roche. Open for respectful visits and worship from May to Oct.

where to stay

Briars Resort & Spa. 55 Hedge Rd., R.R. 1, Jacksons Point; (905) 722-3271, (800) 465-2376; www.briars.ca. This historic resort was originally a Sibbald home and has been transformed into one of Ontario's most beloved hideaways, where guests come back again and again. There's elegant white linen dining, an excellent golf course, a full-service spa, and many nature activities. Briars trademarks include a peacock house, the cedar hedges that give Hedge Road its name, and a picturesque avenue of huge spruce and pine that leads to the dining room. Open year-round. $$$

Whispering Pines Bed & Breakfast. 992 Lake Dr. East, Jacksons Point; (905) 722-3998; www.whisperinginn.com. This comfortable and rambling inn has a large main house and separate cottages. It is particularly popular with the fishing crowd, especially in the winter during ice fishing season. Open year-round. $$

georgina

getting there

Georgina is a 10-minute (7.4-km or 4.5-mile) drive from Jacksons Point. Turn right on Metro Road and drive to Civic Centre Road. Turn left at Civic Centre Road and in 1.2 km (0.7 mile), take the second left, which will bring you into Georgina.

where to go

Blue Willow Garden & Butterfly Conservatory. 23834 Highway 48, Baldwin; (905) 722-5849; www.bluewillowgarden.com. There are both indoor and outdoor gardens here, replete with caterpillars, butterflies, and flowers. This is one of those places that is instantly calming. Open June 1 to Sept 30.

Georgina Arts Centre and Gallery. 149 High St., Sutton; (905) 722-9587; www.gacag .com. This small gallery hosts artists exhibits, workshops, and art displays and sells art-works and gifts. Open daily.

Georgina Chamber of Commerce. 22937 Woodbine Ave., Keswick; (888) 436-7446; www.georginachamber.com. The Georgina Chamber of Commerce is a member-driven business organization providing value and support to its membership.

Georgina Pioneer Village and Museum. 26557 Civic Centre Rd., Keswick; (905) 476-4305 ext. 284; www.georginapioneervillage.ca. This 10-acre site is home to 14 buildings that interpret the history of Georgina between 1850 and 1920, including a one-room school-house, a general store, a train station, a blacksmith shop, and an apothecary. Open June to Aug, Mon to Sun. Admission by donation.

Roche Point Anglican Church. 12 Turner St., Box 1066, Roches Point; (905) 476-3491. This is considered by many to be one of the most beautiful and historic buildings in Georgina. Reverend Walter Stennet of Upper Canada constructed the building in 1862 and gave the first service in 1863.

where to eat

Lake Simcoe Arms. 21089 Dalton Rd., Jacksons Point; (905) 722-5999; www.lakesimcoe arms.com. This is a "pubby" place, with the kind of pub grub you would expect—ribs, steaks, roast beef—but it is done well. The ambience is friendly, and the building is historic. The Sunday brunch is popular, and the restaurant is very family friendly. Open daily. $$

georgina island

Georgina Island (www.georginaislandtourism.ca) is the largest island in Lake Simcoe and, along with Fox and Snake Island, belongs to the First Nations. The lake is dotted with several smaller islands, including Thorah Island (a cottage destination) and Strawberry Island (a Basilican retreat, which hosted Pope John Paul II for 4 days just before World Youth Day 2002).

getting there

From Jacksons Point, head west on Dalton Road. Turn left at Black River Road and drive 2.3 km (1.5 miles) to Virginia Beach where you can catch the Aazhaawe ferry to the island. At Virginia Beach Marina and Restaurant you can park your vehicle and board the ferry. It is a 15-minute trip. The ferry boat travels from Apr through to Dec. You can also catch a ride over on the Georgina Island Water Taxi. To book a trip on the water taxi, call (877) 524-6336.

where to go

Nanabush Trails. Georgina Island is a Chippewa First Nation reserve. Not far from the ferry dock, the Nanabush Trails are four themed routes that guide visitors on a cultural exploration of the island, its culture, flora, and fauna. You can get maps and information at the Trail Centre, but the trails are essentially self-guided. There are four trails, colour coded to match the colours of the medicine wheel, and named to reflect the four sacred offerings of

Mother Earth. Each trail offers different lessons to be learned and a unique opportunity to view plants and animals along the way.

where to stay

Neezh Meegwunun Family Campground. 317 Bear Rd., Georgina Island, Lake Simcoe; (905) 715-8730, (705) 437-3025; www.neezh.com. For those more hardy travellers, there's this aboriginal campground experience on the south shore of Georgina Island. There are hiking and biking paths, swimming, fishing, and boating. The washrooms and showers are heated, and there is year-round fishing. Call for hours and rates.

day trip 02

northeast

the kawarthas—"land of shining waters"
kawartha lakes, peterborough, lakefield, bobcaygeon

The Kawarthas is known for its more than 250 fresh water lakes, as its Indian name would suggest. It is also famous for the Trent Severn Waterway, a system of locks and dams that connects Georgian Bay to Lake Ontario and runs through many of the water bodies in the area. The Trent Severn is a popular waterway for houseboats and boating in general, and many people take a leisurely cruise up or down the waterway stopping to camp or to stay at small resorts along the way. It is an area known for its diversity of fish and wetland species as well as being a desirable destination for nature-based holidays and for cottagers. Pine forests, clear lakes, and rolling farmland make up the geography of this idyllic part of Ontario.

kawartha lakes

Pigeon Lake, Stoney Lake, Buckhorn Lake, Balsam Lake, Rice Lake—those are just some of the lakes in this watery destination, The area around the lakes is studded with cottages, small towns and parks. This is vacation country, and there are rustic resorts as well as luxurious inns, campgrounds, and small museums. While the area is far away from the urban development of Toronto, it has a long history.

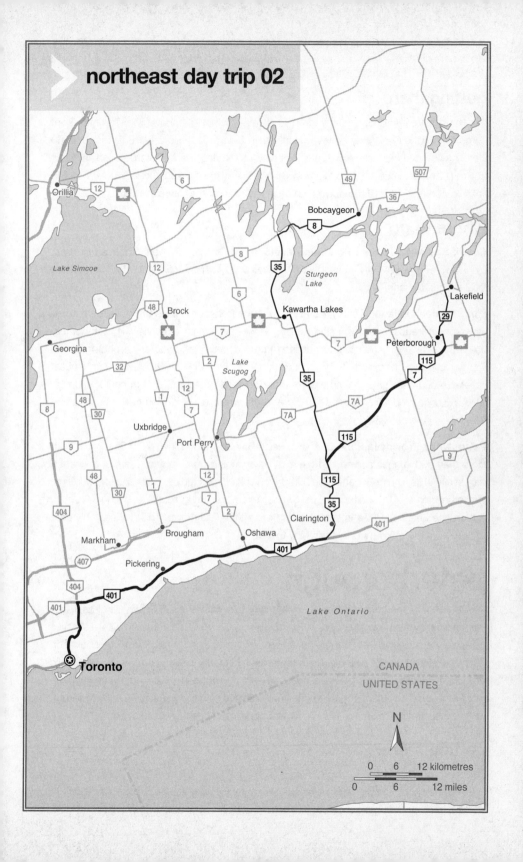

getting there

The Kawarthas are about a 90-minute (130 kilometre or 81 mile) drive from Toronto. From Toronto, take the Don Valley Parkway North to Highway 401. Follow 401 East for about 60 km (37 miles) and then take exit 436 to Highway 115 North towards Peterborough. In about 20 km (12 miles), keep left onto Highway 35 and follow the signs for Orillia/Minden/Fenelon Falls. In about 30 km (19 miles), you will be in the heart of the City of Kawartha Lakes.

where to go

City of Kawartha Lakes Economic Development Office. 180 Kent St. West, Lindsay; (866) 397-6673; www.city.kawarthalakes.on.ca. Drop in here Mon to Fri for news about local events and attractions.

Lang Pioneer Village. County Road 34, east of Peterborough; (705) 295-6694; www .langpioneervillage.ca. An excursion to Lang Pioneer Village includes viewing 19th-century buildings, exploring gardens, and admiring farmyard animals. If you are a photographer, you will love this place, with its lanes and pathways, farm animals, rail and stump fences, vegetable and herb gardens, as well as other authentic details of a 19th-century hamlet, including costumed interpreters. Guided tours are available. Open Mon to Fri in spring and fall, daily in summer. $$

Petroglyphs Provincila Park. 2249 Northey's Bay Rd., Woodview; (705) 877-2552. With more than 900 images carved into the rock by aborigines hundreds of years ago, it is the largest site of its kind in Canada. The 900 petroglyphs depict turtles, snakes, birds, humans, and other images. In addition to the glyphs, there are hiking routes and canoe routes. Explore the Learning Place Interpretive Centre and the Park Store. This day use only park is open 10 a.m. to 5 p.m. daily from May to Oct.

peterborough

Peterborough is the home of Trent University and nicknamed the "Electric City," as it was the first town in Canada to use electric streetlights. George Street is filled with distinctive galleries and shops as well as the Market Hall Performing Arts Centre. Water transportation is key to Peterborough's history. The Peterborough Lift Lock is the world's highest hydraulic lift lock. It routinely moves pleasure boats up and down the Trent-Severn Waterway. The city's reputation as a canoe building capital is solidified with the Canadian Canoe Museum, where visitors can explore the world's largest collection of canoes and kayaks.

getting there

Peterborough is about a 1.5 hour drive (140 kilometres or 87 miles) from Toronto along main roads. Follow the Don Valley Parkway North to Highway 401 East and drive about 60

for more information

Peterborough & the Kawarthas Tourism. *1400 Crawford Dr., Peterborough; (705) 742-2201, (800) 461-6424; www.thekawarthas.net. This large and informative visitor centre is open Mon to Sat.*

km (37 miles). Take Highway 115 from Highway 401, and it will take you to Television Road which will bring you into Peterborough.

where to go

Art Gallery of Peterborough. 250 Crescent St., Peterborough; (705) 743-9179; www .agp.on.ca. The gallery is located in a historic building on the shore of Little Lake beside Del Crary Park and features 1,300 pieces from around the world. The gallery is dedicated to exhibiting and collecting visual works of art, with an emphasis on works on paper—drawings and prints. Closed Monday in winter. Admission is free.

Canadian Canoe Museum. 910 Monaghan Rd., Peterborough; (705) 748-9153, (866) 342-2663; www.canoemuseum.ca. The Canoe Museum is about as iconically Canadian as a museum can get. And it is a fascinating place, which displays the canoe that our Prime Minister Pierre Elliott Trudeau famously paddled. It is a national heritage centre that explores the enduring significance of the canoe to the peoples of North America. The museum holds the largest collection of canoes in the world, with more than 600 canoes and kayaks, as well as a thousand related artifacts. Open daily.

Peterborough Centennial Museum & Archives. Ashburnham Memorial Park, 300 Hunter St. East, Peterborough; (705) 743-5180; www.peterboroughmuseumandarchives .ca. The historical museum is the oldest in Peterborough and contains a large collection of artifacts pertaining to the area, including maps, architectural drawings, books, diaries, photographs, and paintings. The Archives collection includes items from Catherine Parr Trail. Open daily. Admission by donation.

where to stay

King Bethune Guest House & Spa. 270 King St., Peterborough; (705) 743-4101; www .kingbethunehouse.com. There are 2 guest rooms and a spa suite in this heritage property that also is home to an in-house spa. $$–$$$

Summit Bed and Breakfast. 1167 Summit Dr., Peterborough; (705) 743-2777, (800) 297-6105; www.summitbedandbreakfast.ca. This bed-and-breakfast is plain but cosy, borders the second hole of the Kawartha Golf and Country Club, and is minutes from downtown. There are four styles of rooms to choose from. $$

where to eat

Black Honey Desserts. 221 Hunter St. West, Peterborough; (705) 750-0014, (877) 350-0014; www.blackhoneydesserts.com. Stop in here for fair trade coffee, specialty teas, light lunches, and wonderful desserts. The cafe uses fresh and local ingredients as much as possible and is a good place to find out what is happening in the culture department in town. Open daily. $–$$

Parkhill on Hunter. 180 Hunter St. West, Peterborough; (705) 743-8111; www.parkhill onhunter.com. This pretty restaurant, done in soft yellows and very inviting, serves classic European cuisine, like pumpkin seed crusted rack of lamb, but spiced up with some fusion dishes. Closed Sun and Mon. $$$

Rare Grill House. 166 Brock St., Peterborough; (705) 742-3737; www.raregrillhouse .com. If you are looking for substantial fare without surprises, this casual restaurant excels at steaks, seafood, and pasta, with an emphasis on fresh and local. Open only for dinner. Closed Sun and Mon. $$$

lakefield

This bucolic town, just north of Peterborough, has always been important to me because one of my favourite authors, Margaret Laurence, chose this town to live in, and it's where she eventually committed suicide after a diagnosis of incurable cancer. Lakefield's streets are lined with historic original homes and churches, many of which date back to the 1800s. Try a hike along the boardwalk which traces the path of the Katchewanooka River, or bike, hike, or roller blade for miles along the Rail Trail. Near the village is legendary Lakefield College School which Prince Andrew, Duke of York, attended in 1977. There are golf courses, museums, and galleries as well as great fishing and a good beach scene. The town's Victorian past can be explored on a walking tour that visits several historic points of interest, including the 19th-century homesteads of prominent Lakefield citizens.

getting there

Lakefield is about 20 minutes (14 kilometres or 9 miles) from Peterborough. Follow Lakefield Road/County Road 29 directly onto Lakefield.

where to go

Stony Lake Boat Cruises. R.R. 4, Lakefield; (705) 654-LAKE (5253); www.stonylake cruises.on.ca. Take a leisurely 15-kilometre cruise on Stony (also spelled Stoney) and Clear

Lakes, through thousands of charted islands. The cruise includes a commentary on sites on the cruise, like St. Peter's Church on the Rock, which is only reachable by boat, Ronnie Hawkins' 22-acre estate, and the Davis Island Manor. There are also dinner cruises offered. Cruises run spring through fall, weather permitting.

Winslow Farm. 779 Zion Line, Lakefield; (705) 932-4445, (800) 814-0055; www.4thline theatre.on.ca. Described as "idyllic, rural, and quintessentially Canadian" this theatre company presents Canadian plays in an outdoor venue at the Winslow Farm. The playwrights are some of our best, and the quality of the performances is excellent, somehow more special because of being performed in nature. Performances run June and July. Ticketing offices are at 4 Tupper St., Millbrook. The box office is open 9 a.m. to 5 p.m. Mon to Fri.

where to stay

Irwin Inn on Stoney Lake. 1390 Irwin Rd., R.R. 2, Lakefield. There are cottages, suites and bed-and-breakfast rooms in this resort, with lakeview dining and wonderful views of sunsets over Stoney Lake. Amenities include: a 9-hole golf course, full English riding stable, tennis, whirlpool, sauna, pool, and sandy beach. Open year-round. $$$

Village Inn. 39 Queen St., Lakefield; (705) 652-1910, (800) 827-5678; www.villageinn.ca. While this is a standard North American style hotel, the rooms are large and the premises are new and well cared for. There are 26 rooms and 2 suites. $$

where to shop

Cottage Toys Lakefield. 9 Clementi St., Lakefield; (705) 652-6852; www.cottagetoys .ca. A perfect place for cottage fun, this store features everything you might want for water sports, skiing, or adventure, either for purchase or rental. You can rent a kayak and explore the lakes and rivers for the day. Open daily.

Young's Point General Store. 2095 Nathaway Dr., Young's Point; (705) 652-3731. This is a general store like the ones you have seen in the movies—with the old crooked wooden floors, original tongue and groove ceilings, and some of the decades-old handmade wooden displays and shelving. But the stock is amazing—just about everything you might need, with a lot of things you didn't know you needed—like free run eggs, artisanal cheese, a wool blanket, or a canoe. Open daily.

bobcaygeon

getting there

Bobcaygeon is about 2 hours and 15 minutes (166 kilometres or 103 miles) from downtown Toronto. Follow the Don Valley Parkway North to Highway 401 East and drive about 60 km

(37 miles). Take Highway 115 from Highway 401 to Highway 35 North to Lindsay. Turn right, towards Fenelon Falls, and drive on Highway 8 which will take you right into Bobcaygeon.

where to go

Bobcaygeon & Area Chamber of Commerce. 21 Canal St. East, Bobcaygeon; (705) 738-2202; www.bobcaygeon.org. This visitor centre is located next to the locks and has reading material and maps about the area.

Boyd Heritage Museum. 21 Canal St. East, Bobcaygeon; (705) 738-9482; www.theboyd museum.com. This historic home has been made into a museum to conserve and display the lives and enterprises of the Mossom Boyd family from the 1830s. In addition to the museum, there is an art gallery for local artists, educational programs, and events. Open weekends only May, June, and Sept, daily in July and Aug. Admission by donation.

Kawartha Settlers' Village. 85 Dunn St., Bobcaygeon; (705) 738-6163; www.kawartha settlersvillage.com. A collection of heritage buildings that have been carefully preserved makes up this unique village which was a project begun and maintained by the Kawartha Region Arts and Heritage Society. In summer, costumed guides give guided tours that re-create the history of pioneer life in the area. There are also frequent art shows, events, and performances. Open daily for guided tours in summer. Admission by donation.

sail a houseboat through the locks

There are several places that rent houseboats for the perfect family vacation— promising long days on the water, but your hotel comes with you. There are parks, small historic towns, and many attractions along the way. While you need some knowledge of boating to sail one, the company will help you get accus- tomed to the boats and they are quite easy to maneuver. Here are two compa- nies in Bobcaygeon that do seasonal rentals of houseboats on the Trent-Severn Waterway:

***Happy Days Houseboat Rentals.** R.R. 2, Bobcaygeon; (705) 738-2201; www .happydayshouseboats.com. This company rents several sizes of houseboat, sleeping up to 12 people. May to Oct. $$$*

***R & R Houseboat Rentals.** 54 Prince St., Bobcaygeon; (705) 738-4800, (888) 784-2628; www.rrhouseboats.com. Houseboats come equipped with everything you will need for a holiday on the water with your family.*

Lock 32 on the Trent Severn Waterway and the Lockmasters Watch House. Canal Street, Bobcaygeon. Lock 32, built more than 160 years ago, was the first lock constructed on the Waterway. Located in the heart of Bobcaygeon, it is a great place to watch the boats traverse the locks. Peak in at the Lockmasters Watch House. Its prime location makes this lock one of the busiest ones along the Trent-Severn Waterway. Overnight mooring is available above and below the lock.

Trent-Severn Waterway and Locks. www.pc.gc.ca/eng/lhn-nhs/on/trentsevern/index .aspx. The Trent-Severn is one of Canada's most beautiful waterways. It extends from the Bay of Quinte on Lake Ontario all the way to Georgian Bay, and it is a delight for boaters who either travel the complete waterway or do sections of it. It covers 386 kilometres (240 miles) through a chain of rivers and lakes linked by more than 40 locks and excavated canals. There are 5 locks that are part of the Trent-Severn national historic site, and one of them is in Bobcaygeon. The locks operate from May through Oct.

where to stay

Elmhirst Resort. R.R. 1, Keene; (705) 295-4591, (800) 461-1940; www.elmhirst.ca. Presently there are four generations of the Elmhirst family living and working on the resort, which tells you a bit about the kind of homey and welcoming atmosphere you will find here. There are 30 cottages bordering on Rice Lake, all with full kitchens, though guests often elect to dine in the main dining room. The food is local as much as possible, with eggs collected daily from the resort's own free-range laying hens. You can visit the chickens enroute to the stables to see the horses and new calves. There are riding stables, a spa, nearby golf, and sightseeing flights are available. Open all year. $$–$$$

Viamede Resort. General Delivery, Woodview; (705) 654-3344, (800) 461-1946; www.via mede.com. Known as "the Grand Lady" of Stoney Lake, Viamede has been a vacation destination for more than a hundred years. Rooms are large and comfortable, country casual rather than sophisticated, and there are lakeside cottages as well. There are three dining rooms, including the Boathouse Lounge which was recently featured on the *Restaurant Makeover Show*. Good basic food and accommodations alongside a fabulous lake. Open all year. $$–$$$

where to shop

Bigley's Shoes and Clothing. 35-45 Bolton St., Bobcaygeon; (800) 231-6365; www .bigleyshoes.com. A large and sprawling store that specializes in shoes, this 98-year-old emporium located right next to the locks has branched out to include clothing and accessories. Open daily.

day trip 03

northeast

hit the trails in uxbridge
uxbridge, port perry

Uxbridge Township is officially known as the Trail Capital of Canada, with good reason. There are hundreds of kilometres of trails running through the area's forests and rural districts, including the Oak Ridges and Trans Canada Trails, and trails that meander through 8,000 acres of conservation lands. Uxbridge Trails run through historic villages, mixed forests, streams, wetlands, and meadows with an abundance of flora and fauna. It is a wonderful destination for day trips to enjoy biking, hiking, or horseback riding. Port Perry is one of those lakeside villages that will charm you with its marina and shopping area.

uxbridge

The area was settled in the early 1800s by Quakers and farmers, and still retains its rich historical culture and architecture. There are 9 heritage buildings in the area, including a 1929 brick schoolhouse on its original site, as well as an 1850s house, 1870s board and batten church, 1859 Orange Lodge Hall, the 1860 Scott Township Municipal Hall, a print shop, and various agricultural sheds.

getting there

Uxbridge is about an hour's drive (71 kilometres or 44 miles) from Toronto. Take the Don Valley Parkway North and continue on to Highway 404. Take exit 26 onto Toll Road 407 and

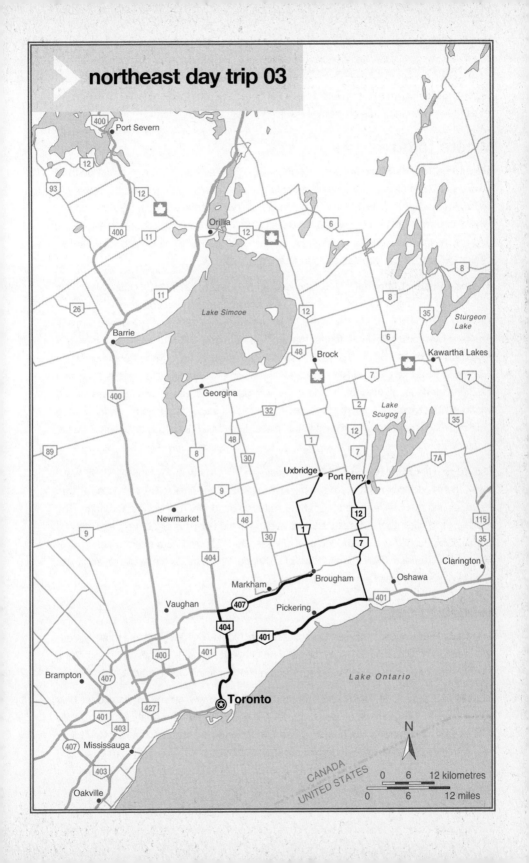

northeast day trip 03

drive for 34 km (21 miles). Turn left at Regional Road 1/Brock Road and drive for 16 km (10 miles), then bear right onto Highway 47 which will take you into Uxbridge.

where to go

Leaskdale Manse Museum. Main Street, R.R. 1 in Leaskdale, 8 km (5 miles) north of Uxbridge; (905) 852-5854; www.100yearsofanne.ca. The Manse was home to one of our most famous authors, Lucy Maud Montgomery, author of *Anne of Green Gables,* and it is where she wrote many of her well-loved books. The manse is in the process of restoration, and the museum is growing, so visiting is problematic but a definite pleasure. If you are an "Anne with an 'e'" fan, you can call and arrange to visit.

Thomas Foster Memorial. 9449 Concession 7, Durham; (905) 852-0095; www.foster memorial.com. This is the last thing you would expect to see in the countryside in eastern Ontario—a Byzantine Taj Mahal-like building that fairly glows with exotic colour and forms. It was built by Thomas Foster, a former mayor of Toronto from 1925 to 1927, as a memorial to his ancestors and other local pioneers in the cemetery of his boyhood community. He was indeed inspired by the design of the Taj Mahal, and the building is a glorious thing with solid bronze doors and a domed roof of solid copper pierced with 12 stained glass leaded windows. The floors are coloured terrazzo and marble mosaics. It's a unique and fascinating building, more so for its strangeness in this place. Lucy Maud Montgomery's son is buried in the nearby cemetery. The building is open for public tours in July, Aug, and Sept.

Uxbridge Historical Centre. 7239 Concession 6, Uxbridge; (905) 852-5854; www .uxbridgehistoricalcentre.com. The museum is situated on Quaker Hill and is dedicated to preserving the Quaker heritage and the history behind the Township of Uxbridge. The museum collection contains many artifacts relating to the Uxbridge-Scott area, and facilities are available for family tree and local history research. The museum offers a spectacular view of the Uxbridge valley and the town of Uxbridge. Picnic tables are available, and there is an herb garden. Open Wed to Sun, May to Oct.

where to eat

Frankie's Ristorante. 1 Main St. South, Uxbridge; (905) 852-1011. This is a totally gluten-free restaurant with an Italian style for the food challenged, but it is also very good. Try a Caesar decorated with pickled asparagus and a veggie panini. Open daily. $$–$$$

Tin Mill. 53 Toronto St. North, Uxbridge; (905) 862-0553; www.tinmill.ca. Famed for their carrot cake and homemade desserts, the Tin Mill does a great job with their sweet potato fries, soups, and entrees like the fresh Lake Erie Pickerel. It is located in a renovated flour mill, with a relaxed ambience and good service. $$–$$$

> ## the japanese are in love with a red-haired canadian girl

Anne of Green Gables *has a surprising and large fan base—in Japan. The red-haired Canadian adventuress became a darling of Japanese readers when, after World War II,* Anne of Green Gables, *translated by Hanako Muraoka, was eagerly embraced by the Japanese people in order for them to learn English. It became a country-wide favourite and continues to be a popular read. Many groups in Japan get together to discuss LMM's books and to go on field trips. One of these groups "The Buttercups," came to Leaskdale in July 1998 for a tour of the Leaskdale area and a Victorian tea. When the historic manse was opened, in its unrestored state in the summer of 1997, there were more than 500 visitors from Canada, the USA, Europe, and Japan over 46 days. Since then, the manse has undergone repair and development as a museum.*

The love affair continues with the release of Before Green Gables (Konnichiwa Anne), *an animated TV series adapted from Budge Wilson's "prequel." The story details Anne's hard-luck life in a string of Nova Scotia foster homes and orphanages before she ends up at age 11 at Matthew and Marilla Cuthbert's farm in Avonlea.* Konnichiwa Anne *is produced by Nippon Animation, the same studio behind the Japanese version of* Anne of Green Gables *that still airs on Japanese TV, some three decades after its creation.*

where to stay

Lavender Cottage B&B. 6 Deerfoot Dr., Uxbridge; (905) 852-1971; www.lavendercottage .ca. This 1820 log house featured in *Century Home Magazine* is a comfy place for an overnight. There's a big stone fireplace, two kitty cats, and antique furnishings. The owner is a quilter, and the house is full of examples of her work. There are also special quilter workshops and weekends. $$

Rolling View Highlands B&B. 875 Scugog Line 12 R.R. 3, Uxbridge; (647) 668-0875; www.bbcanada.com. There's a great view of the surrounding countryside from this B&B that is situated on top of the Oak Ridge Moaraine. There is one 2-bedroom suite with high wood ceilings, a kitchen dining room, and washer and dryer. $$

port perry

This is the quintessential perfect small Ontario town. It has a marina, a great historic main street with a nice shopping district, a lovely town hall, and a town ghost. Walk along the boardwalk, hang out at the marina, gamble in the casino, or dine in one of the many little restaurants—the perfect destination for a quiet getaway.

getting there

Port Perry is about 1 hour and 10 minutes, 79 kilometres (49 miles) from Toronto. Follow the Don Valley Parkway to the 401. Take Highway 401 East to Brock Street/Highway 12 in Whitby. Proceed North on Brock Street/Highway 12 and then take Highway 7A East into Port Perry. Highway 7A becomes Queen Street, which is the main street of downtown Port Perry.

where to go

Great Blue Heron Casino. 21777 Island Rd., Port Perry; (888) 29-HERON (43766); www .gbhcasino.com. This large and lively casino is owned by the Mississaugas of Scugog Island First Nations. In addition to gaming tables and slot machines there are two restaurants and two bars. Open 24 hours a day, 7 days a week.

Northwood Zoo & Animal Sanctuary. 2192 Cookson Lane, Seagrave; (905) 985-2738; www.northwoodzoo.com. Northwood is an animal sanctuary dedicated to giving a safe and healthy habitat to many types of animals, including tigers, lions, primates, bears, wolves, buffalo, eagles, owls, and many others. See a great collection of sleek exotic members of the cat family, which have been lovingly raised and were chosen to appear in many movies and commercials. The cats are a thrill to watch. Open daily May to Oct.

Scugog Island Cruises. 16100 Old Simcoe Rd., Port Perry; (905) 982-1106, (877) 877-2091; www.scugogcruises.com. The double decker cruise ship *The Woodsman* takes guests out on guided tours of Lake Scugog. They offer lunch cruises, brunches, sunset dinner cruises, and entertainment cruises. Operating from May to Oct.

Scugog Shores Historical Museum and Archives. 16210 Island Rd., Port Perry; (905) 985-3589; www.scugogshoresmuseum.com. Eleven authentically restored buildings in a peaceful rural setting are furnished to reflect life in the mid- to late-19th-century. Realistic displays re-create the lifestyles, commerce, and industry of the period. This is an attraction that could keep a family happy for a whole day, touring the village buildings and enjoying a pleasant stroll through heritage gardens. Open year-round.

where to shop

Anja of Sweden Boutique. 229 Queen St., Port Perry; (905) 985-9550; www.anjaof sweden.ca. You'll enjoy browsing through this beautiful store to shop for unique upscale clothing, shoes, and accessories. Closed Monday.

Caviar and Cobwebs Garage Sale. 235 Queen St., Port Perry; (905) 985-6929. C&C is an interesting consignment store offering collectibles, antiques, and furniture, with new stock arriving weekly. Glass, china, linens, jewellery, art, clocks, Canadiana, retro, depressions, and early 1900s furniture are just a few items offered. Open daily.

Petite Images—Dollhouses & Miniatures. 223 Queen St., Port Perry; (905) 985-6748; www.petiteimages.com. Ever since I gave my daughter a dollhouse, I have been collecting good miniatures and am always looking for places to find unique items. This is a treasure of a store for anyone who collects miniature dollhouse furniture and accessories. Open daily.

where to eat

Hank's Pastries. 204 Queen St., Port Perry; (905) 985-2172. Stop in for a quick bite for breakfast or savour the aromas of freshly baked pies, tarts, and European pastries over a steaming pot 'o tea with friends. Their pumpernickel loaves are famous. Open daily. $$

Pantry Shelf. 172 Water St., Port Perry; (905) 985-1409. The Pantry Shelf is in the perfect location overlooking Palmer Park and is a good stop for breakfast or lunch, offering a good selection of sandwiches, soups, coffee and tea, and pastries. There are cafe-style tables outdoors during the warmer seasons. Open daily. $$

Salvatore's Trattoria & Cafe. 263 Queen St., Port Perry; (905) 985-3500. This Italian-style family run cafe offers fresh specialties for lunches and dinner. Open daily. $$

where to stay

Nestleton Waters Inn. 3440 Beacock Rd., Nestleton; (905) 986-0670; www.nestleton watersinn.com. The Nestleton is a classically beautiful inn, family run and expertly decorated. Guests can enjoy a salt spa hot tub for 7 on a covered deck overlooking the water, volleyball, bocce ball, beautiful gardens, fountains, hiking, and bird watching. $$–$$$

Piano Inn 1884 Address. 217 Queen St., Port Perry; (905) 985-6060; www.pianoinn.ca. This historic inn, in downtown Port Perry has 3 spacious and elegant suites with kitchenettes, Wi-Fi, and flat screen TVs. $$

north

day trip 01

north

pioneers & painters
black creek pioneer village,
woodbridge, vaughan, kleinburg

One of the true benefits of living in a large urbane city is that the surrounding area is almost as rich in adventure as the city itself. Perhaps this is because there are many artists, museums, and entrepreneurs who like to be near, but not in, a city. The benefit for Toronto-nians is that, within a short drive, some great adventures are in easy reach, especially along the northern corridor to cottage country. The world famous McMichael Gallery, the Space Museum, ski hills, and nature preserves beckon the day tripper and promise a memorable experience.

black creek pioneer village

A visit to Black Creek is a kind of time travel—within a very short time of leaving the modern bustle of downtown Toronto, you are in the middle of an authentic pioneer village. It's living history at its best and a visit here provides great entertainment as well as solid historical fact. Plan on spending a full day here, immersed in another century.

getting there

Pioneer Village. 1000 Murray Ross Pkwy.; (416) 736-1733; www.blackcreek.ca. The village is about a half-hour drive (33 kilometres or 20 miles) from downtown Toronto. The fastest way to get there is by following the freeways. Take the Gardiner Expressway West to Highway 427. Take the 427 North to Highway 401 East. Follow the 401 to Highway 400

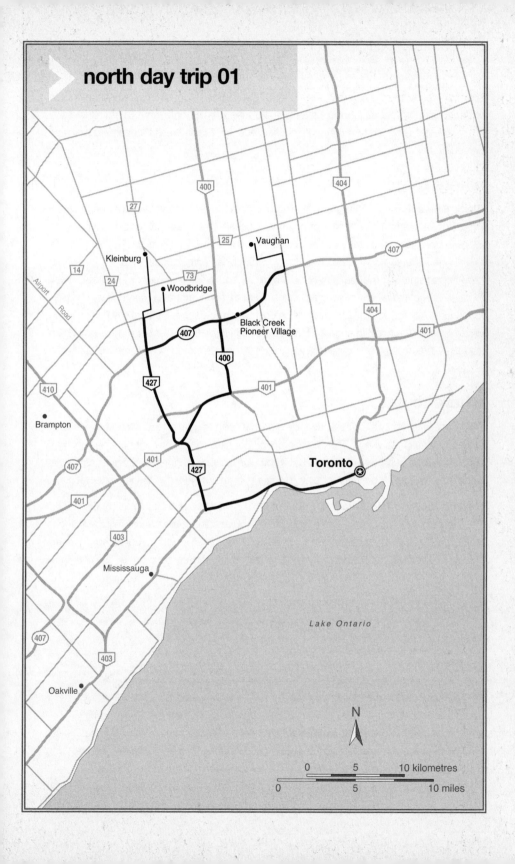

north day trip 01

North. In about 4 km (2.5 miles), take exit 25 toward Finch Avenue East. Continue a short while, about 800 metres (about half a mile) and then turn left onto Jane Street. Drive for 2 km (1.2 miles) and then turn right onto Steeles Avenue. Black Creek Pioneer Village will be on your right.

where to go

Black Creek Pioneer Village is a restored model of a working pioneer village, a living history museum on 30 acres of country landscape, with farm animals and costumed interpreters. The centre makes a lively place to spend a day, particularly with young family. The village features heritage buildings from communities across south central Ontario that have been faithfully furnished with original furniture and artifacts. Every day at Black Creek Pioneer Village is different offering its own schedule of demonstrations, activities, and performances. Ask for details at the admission desk when you arrive. Authentic buildings in the village include: the tinsmith shop and Masonic Lodge (ca. 1850), Daniel Strong's grain barn (ca. 1825), Henry Snider's cider mill (ca. 1840), an apple storage cellar (ca. 1850), and a chicken house (ca. 1860), plus many more. Open daily, May to Dec.

where to eat

The village is an entity all to itself, and it is a bit of a drive to go elsewhere to eat so it is best to plan to dine in the village. The Pavillion Snack Bar sells snacks and light lunches and has outdoor seating suitable for a picnic. But if you plan on spending a real "pioneer" day, have lunch in the authentic brewery, or plan to linger over their high tea in the late afternoon.

Historic Brewery Restaurant & Pub. Located in the Half Way House; (416) 667-6295. The brewery is a cosy place, with a large stone fireplace and rustic charm. Try the Ploughman's Lunch, a cold platter with local cheese, cured meat, chicken, boiled egg, pickled onions, sour pickle, maple mustard, and a crusty chunk of bread and butter. It's filling and

is it inherently canadian to have a hankering to head north?

There is a persistent draw that takes people in this direction, seeking perhaps for that clean fresh air, those forests, the uncompromising rocky shield, and those hard blue skies that seem to symbolize a more pure life than that to be found in urban centres. Whatever the reason, on most Fridays, as work finishes for the week, there are steady streams of cars heading out of the city for the sanctuary of the north. It's impossible not to want to join them.

deliciously fresh. The food in the restaurant is designed in the style of basic fare that would be found in a 19th-century rural setting. All of the produce and meats are locally grown and raised in Ontario. The chicken comes from Bradford, the pork chops from Mitchell, the bison from Thornbury, and the pulled beef from Guelph, Ontario. Open daily in summer for lunch and tea, seasonal hours otherwise. $$

woodbridge

Set in the rolling hills north of Toronto, this once small village has been pretty well consumed by upscale developments and city encroachment, but there are still some special things to see and do here that are unique. The racing enthusiast can watch the thoroughbreds at Woodbine, and the nature lover can enjoy the lovely Kortright Centre. Historic shopping complex Market Lane is situated here and, in summers, is the location of the Woodbridge Village Farmers Market. There is a large Italian community here, so dining is excellent.

getting there

It is about a 30-minute drive (34 kilometres or 21 miles). Take the Gardiner Expressway West to Highway 427. Take the 427 North for about 20 km (12 miles), and then turn right on Regional Road 7. Turn right onto Martingrove Road, which will take you in to Woodbridge.

where to go

Boyd Conservation Area. 8739 Islington Ave., Vaughan; (905) 851-0575; www.trca.on .ca/enjoy/locations/boyd-conservation-area.dot. The Boyd is situated in the lovely Humber River Valley, and is popular for picnics. There are bocce courts, volleyball and basketball courts, soccer fields, and children's playgrounds found within the park. There is also bird watching, nature hikes, and music concerts. Open Apr to Oct.

Kortright Centre. 9550 Pine Valley Dr., Woodbridge; (905) 832-2289; www.kortright.org. This important Centre for Conservation offers hiking and cross-country ski trails, environmental demonstrations, maple syrup making in season, a unique gift shop, cafe, picnic facilities, a kite festival, bird watching, and earth energy workshops. Open daily year-round.

Woodbine Racetrack. 555 Rexdale Blvd., Toronto; (416) 675-7223; www.woodbine entertainment.com/woodbine. Experience the excitement of thoroughbred racing, try your luck at the slots or dine trackside. Admission and parking are free. Open year-round.

where to eat

Oca Nera Restaurant. 8348 Islington Ave., Woodbine; (905) 264-7152; www.ocanera .com. Pleasant Italian dishes, fresh ingredients, and a small and unpretentious space make this a good choice for a casual lunch or dinner. The Panzanella Tuscan salad is a fresh and filling dish. Closed Sunday. $$–$$$

Tremonti Restaurant. 3850 Steeles Ave. West, Woodbridge; (905) 856-6600, (877) 878-6692; www.tremontirestaurant.com. This Italian restaurant serves the standard dishes but does them well. If there are two of you, try the Zuppa Di Pesce Adriatica for two, with fresh seafood, white wine, garlic and herbs in a light spiced tomato broth. Closed Sunday. $$$

vaughan

This is a bustling city best known for Wonderland, but also home to great shopping and dining.

getting there

It's about a half hour drive (38 kilometres or 24 miles). Take Highway 427 to toll road Highway 407. Follow the 407 East and then take exit 73 for Dufferin Street/Regional Road 53. Turn left at Langstaff Road/Regional Road 72. Take the third right onto Planchet Rd. and then take the first right onto Basaltic Road which will take you into Vaughan.

where to go

Canada's Wonderland. 9580 Jane St., Vaughan; (905) 832-8131; www.canadaswonderland.com. This colossal premium amusement park has more than 200 attractions, and 65 rides, many of them the latest, fastest, or scariest. While it is undeniably commercial, it is also great fun for families. There are rides just for the younger ones, many places for fast food, and midway booths, shops, and music concerts. Because it is a drive to get to, most people plan to spend the day there. The park sells day passes and family passes. Be prepared to be thrilled. Open Apr to Nov.

Canadian Air & Space Museum. Downsview Park, 65 Carl Hall Rd., Toronto; (416) 638-6078; www.casmuseum.org. The building is the original 1929 home of the de Havilland Aircraft of Canada Ltd. (one of Canada's most successful aircraft manufacturers), and also the original home of Canada's leading space technology company best known as SPAR. The site contains the oldest surviving aircraft factory in Canada, and is the birthplace of the famous Beaver and Otter bush planes which opened the Canadian North. There are exhibits here of full-size iconic airplanes for the aviation buff. Closed Mon and Tues.

Vaughan Mills Shopping Centre. 1 Bass Pro Mills Dr., Vaughan; (905) 879-1777; www.vaughanmills.com. This huge indoor mall with bowling alley, Bass Pro Shop anchor, and many fashion outlets is a well-known shopping destination. Savvy shoppers can search a carefully curated mix of factory outlets and concept stores that make the mall a shopping paradise for fashionistas and bargain hunters. Open daily.

kleinburg

This small and affluent town is home to one of Ontario's most important art galleries, the McMichael. The historic centre of town offers shopping and fine dining, and there is a historic self-guided walking tour booklet available from the Kleinburg National Historic Archives. Kleinburg is also home to the Toronto International Film Studios, a television and movie production centre, an explanation for the many movie stars that are often spotted around town. Kleinburg was home to Canadian author Pierre Burton for nearly 50 years until his death in 2004. Kleinburg was also the home of former Prime Minister Lester B. Pearson.

getting there

It's a 40-minute drive (45 kilometres or 28 miles). Take the Gardiner Expressway West to Highway 427. Take the 427 North. Turn right at Zenway Boulevard and then take the third left onto Regional Road 27. In about 7 km (4 miles), turn right at Nashville Road/Regional Road 49 (signs for Kleinburg/Nashville Road). That takes you into Kleinburg.

where to go

McMichael Canadian Art Collection. 10365 Islington Ave., Kleinburg; (905) 893-1121, (888) 213-1121; www.mcmichael.com. Canada's best known gallery devoted to Canadian art, the McMichael consists of 13 exhibition galleries, outdoor paths, and hiking trails enlivened with sculptures. It is a thrill for art lovers to wander the McMichael Cemetery where six Group of Seven members and gallery co-founders Robert and Signe McMichael have been laid to rest. There are frequent lectures, movies, hands-on art activities, and major exhibitions. There is also a library, archives, gift shop, and restaurant. It sits in the middle of 100 acres of conservation land.

where to eat

Doctor's House. 21 Nashville Rd., Kleinburg; (416) 234-8080; www.thedoctorshouse.ca. The restaurant can seem a bit touristy and maybe somewhat impersonal, but the decor is lovely and the food is good, though on the pricey side. It concentrates on the regular favourites like steaks, seafood, and chicken. The Doctor's House is a convenient place to dine when you are visiting the McMichael. Open daily. $$$

Dolcini by Joseph. 10462 Islington Ave., Kleinburg; (905) 893-5499; www.dolcini.ca. Stop in for some exquisite pastries, cakes, and biscotti, all beautiful and jewel-like but delicious too. Open daily. $

where to stay

Eaton Hall Inn & Conference Centre. 13990 Dufferin St., King City; (905) 833-4500; www.eatonhall.ca. This Normandy-style French chateau once belonged to the Eaton family and is now available for guests to stay in. The 700-acre estate sits on a private lake, featuring Eaton Hall and 3 chalets with a total of 34 guest rooms on site. While it is often used for conferences, it's still an elegant place to stay. Open all year. $$$

20 Bells Lake Bed & Breakfast. 20 Bells Lake Rd., Nobleton; (905) 859-1555; www.20 bellslake.ca. This large inn/b&b has all nonsmoking suites as well as an in-house spa. The breakfast jackfruit muffins are delicious. Open all year. $$

day trip 02

north

mountains to ski, hike & zip-line
barrie, penetanguishene,
collingwood

This is the part of Ontario that calls to the active adventurer. Here you'll find miles of hiking trails, ski hills, cross country skiing, boating, and zip-line runs. Collingwood, Blue Mountain, and Horseshoe Valley draw skiers every weekend during the winter season when the ski hills are open, for the skiing as well as for affluent dining, a great Scandinavian spa, a lively party scene, and chalet stays. And then there is the longest fresh water beach in the world, Wasaga Beach.

barrie

Barrie is the doorway to cottage and ski country. It's really the last big provisioning outpost before you head out—the small towns farther north are great but they don't have everything. It also has an interesting downtown area and many adventures of its own.

getting there

This is a 1 hour and 15 minute drive (94 kilometres or 58 miles), but I have done it in an hour in good traffic. It's a straight run from Toronto. Just get on Highway 400 North and it takes you right in to Barrie.

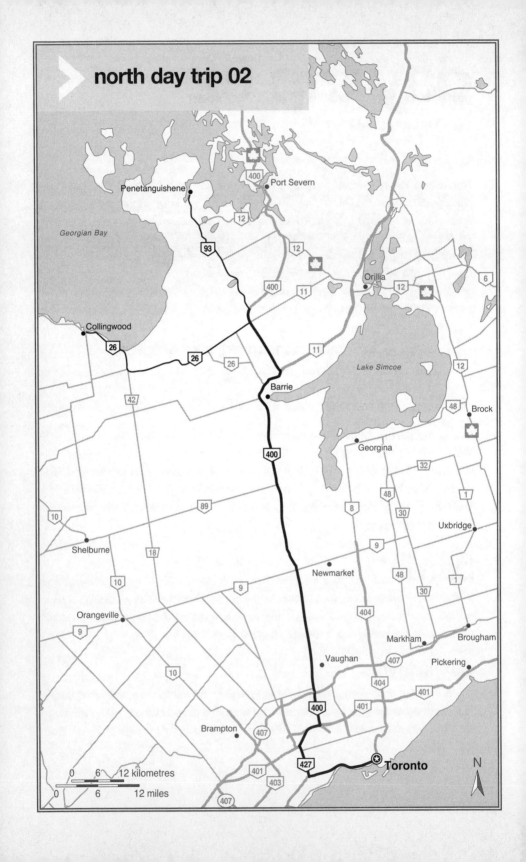

north day trip 02

where to go

Highview Farms. 1992 Sandhill Rd., Waubaushene; (705) 538-0052; www.highviewfarms .ca. The Equestrian Centre not only boards horses, it runs trail rides along groomed trails through idyllic forested country. Open year-round.

Horseshoe Valley Resort. 1101 Horseshoe Valley Rd., R.R. 1, Barrie; (705) 835-7600; www.horseshoeresort.com. There's almost too much to do at this all-season upscale resort—25 Alpine ski and snowboard runs, 35 km (22 miles) of groomed double track set Nordic trails, competition level half pipe, terrain park with more than 20 features, 2 full championship golf courses, 4 restaurants, Shizen Spa and salon, hot tubs, saunas, Segway Off-road Adventures, Yamaha Riding Adventures, Treetop Trekking, indoor and outdoor pools, fitness facilities and weekly classes, 4-hectare (10-acre) driving range, putting green, hiking and biking trails, Kids Korral, and the Horseshoe Adventure Park. A lovely place to stay in both winter and summer.

MacLaren Art Centre. 37 Mulcaster St., Barrie; (705) 721-9696; www.maclarenart.com. This important public gallery is one you should not miss. The MacLaren houses a permanent collection comprising 26,000 works of art, including a unique archive of 23,116 vintage Soviet press photographs. The balance of the collection represents visual culture in Canada with an emphasis on contemporary art. Open daily.

Self-Guided Walking Tours. (Download tours from the Tourism Barrie site at www.tourism barrie.com.) As the centre of commerce and county government, Barrie was the location of choice for many prominent families in the 19th and early 20th century. Their stylish homes, businesses, and landmarks survive along Barrie's modern streetscapes, and their stories can be uncovered by taking a self-guided walking tour.

where to eat

Cravings Fine Food. 131 Commerce Park Dr., Unit A, Barrie; (705) 734-2272; www.cravings finefood.ca. Cravings is the place to stop for the gourmet additions to your picnic, for lovely culinary surprises to enjoy at the cottage, or for food finds to bring home. This is the place to pick up duck confit, truffled lamb chops, and French *tortiere*. Their prepared foods will solve dinner problems for you. Closed Sunday. $$

Oscar's Restaurant. 52 Bayfield St., Barrie; (705) 737-0522; www.oscarsrestaurant.ca. The decor is sophisticated, and there's an extensive cheese bar comprised of Canadian Artesian cheeses that you really should try, along with a glass of wine from the large wine list. The beef cheek ravioli with tomato confit is rich and filling, or try a tasting menu. Open daily. $$$

for more information

Tourism Barrie. 205 Lakeshore Dr., Barrie; (705) 739-9444, (800) 668-9100; www.tourismbarrie.com. This visitor centre is open all year and has maps, brochures, and up-to-date information on local attractions.

Georgian Triangle Tourist Association Visitors Centre. 30 Mountain Rd., Collingwood; (705) 445-7722, (888) 227-8667; www.visitsouthgeorgianbay.ca. The visitor centre can help with maps, brochures, and planning a visit.

Shirley's Bayside Grill. 150 Dunlop St. East, Barrie; (705) 735-0035. It can be noisy and it's always busy, but the view from the patio is fantastic. The food is predictable, but good. Try the warm spinach salad or the apricot chicken. Open daily. $$$

where to stay

Flavours Country Inn. 8288 Eleventh Line, Barrie; (705) 726-8020; www.flavourscountry inn.com. In addition to 4 comfortable bedrooms, this Swiss run inn offers an in-ground pool, workout room, infrared sauna, mega trampoline, bonfire, and walking trails. $$

where to shop

Cookstown Outlet Mall. 3311 Simcoe Rd. 89, Cookstown; (705) 458-1371; www.cooks townoutletmall.ca. The mall has a large number of brand name outlets, so be prepared to spend some time here. There are good bargains on well-known brands. Open daily.

penetanguishene

The Ojibwa name is often shortened to Penetang. This bilingual town is located on the southeast tip of Georgian Bay and is the gateway to the 30,000 islands. It is a small but historic town with much natural beauty, a place for appreciating the splendour that is northern Ontario.

getting there

It's about a 1-hour drive from Barrie to Penetang (58 kilometres or 36 miles) and about 2 hours from Toronto. From Barrie, take the Highway 400 North toward Sudbury/Parry Sound. Take exit 121 onto Penetanguishene Road/ON-93 North toward Midland/Penetanguishene. Continue to follow ON-93 North and follow signs which will take you into town.

where to go

Awenda Provincial Park. Box 5004, Penetanguishene; (705) 549-2231. Good hiking trails, lovely beaches and abundant camp sites (approximately 365) are featured at Awenda Provincial Park. The many recreational options in the park include canoeing, swimming, and cross-country skiing. Across the water is Giant's Tomb, an island where the spirit Kitchikewana rests. There are forest fens, spirit walks, and owl prowls.

Discovery Harbour. 97 Jury Dr., Georgian Bay, Penetanguishene; (705) 549-8064; www .discoveryharbour.on.ca. This 19th-century site features the early days of the British Navy and military on Penetanguishene Bay, with tours of the historic ships H.M.S. *Tecumseth* and *Bee*. Visitors can see 15 historic buildings including the original Officer's Quarters (ca. 1845). Open May to Sept.

Georgian Bay Island National Park. 901 Wye Valley Rd., Box 9, Midland; (705) 526-9804; www.pc.gc.ca/eng/pn-np/on/georg. In southern Georgian Bay you will discover spectacular landscapes, time-worn rock faces, diverse habitats, and the rugged beauty of the Canadian Shield. These magnificent islands are accessible by boat only. The largest island, Beausoleil, offers tent camping, overnight and day docking, heritage education programs, and hiking trails. For a great day trip, spend a Saturday exploring the scenic north end of Beausoleil Island to see classic Georgian Bay scenery. Boats depart from Honey Harbour at 9:30 a.m. to take you to a dock in Chimney Bay, returning at 3:30 p.m. You can spend the day hiking the trails, enjoying a picnic lunch, swimming, and bird watching. Though the park is open year-round it is only serviced from May to Oct.

Huronia Museum. 549 Little Lake Park, Midland; (705) 526-2844; www.huroniamuseum test.wordpress.com. The Huron Village recreates Huron life from the years between 1500 and 1600, just prior to the arrival of Europeans. There is a longhouse, sweat lodge, a shaman lodge, and many other artifacts of life from that time. There is also the Historic Art of Huronia Gallery, displaying important works of Canadian artists. Open year-round.

King's Wharf Theatre. Discovery Harbour, 97 Jury Dr., Penetanguishene; (705) 549-5555. The King's Wharf presents summer theatre in the historic surroundings of Discovery Bay. After the performance you can have dinner at Captain Robert's Table Restaurant just nearby. Open May to Sept.

Sainte Marie among the Hurons. Highway 12 East, Midland; (705) 526-7838; www .saintemarieamongthehurons.on.ca. Visit this 17th-century fortress and headquarters for the French Jesuit mission to the Huron nation, Ontario's first European community and marvel at a world that existed more than 350 years ago. Begun in 1639, this reconstructed, palisaded community includes barracks, a church, workshops, and residences. The site features an introductory audio-visual show, award-winning interpretive museum, on-site restaurant, and museum gift shop. Open daily Apr to Oct.

collingwood

Collingwood is situated on Nottawasaga Bay at the southern point of Georgian Bay. It's an important town for cottagers who visit regularly during the season. There's a very popular Elvis Festival in July, and there are numerous heritage properties in the town itself that make a walk here fascinating.

getting there

It's a 1.5- to 2-hour drive (148 kilometres or 92 miles) from Toronto to Collingwood. You can make it in less time if the traffic is light. Take Highway 400 North through Barrie. Past Barrie, take exit 98 for ON-26 West toward Wasaga Beach/Stayner/Bayfield Street. Turn left at Bayfield Street/ON-26 West (signs for Bayfield Street/Wasaga Beach/Stayner) and in 6 km (4 miles), turn left at ON-26 West. Continue on ON-26 West and then turn left at Hurontario Street/County Road 124 (signs for Simcoe) which will take you into Collingwood.

where to go

Collingwood Museum. 45 St. Paul St., Collingwood; (705) 445-4811. The museum offers exhibits, special events, education programmes, archives and research facilities, and a store. There are changing exhibits throughout the year that celebrate in-depth the heritage of Collingwood. Open daily. Admission by donation.

Heritage Walk. At Heritage Collingwood; www.heritagecollingwood.com. You can download a map that gives the location and history of the heritage buildings in Collingwood.

Mount St. Louis Moonstone Ski Resort. 24 Mount St. Louis Rd., R.R. 4, Coldwater; (705) 835-2112, (877) 835-2112; www.mslm.on.ca. This popular ski destination has 40 different slopes and 12 state-of-the-art chair lifts. There are restaurants and bars, rental services, and a ski school. Open during snow season.

Scandinave Spa Blue Mountain. 152 Grey Rd. 21, Blue Mountains; (705) 443-8484. This is an experience you will want to have. While spas are lovely relaxing places, this one takes everything a bit farther, in true Scandinavian style. There is a Finnish sauna, Norwegian steam bath, thermal & Nordic waterfall, as well as hot baths & cold plunges, as well as a solaria, relaxation areas, and outdoor fireplaces. Open year-round.

Scenic Caves Nature Adventure. 260 Scenic Caves Rd., Collingwood; (705) 446-0256; www.sceniccaves.com. This attraction offers self-guided tour of caves, caverns, and lookouts on the highest point of the Niagara Escarpment. It has Ontario's longest suspension footbridge with views of Georgian Bay and the surrounding countryside. There's also gemstone mining, minigolf, a trout pond, picnic areas, snack bar, and gift shop. Open daily May to Oct.

Wasaga Beach National Park. Wasaga Beach; (866) 2WASAGA; www.wasagabeach
.com. This remarkable beach has been a Biosphere Reserve since 2004. It is the world's
longest fresh water beach, 14 km (9 miles) of white sand spread out along Nottawasaga
Bay. If sun-tanning or a more lively activity is your thing, then the recreational areas of
Beaches 1 & 2 are the place to be. Families and those looking for a quieter place to relax or
play in shallow, sandy waters will enjoy the beaches to the east or the west of the two main
beaches. Don't forget to visit the Nancy Island Historic Site, near Beaches 1 & 2, where a
preserved schooner from the War of 1812 is on display.

where to stay

Blue Mountain Resort. 108 Jozo Weider Blvd., Blue Mountains; (705) 445-0231; www
.bluemountain.ca. The Resort Village of Blue Mountain offers year-round adventure, with
skiing, golf, tennis, mountain biking, and numerous other outdoor activities. There are several types of lodging, many restaurants, and bars. In short, you can check in here anytime
and find everything you need for a holiday. Open year round.

day trip 03

north

ontario's famous cottage country

While a visit to Cottage Country for a day is do-able, it is much nicer to stay over and enjoy the full experience. The small towns along the lakes are a complete surprise—still small and quirky but decidedly upscale because of the preponderance of wealthy cottagers who make Muskoka home for the summer. You can dine in sophistication or in rustic simplicity in the many restaurants. Decor stores are beautiful, filled with quilts, sculpture, overstuffed sofas, and distressed whitewashed cupboards designed for the cottage. There are artist galleries and farmers' markets, as well as large resorts that have been here for decades and small ones too. This is mellow country, where everyone lives in the outdoors. At sunset, drinks and nibbles on the lakeside veranda are a daily ritual. There are times in January that I dream of this place so vividly that I can almost feel the Muskoka sun on my face. But winter is good up here too, with skiing, snowmobiling, and snowshoeing being the big activities.

getting there

Once you pass Barrie, you are basically in cottage country, and there are dozens of small town and cottage communities clustered around the lakes. Lake Muskoka, Lake Rosseau, and Lake Joseph are the most well known. Tred in the footsteps of famous cottagers like Eddie and Alex Van Halen, golfer Mike Weir, Steven Spielberg, Tom Hanks, Martin Short, Goldie Hawn, and Kurt Russell.

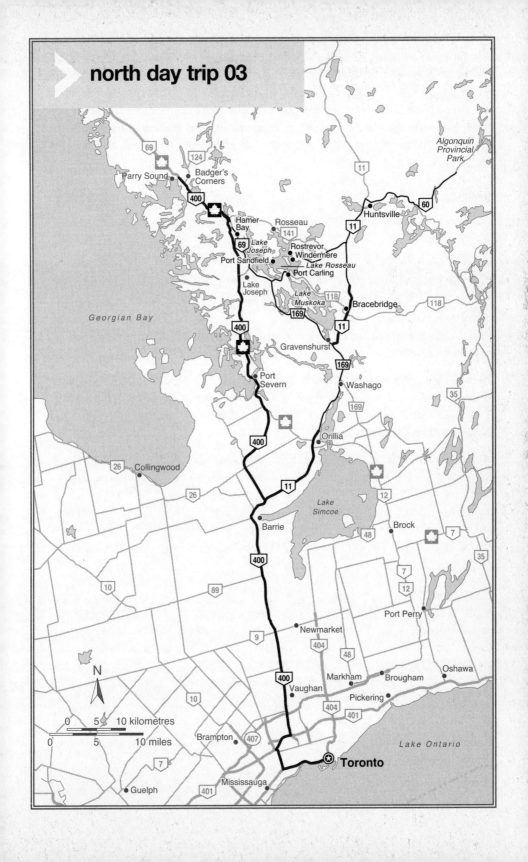

The best plan is to choose a lake, either Muskoka, Lake Joseph, or Lake Rosseau and find a good place to stay and then head out to explore. There are many resorts and historic hotels in the area (see below). Towns like **Windermere, Port Carling, Port Sandfield, Rostrevor, Hamer Bay,** and the large ones of **Bracebridge** and **Huntsville** are great places for shopping, dining, and exploring.

where to stay

Clevelands House Resort. 1040 Juddhaven Rd., Minett; (705) 765-3171, (888) 567-1177; www.clevelandshouse.com. Another sprawling lakeside resort with a long history, this one has several lodges and cottages. It is a family friendly resort with all the amenities. $$$

Deerhurst Resort. 1235 Deerhurst Dr., Huntsville; (705) 789-6411; www.deerhurstresort .com. This elegant all season resort was the site for the G5 Summit and is a great place for a wilderness getaway with all the luxurious trimmings. The resort has a golf course, swimming pools, tennis courts, and many other activities, including a spa and some very good restaurants. $$–$$$

Rosseau Muskoka Resort & Spa. 1050 Paignton House Rd., Minett; (705) 765-1900; www.marriott.com. This sprawling resort is styled after the traditional resorts in the area, and has just about everything you might need for a getaway vacation, including pools, a beach, and an in-house spa. $$–$$$

Windermere House. 2508 Windermere Rd., Windermere; (705) 769-3611, (888) 946-3376; www.windermerehouse.com. This fine hotel looks out on Lake Rosseau. It is a handsome white clad hotel with a broad veranda and lots of history. The dining room is a good bet for a meal, and the patio is a popular place for light lunches. You can sit here and watch the cottagers load their boats and head off for their island homes. Book a lakeview room and go to sleep with the clean northern air and the sound of the water. There are also cottages for rent. $$$

northwest

day trip 01

northwest

ontario's limestone villages
elora, fergus

elora

Elora is a country village that has never lost its rustic appeal. The town perches on the edge of the spectacular limestone gorge for which it is famous. Many original stone buildings from the 1800s are still part of the village centre, and the old buildings have been turned into galleries, gift shops, artists studios, and restaurants. This is a perfect destination for antiques shopping. At the foot of Mill Street stands the Elora Mill, one of the few early Ontario 5-storey grist mills still in existence, now an inn and restaurant (in the process of renovations). One-of-a-kind shops and interesting cafes make this a town in which to linger.

getting there

Elora is an easy 1.5-hour (115-kilometre or 71-mile) drive from Toronto. Follow the Gardener Expressway West to Highway 427 North. Take the 427 North to Highway 401 West. Drive about 53 km (33 miles) and then take exit 295 onto Highway 6 North. It does a little jog in Guelph, where the 7 and 6 merge, but just keep on Highway 7 and signs for Elora. Once you enter town, turn right at McNab Street, and then left at Metcalfe Street, which will take you into the centre of town.

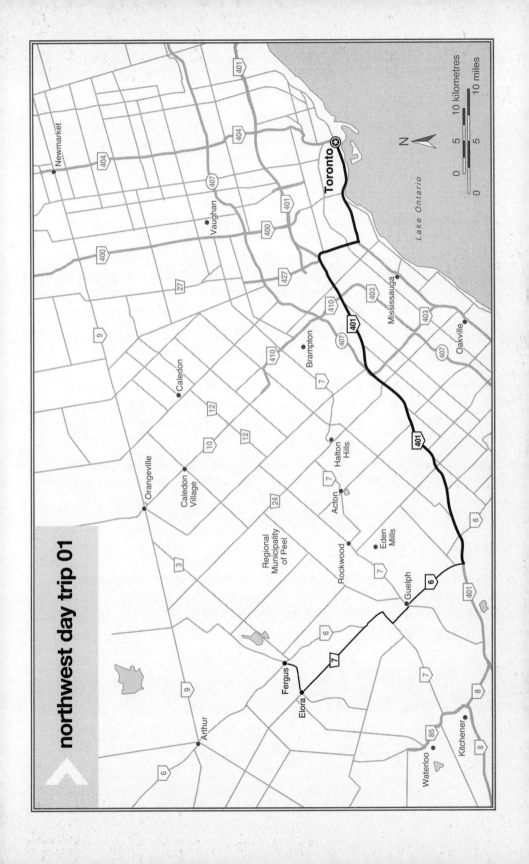

northwest day trip 01

where to go

Elora Gorge Conservation Area. 7400 Wellington County Rd. 21, Elora. The Grand River rushes through the Elora Gorge with its 22-metre high cliffs, and it's a spectacle to behold— whitewater rushing between limestone walls. Riverside trails and scenic overlooks provide hikers with stunning views of the river. Visitors can kayak or enjoy tubing down the river, if walking doesn't hold enough excitement. Open Apr to Oct.

Elora Quarry Conservation Area. East Mill St., County Road 18/County Road 8, Elora. Once a limestone quarry that supplied the stone for the sturdy buildings in the area, the stone quarry is now a swimming destination, with clear clean water and a small sand beach. The water is deep and cold, supplied by underground springs, making it the ideal day-trip destination on a hot summer day. There are washroom facilities, changing rooms, and pic-nic areas. Within a short walk is the start of the Elora Cataract Trailway which provides easy walking or cycling all the way to Fergus, and beyond.

where to eat

Shepherd's Pub. 8 Mill St. West, Elora; (519) 846-5775. This is an authentic pub, in a 125-year-old building with stone walls and fine views of the river. Imported and local draft beers are sold, as well as standard British pub dishes like bangers & mash, and beef and Guinness pie. This is a happy and welcoming place for a casual meal. Open daily. $$

Whispers Restaurant. 14 Mill St. East, Elora; (519) 846-1104; www.whispersrestaurant .ca. Chef Dean Michielsen offers cuisine that is focused on local and fresh ingredients, including vegan dishes and homemade pasta. There are frozen meals available for takeout, and a very nice patio to dine outside in good weather. $$

where to stay

Drew House. 120 Mill St., Elora; (519) 846-2226; www.drewhouse.com. Eleven bedrooms in a restored historic limestone home that was once the home of Ontario Premier George Drew, this inn is close to all the main attractions of Elora. $$

for more information

Elora BIA. 9 Mill St. East, P.O. Box 814, Elora; (519) 846-9841; www.elora.info. Stop in here for tourism information, brochures, and maps.

Elora Mill Inn & Spa. 77 Mill St. West, Elora; (519) 846-9118, (866) 713-5672; www.elora mill.com. The heritage property, unfortunately, fell into receivership and closed in November 2010, but the property has been purchased by the same owners who have brought The Old Mill in Ancaster to fame, and who have rejuvenated the Mill in Cambridge. They have great plans to repair and refurbish the inn. Check the website before you go to see if the new place is up and running. It is such a lovely location, and for years it was the best place to stay in town. Hopefully it will be again.

Log Cabin Heaven. 7384 Middlebrook Rd., Elora; (519) 846-9439. Only one bedroom in this b&b but it is lovely. There is also an indoor pool, spa, private deck, and an in-house blue ribbon chef. $$

where to shop

Grand Gourmet. 42 Mill St. West, Elora; (519) 846-5771. This colourful kitchen store features Emile Henry, Cuisipro tools for cooks, linens from Danick & Soma, hand blocked vegetable dye cloths, and machine washable carpets from Belgium. Closed Mon and Tues in the winter months.

Karger Gallery. 45 Mill St., Elora; (519) 846-2921; www.kargergallery.com. Located in an old stone building, this gallery features works of Canadian and international artists and artisans working in metal, wood, glass, textiles, clay, and fine art. Open daily.

Mermaid Antiques. 105 Metcalfe St., Elora; (519) 846-2504. This eclectic shop has four rooms stuffed with antiques, vintage jewellery, weathervanes, doorknockers, books, Persian rugs—the gamut. You are sure to find a treasure. Open daily.

fergus

Another stone and limestone village, Fergus has preserved and celebrated its Scottish heritage. The Highland Games and Scottish Festival are just two of the highlights of the Scots' flavour in the area.

getting there

Fergus is just a 10-minute drive, about 6 km (4 miles), from Elora. County Road 18 takes you from Elora right into Fergus.

where to go

Belwood Lake Conservation Area. Wellington Road 18, Fergus; (519) 843-2979. Belwood Lake was created in 1942 with the construction of the Shand Dam. Visitors can stand on the top deck of the dam and see the vista of the Grand River valley below. A stairway along the face of the dam allows visitors to walk down to its base. The 12 km lake (7.5 miles) offers excellent boating, fishing, and water-skiing, while a small spring-fed quarry offers an ideal spot for people to cool off on hot summer days. No overnight camping.

Fergus Market/Fergus Marketplace. 105 Queen St., Fergus; (519) 843-5221. Located on the banks of the Grand River, this former old market has been renovated and is home to a number of merchants, restaurants, and more. The marketplace is housed in one of the town's most architecturally significant buildings, the historic Beatty Brothers Farm Implement Manufacturing building, that was built in the early 1870s. Open daily.

Fergus Stone Heritage Houses. Fergus is very well known for its wide variety of older houses, from the late 1800s. It is a good excuse to take a walk through the streets of this limestone village on the banks of the Grand, formerly known as "Little Falls."

Wellington County Museum & Archives. R.R. 1, 0536 Wellington Rd. 18, Fergus; (519) 846-0916, (800) 663-0916; www.wcm.on.ca. The museum overlooks the Grand River between the towns of Fergus and Elora. Built of locally quarried limestone in 1877 as the House of Industry and Refuge, this landmark structure provided shelter for the "deserving poor," the aged, and the homeless for almost a century. Twelve galleries of museum exhibits reflect the life stories of Wellington County people over the past centuries. Enjoy displays that focus on the decorative arts and the museum's superb textile collection, as well as travelling exhibitions, historical displays, and installations by local artists. Open daily. Admission by donation.

where to stay

Breadalbane Inn. 487 St. Andrew St. West, Fergus; (519) 843-4770, (888) 842-2825; www.breadalbaneinn.com. The inn was built in 1860 by one of the founders of Fergus and offers a Victorian garden, solarium, 2 restaurants—The Breadalbane Street Bistro and The Fergusson Room—a spa, and 12 suites with Jacuzzi tubs and fireplaces. The Carriage House, adjacent to the inn, has 4 additional suites. $$

where to shop

I Love Chocolate! 128 St. Andrew St. West, Fergus; (519) 843-7906, (800) 830-7881; www.ilovechocolate.ca. This little jewel box of a store will confound you—you won't be able to choose between the many delights. Go for the Belgian chocolate truffles, or the almond buttercrunch, the chewy praline fudge, or the cocoa dusted Belgian chocolate covered almonds. All the products are handmade on the premises. None of your choices will be the wrong one. Closed Sunday.

where to eat

Fergusson Room, Breadalbane Inn, 487 St. Andrew St. West, Fergus; (519) 843-4770, (888) 842-2825; www.breadalbaneinn.com. The main dining room is pretty in a rustic way and the food is good, with a strong emphasis on local produce. The wine list is preponderantly Canadian, with some good choices available. Open daily. $$

Fountainhead Veggie Cafe. 212 St. Andrew St. West, Fergus; (519) 787-5123. Super lattes and delicious homemade soups, wraps, and sandwiches make this a good place for lunch. The store also carries a full range of vitamins and health supplements. Closed Sunday. $$

day trip 02

northwest

privileged estates & paddocks
arthur, caledon & caledon village,
headwaters country

To the northwest of Toronto lies this gracious area of rolling hills, rich farmland, horse farms and large private estates. It promises seclusion amid heavily treed hills, while still being easily accessed from the city. Artists, chefs, and antique dealers have created businesses here, and the shopping and dining is exceptional.

arthur

Learn to soar and glide in this small town with an intriguing little airport.

getting there

It is about a 1 hour and 45 minute drive (118 km or 73 miles) to Arthur. Take the Gardener West to Highway 427 North. Follow 427 to Highway 401 West. Follow the 401 for about 50 km (31 miles), and then take exit 295 onto Highway 6 North. Follow the signs for Highway 6 through Fergus. Highway 6 will take you right into the centre of Arthur.

where to go

York Soaring Association. Highway 9 and 5th Line West, Garafraxa, Airfield; (519) 848-3621, or Toronto offices (416) 223-6487; www.yorksoaring.com. The small airport in Arthur is one of the few places in Ontario where you can experience the thrill of gliding. If you haven't tried it, consider calling and arranging a demonstration run. It is akin to flying like the

144

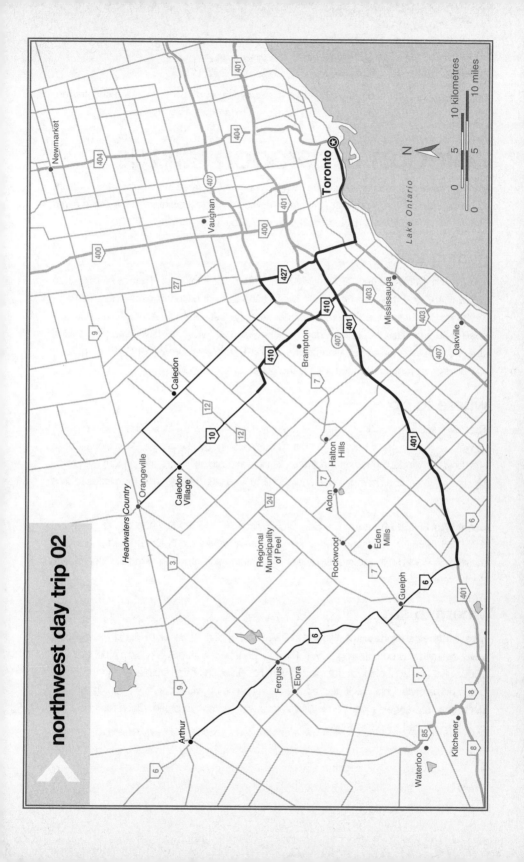

northwest day trip 02

birds, silent, smooth, and peaceful, with a "bird's eye view" of the surrounding countryside. Throw in a good lunch on the way and it makes a memorable day trip.

caledon & caledon village

Many of Toronto's wealthiest citizens own large country estates in the area, among them many members of the Eaton Family, Norman Jewison, and the inventors of the board game Trivial Pursuit. It is a small historic town surrounded by rolling farmland.

getting there

It is about a 45-minute drive (60 km or 37 miles) from Toronto. Take Highway 427 North to Highway 407 (toll). Take the Goreway Drive exit and turn right. Continue onto Humber Parkway West. Turn left at Castlemore Road then take the first right onto Airport Road/Regional Road 7. Turn right at Old Church Road/Regional Road 22, which takes you into the Caledon area. For Caledon Village, continue along Airport Road, then turn left at Charleston Road and drive to Hurontario Street, which is the centre of Caledon Village.

where to go

The main reason for visiting Caledon is to enjoy the small-town-Ontario charm of the place, as well as hike the many trails in the area. There is also good skiing here. It's a nice place to stay to visit surrounding towns like Arthur, Elmira, and Albion. In fall, the colours are amazing, there are small artist's galleries and shops tucked into the hills, and the places to dine are numerous.

Great War Flying Museum. c/o Brampton Flying Club, 13691 McLaughlin Rd., Caledon; (905) 838-4936; www.greatwarflyingmuseum.com. This is the only Great War flying aircraft museum in Canada. It displays airplanes, uniforms, medals, and much more. Open May to Sept. Free.

where to eat

Mrs. Mitchell's Restaurant. Highway 89 West of Airport Rd., Violet Hill; (519) 925-3627; www.mrsmitchells.com. Dining at Mrs. Mitchell's is a bit like stepping back in time. Set in an 1800s historical schoolhouse, the dining room has an open hearth fire place, and the food is down-home style. Enjoy rack of lamb, traditional prime rib with Yorkshire pudding, or roast ducking with orange sauce. You will fall in love with the spoon bread. Open for lunch, tea, or dinner. Closed Monday. $$$

where to stay

Erin Country Inn & Conference Center. 5483 Wellington Rd. 24, Erin; (519) 833-1000, (800) 837-6599; www.erincountryinn.com. The inn is situated in a country mansion on 12 acres of forested property. There are 7 en suite rooms, 2 with their own deck and fireplace. $$

Millcroft Inn & Spa. 55 John St., Alton-Caledon; (800) 383-3976; www.vintage-hotels .com. This inn could easily act at the home base for your exploration of the area. It is an upscale and well-appointed resort, with a fine spa and an exceptional dining room. Set in a wooded and quiet country scene, the hotel is a place of retreat and renewal. $$$

where to shop

Inglewood Antique Market. 16083 Hurontario St. (Highway 10), Caledon; (905) 838-4000; www.inglewoodantiquemarket.com. The antique market is housed in an old apple barn and shows the wares of several dealers. You will find a wide range of antiques and collectibles, and can spend most of a day poking around in the different stalls. In addition to venerable antiques, the market features shabby chic pieces—old white ironstone and graniteware, discontinued china, lighting, jewellery, vintage clothing, hats, purses, sterling silver, books, art, and a good selection of doors, windows, and tin ceiling tiles. Open daily.

Merle Harstone Studio. 16797 Kennedy Rd., Caledon; (519) 927-5894; www.silvercreek studios.ca. Harstone's paintings are soulful and colour-filled abstractions perhaps inspired by the Caledon Hills. The gallery is open the first Sun monthly from noon to 4 p.m. or anytime by appointment.

headwaters country

Headwaters Country is the highest geographic location in Ontario and is the source of four river systems, the Grand, Humber, Nottawasaga, and Credit. The Niagara Escarpment adds beauty and elevation to the scenic drives that grace our region. The area is host to many inns, bed-and-breakfasts, rustic villages, art studios, parks, and theatres.

getting there

From Toronto, take Highway 401 West to Highway 410 North. The highway becomes 10 (Hurontario Street) and continues right up into the Headwaters country.

where to go/where to stay

Hockley Valley Resort. 793522 Mono Third Line, R.R. 1, Orangeville; (519) 942-0754; www.hockley.com. Nestled inside 300 acres of the rolling hills of Hockley Valley, the

for more information

Headwaters Country Tourism Association. 1 Buena Vista Dr., Orangeville; (519) 942-0314. Contact the association for tourism information about the Head-waters area.

property's natural beauty is quiet, relaxing, and a perfect respite from the daily grind. This resort has just about everything you will ever want—dining rooms, spa, golf course, ski hills, fitness centre, squash courts, and indoor and outdoor pools. $$$

where to shop

Farmhouse Pottery. 307115 Hockley Rd, R.R. 1, Orangeville; (519) 941-6654; www.pace pottery.com. The studio gallery is nestled on the banks of the Nottawasaga River. This log construction studio provides a beautiful setting for Al's pottery and also a home for Al and his family.

where to eat

Black Birch Restaurant. 307388 Hockley Valley Rd., R.R. 1, Orangeville; (519) 938-2333; www.blackbirchrestaurant.com. The Black Birch provides upscale country bistro cuisine, both dine in and take home. Ingredients are local and organic whenever possible, and chef Mark Mogensen creates traditional and vegetarian dishes with flair. There are lovely views from the cosy dining room, and the patio is a good bet for fine weather dining. You can pick up a picnic lunch here to take on a hike through the Bruce Trail or on the hills of Hockley Valley. Closed Monday. $$$

day trip 03

northwest

the urban countryside
the halton hills, acton

This area of small but smart villages is definitely rural but it has an urban sophistication that combines the best of both worlds. It is a highly productive farming area but also provides cosy pubs, live theatre and great shopping.

halton hills

It doesn't take long to hit pristine countryside outside of the urban development of Toronto, and one of the easiest areas to access is the agriculturally rich area of the Halton Hills. Here, amid the large farms, the Niagara escarpment and the Bruce Trail, quiet back roads and rolling wooded hills beckon the visitor who is looking for an antidote to the busy modern life. You can capture the bounty of the season with a visit to a "Pick Your Own" farm, enjoy a picnic at Fairy Lake in Acton, experience a traditional Farmers' Market in downtown Georgetown, visit tea rooms or pubs, see live theatres, and participate in local festivals. Halton Hills is often called the "urban countryside." It includes the towns of Georgetown and Acton and several smaller villages.

getting there

It is about a 45-minute drive (58 km or 36 miles) from Toronto to the Halton Hills area. Take the Highway 401 West to take exit 328 for Regional Road 3/Trafalgar Road and follow Trafalgar Road North which will bring into the Halton Hills area.

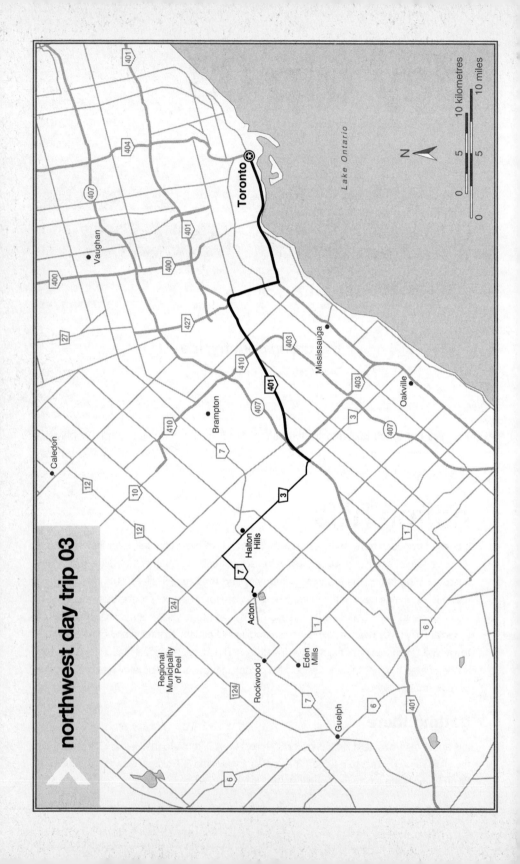

northwest day trip 03

where to go

Andrews Scenic Acres/Scotch Block Winery. Tenth Side Rd., 7 km (4 miles) West of Trafalgar Road, Milton; (905) 878-5807; www.scotchblock.com, www.andrewsscenicacres .com. This family operated farm located in Halton Hills was established in 1980. The farm produces 150 acres of fruit and vegetables. There is a picnic area, a large playground, and a farm animal corral. The Mennonite constructed barn houses a farm market and award-winning winery. Hours are seasonal. Wine tasting is free.

The Gallery. 9 Church St., Georgetown; (905) 877-7915. The gallery, beside the John Elliott Theatre, displays the work of local visual artists. Closed Monday. Free.

Halton Region Museum. 5181 Kelso Rd., Milton; (905) 875-2200; www.halton.ca/museum. This museum is set in the former Alexander family farm, with the barn, log cabin and ancestral home nestled beside a reflective pond. The museum, on the second floor of the barn, displays dozens of area artifacts all on open shelves, easy to see and examine. It is a very visitor friendly museum. Note the wall of shadow boxes, where the flowers and designs are all made of feathers, dried flowers, and human hair. Open year-round Mon to Fri, daily from May to Oct. Free.

Niagara Escarpment Hikes. (905) 877-5191; www.escarpment.org. Halton Hills contains part of the Niagara Escarpment which winds 800 km (497 miles) from Niagara to Tobermory. The escarpment was designated a World Biosphere Reserve in 1990. The Bruce Trail and associated side trails are Ontario's longest and most popular footpaths, for walking, hiking, cross country skiing, cycling, horseback riding, bird watching, nature photography, and painting expeditions.

Ontario Agricultural Museum. Country Heritage Park, 8560 Tremaine Rd., Milton; (905) 878-8151; www.countryheritagepark.com. The museum features historical interpretations of exhibits of agricultural life in the area, a collection of antique tractors, steam engines, farm equipment, and rural life artifacts. Open weekends in July and Aug. Free.

Street Car Museum and Halton County Radial Railway. 13629 Guelph Line, Milton; (519) 856-9802; www.hcry.org. Ride on a scenic 1¼ mile track. The admission price gives

for more information

The Corporation of the Town of Halton Hills. 1 Halton Hills Dr., Halton Hills; (905) 873-2600; www.haltonhills.ca. The corporation can supply tourism information and visitor details for the area.

you access to display barns, authentic historic railway station, and unlimited rides! Open daily in July and Aug, weekends only in May, June, Oct, and Nov.

Willow Park Ecology Centre. Just off Mary Street on Highway 7, Norval; (905) 702-9055; www.willowparkecology.com. A butterfly garden, wetland, snake hibernaculum, and tree trail are some of the ecological features that have been developed here, and children can learn about animals, plants, butterflies, and birds in a natural setting along two water courses. Day use only. Free.

acton

This small country town made its way into the public awareness through an ambitious advertising campaign of its biggest retailer, The Old Hide House, who repeatedly declared in its ads, "It's worth the drive to Acton." And it surely is. The leather store is gone now, a victim of changing tastes, but the town itself is a relaxed and friendly place with interesting architecture.

getting there

From Halton Hills, continue along Trafalgar Road/ Regional Road 3 and turn left onto Highway 7. This road become Queen Street. Turn right at Young Street and then left at Mill Street, which brings you into the town of Acton.

also worthy of a shopping trip

Hamlet of Glen Williams. (www.glenwilliams.org) Hidden in the Credit River Valley between Georgetown and Terra Cotta is "The Glen," as this hamlet is known locally. There are two original mills that have been preserved as well as the Williams Mill Creative Arts Studios. Just up the road is the Beaumont Mill Antiques & Collectibles Market. Rounding out the hamlet's historic charms are the Glen Oven Cafe Bakery, Copper Kettle Pub, and Reeve & Clarke Antiquarian Book Store.

Georgetown. (www.downtowngeorgetown.com) Georgetown has a charming downtown where you can browse antiques shops, art galleries, and farmers' markets. There are a number of historic buildings, including an 1836 train station, still used by GO Transit and VIA Rail. A stroll along Main Street offers views of century homes on a shady avenue, unique stores, and dining options. There is live theatre and an art gallery.

where to shop

The Bergamot. 16 Mill St. East, Acton; (519) 853-0481; www.thebergamot.ca. The shop displays artwork by local artists, as well as home decor, pottery, scarves, jewellery, handbags, birdhouses, quilts, vases, stained glass, candles, original handmade clothing for children, hand-painted T-shirts, and much more. Closed Sun and Mon.

day trip 04

northwest

beer, books & limestone cliffs in eramosa township
guelph, rockwood, eden mills

Eramosa township includes the city of Guelph as well as several small towns, the best known being Eden Mills and Rockwood.

guelph

getting there

It's just over a 1-hour drive (92 km or 57 miles) to Guelph from Toronto. Take Highway 401 West to exit 295 for Highway 6 North. Follow Highway 6 for about 11 km (7 miles) then turn right on Wellington Street which will take you into Guelph.

where to go

Brewery Tours

This is a city that celebrates beer, and a tour of one of the facilities is always informative. Here are 3 that are available in town:

- **F & M Brewery.** 135 Elmira Rd., Guelph; (866) 316-2337; www.fmbrewery.com. Tour lasts 45 minutes.

- **Guelph.** (800) 576-3859; www.wellingtonbrewery.ca. Tour lasts 2 hours.

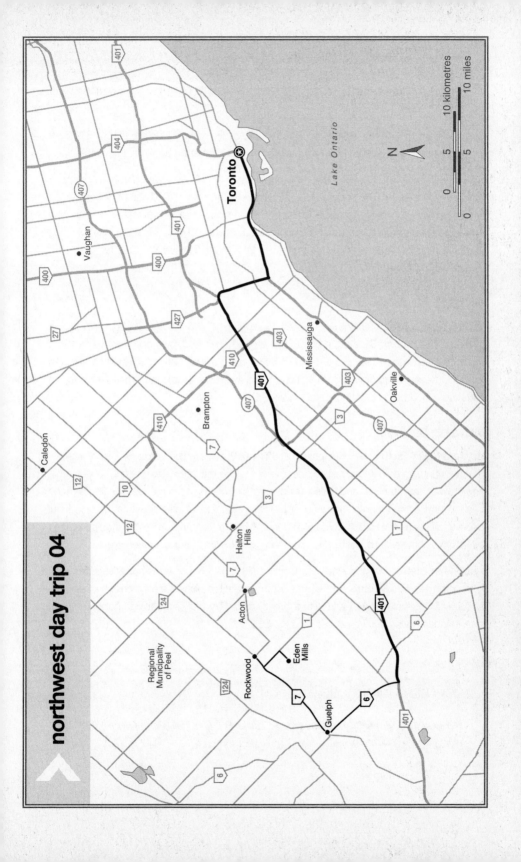

northwest day trip 04

- **Sleeman Breweries.** 551 Clair Rd. West, Guelph; (800) 268-8537, ext. 4454. Tour lasts 2 hours.

- **Wellington County Brewery.** 905 Woodlawn Rd. West, Guelph; (519) 837-2337; www.wellingtonbrewery.ca. Tours are 2 hours and must be booked in advance.

McCrae House. 108 Water St., Guelph; (519) 836-1221; www.guelph.ca/museum. McCrae House is the birthplace of John McCrae, doctor, soldier, and author of the famous First World War poem "In Flanders Fields." McCrae House has permanent and temporary exhibitions that interpret the life and times of Dr. McCrae. There is also an award-winning garden reflecting the time period of the mid to late 1800s. Closed Sat, Dec to June. Otherwise open daily.

where to stay

Willow Manor B&B. 408 Willow Rd. West, Guelph; (519) 763-3574, (866) 763-3574; www .willowmanorbb.com. Situated in an elegant stone house built by stone masons in 1860, this really is an exceptional place to stay. The rooms are large, with high quality linens and feather duvets, the gardens are very nice and the whole house is charming. There is also a separate 3-bedroom coach house available. $$

where to eat

Artisanale. 37 Quebec St., Guelph; (519) 821-3359; www.artisanale.ca. A French restaurant featuring ingredient-inspired cuisine, this is a place that strives to use only local suppliers, drawing from the rich and varied selection of producers in the area. Everything is made fresh in-house, and ingredients are not just site specific but also seasonal. A wonderful place to dine—try the Rabbit Paella with Porcini Mushrooms, and be sure to indulge in a trio of artisanal cheeses as a finishing touch. Open daily for lunch; for dinner on Wed to Sun. $$

BabelFish Bistro. 80 Macdonell St., Guelph; (519) 826-6709; www.babelfishbistro.com. It is a pretty and cosy bistro serving most of the expected dishes, steaks chicken, seafood, and pasta, but doing it well and with a breezy style. Try the Asian spiced pork tenderloin with chipotle-honey demi glaze. Open daily. $$$

for more information

Tourism Services City of Guelph. 1 Carden St., City Hall, Guelph; (519) 837-1335, (800) 334-4519; www.visitguelphwellington.ca.

a strange character with a mysterious past

One of Rockwood's interesting characters was Millicent Milroy who died in 1985 at over 90 years of age. Although the appearance of the home is greatly altered, she lived in this then-poorhouse at 132 Richardson St. and could be seen walking around the village poorly dressed. Millicent maintained that not only was she the daughter of King James of Scotland but that she was married to King Edward VIII of England the Duke of Windsor. Though it is difficult to confirm this information, there are local residents who say that letters, possibly cheques, used to arrive regularly from England. Millicent's tombstone in a cemetery in Cambridge, Ontario, reads: Millicent Mary Maureen Marguerite, Princess of the Royal House of Stuart, wife of Edward VIII, the Duke of Windsor. Millicent claims that she met Edward when he visited Cambridge (then Galt) in 1919 and they entered into a morganatic marriage—a legal arrangement but with the agreement that the wife and any offspring would have no claim on the husband's estate or title. While Millicent's claim cannot be proven, her story remains a cherished part of Rockwood lore.

Story credit: RockwoodHeaven.com

rockwood

getting there

Rockwood is just 15 minutes (12 km or 7 miles) away from Guelph. Follow Highway 7 East to Rockwood.

where to go

Historic Walking Tours. www.rockwoodheaven.com. Visit this site to access a good map outlining the history and details of the many wonderful old houses and factories in Rockwood. Many of the stone houses are still in good condition and they make for an interesting walk through history. Stop at places like Saunders Bakery, which has operated as a bakery since as far back as 1864, the old Rockwood Academy, or Burdaby Cottage or the Mill Owner's House.

Rockwood Conservation Area. 161 Fall St., Rockwood; (519) 856-9543. Visitors come by the thousands to see the towering limestone cliffs, caves, and glacial potholes, including one of the world's largest, that are just a few of the natural wonders at the Rockwood

Conservation Area. You can view them from hiking trails on both sides of the Eramosa River or in a rented canoe. The conservation area is open for swimming, hiking, canoeing, picnicking, and camping from the last Fri in Apr to the Sun following Thanksgiving.

eden mills

It's small and charming, but what has put Eden Mills on the map is its famous literary festival.

getting there

From Rockwood, head out on Alma Street/Highway 7 West to Wellington Street/Highway 44 and turn left. Turn left at Wilson Street and drive to York Street and turn right to get to the centre of the village.

where to go

Eden Mills Writers' Festival. www.edenmillswritersfestival.ca. The Eden Mills Writers' Festival began in 1989 when author Leon Rooke gathered with his friends Michael Ondaatje and Jane Urquhart to mark the publication of his novel, *A Good Baby*. Since then the event has become an annual affair, attracting some of the best Canadian writers who read from their work beside the river, on riverbanks, and along the street side. It takes place the second Sun after Labour Day.

day trip 05

northwest

culinary mecca
creemore, singhampton

It is logical that a country that has such rich farmland would produce great food. So it isn't surprising to come upon a town like Creemore, with its markets, fine little restaurants, and excellent brewery. And in Singhampton, the crown prince of Canadian Cuisine has made the town a destination that the world has sought out in order to sample his cooking.

creemore

Creemore is one of those country towns that has exerted such a pull on artists, chefs, writers, and foodies that they have moved here by the dozens, and that is reflected in the quality of the dining and shopping. The main street is small and quaint, lined with great finds and intimate places to eat.

getting there

It is about a 2-hour drive (119 km or 74 miles) from Toronto to Creemore. Take Highway 427 North to toll road 407 West. Drive along 407 for just about 4 km (2.5 miles) and then exit at Goreway Drive. Head north on Goreway Drive, which becomes Humber Parkway. Turn left at Castlemore Road and then take the first right onto Airport Road/Regional Road 7. Continue for about 68 km (42 miles) and then turn left onto Highway 9. In about 2 km (1.2 miles), turn left at Mill Street and follow it into Creemore.

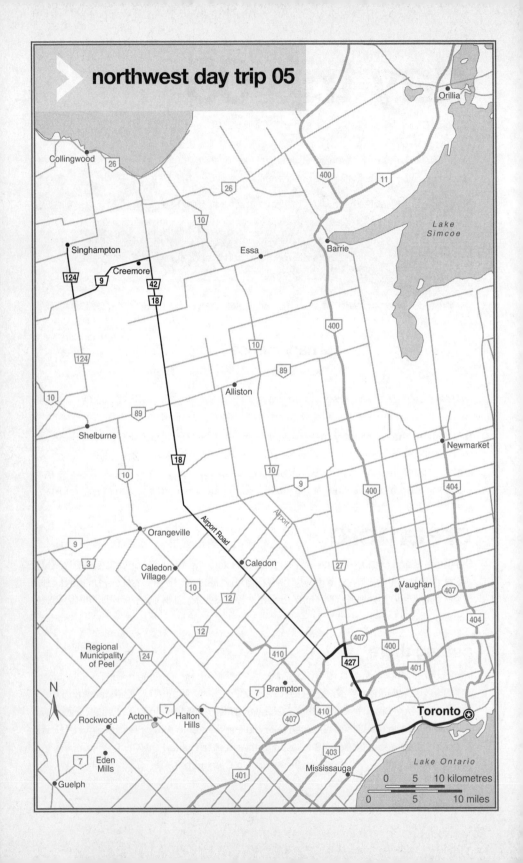

northwest day trip 05

where to go

Affairs Catering Bakery & Cafe Inc. 148 Mill St., Creemore; (705) 466-5621; www.affairs bakery.com. The kitchen in this hundred-year-old building turns out hearty lunches to dine in or take out. Try their pumpkin-spice cookie sandwich with cream cheese filling. There are cupcakes, holiday baskets, and hostess gifts. Open Sat. Sun. & Mon.

Creemore 100 Mile Store. 176 Mill St., Creemore; (705) 466-3514; www.100milestore .ca. The Creemore 100 Mile Store provides local food with a preference for organic or naturally grown. They support small to midsize natural and organic farms and artisanal and fair trade producers. There are specialty desserts and prepared foods made to order. Closed Monday.

Creemore Springs Brewery. 139 Mill St., Creemore; (705) 466-2240; www.creemore springs.com. Creemore Springs Premium Lager is made here in this century-old building in the heart of the village. You can take a tour, have a taste, or just poke about the retail store. In addition to their popular beer, the store has glassware and branded merchandise. Open daily.

SOLA. Corner of Mill & Francis Street East, Creemore; (705) 466-3469. SOLA is a treasure house of specialty food items and kitchenware, offering quality ingredients and international packaged meals. Everything you might need for gourmet entertaining, specialty oils, spices, seasonal products, and organic-oriented options are all available here. Open daily.

singhampton

There is only one really compelling reason to visit Singhampton—and people from all over the world do—and that is to get Michael Stadtlander to cook for you. His farmhouse restaurant, Eigensinn, was named one of the top 10 restaurants in the world—also one of the most expensive—and people made reservations a year in advance. The 12-course meal that I enjoyed there still lingers in my memory and was certainly the best dining experience I have ever had. Now Michael and wife Nobuyo have opened Haisai, a cafe and bakery in Singhampton, that has just been named the best new restaurant in Canada.

getting there

From Creemore, it is a 20-minute drive (22 km or 14 miles) to Singhampton. Take County Road 9 for 9 km (6 miles) to County Road 124 and turn right. Drive for 9 km (6 miles) and then turn right at Gershom Street. Turn left at Church Street and you are in Singhampton. It is a 2-hour drive from Toronto.

where to eat

Haisai Restaurant and Bakery. 794079 Country Rd. 124, R.R. 2, Singhampton; (705) 445-2748; www.haisairestaurantbakery.com. The decor is startling and amusing, but the food—now that is real art. Save up your dollars and your appetite and try out this wonderful place, an example of how an artist can take the best of what is produced in our area and turn it into culinary memories to die for. You can bring your own wine, with a corkage fee. $$$

where to stay

If you drive to Singhampton from Toronto for dinner, you will almost have to stay over, but the choices are few. Here's one you will like.

Avalon Clearview Studio B&B. 1651 County Rd. 124, Clearview Township, R.R. 1 Duntroon; (705) 444-8541; www.avalonclearview.com. This well-designed bed-and-breakfast overlooks the Mad River Valley and Devils Glen Provincial Park and Ski Resort. There are 3 rooms each with its own private entrance and patio. $$

west

day trip 01

west

best of the bard
stratford, shakespeare

I once met a man on a cruise ship off the coast of Gibraltar who reminded me of just how special Stratford, Ontario, is. He was a Californian who told me he had been making the trip to Stratford annually for the last 20 years. "You do realize," he told me, "that the Stratford Shakespeare Festival is producing some of the finest Shakespearean theatre in the world—I would even suggest it's better than the Royal Shakespeare Theatre in Britain." I did sort of know that, but he certainly reminded me.

stratford

There are really two compelling reasons for coming to Stratford. Well, maybe three. It is a mecca for lovers of authentically fine theatre, and it is a culinary gem, thanks to the Stratford Chefs School and some resident chefs with great chops. It is also a really good place for shopping. Stroll along the river, enjoy a picnic on the grass, feed the swans, and try to be in town for the Parade of the Swans in the spring—a funny and charming sight as the birds are herded from their winter quarters down to the river, with great dignity and mirth.

getting there

It's a 1¾-hour drive (149 km or 93 miles) from Toronto to Stratford, though I have made it in much less in good traffic. From Toronto, take the Highway 427 North to Highway 401

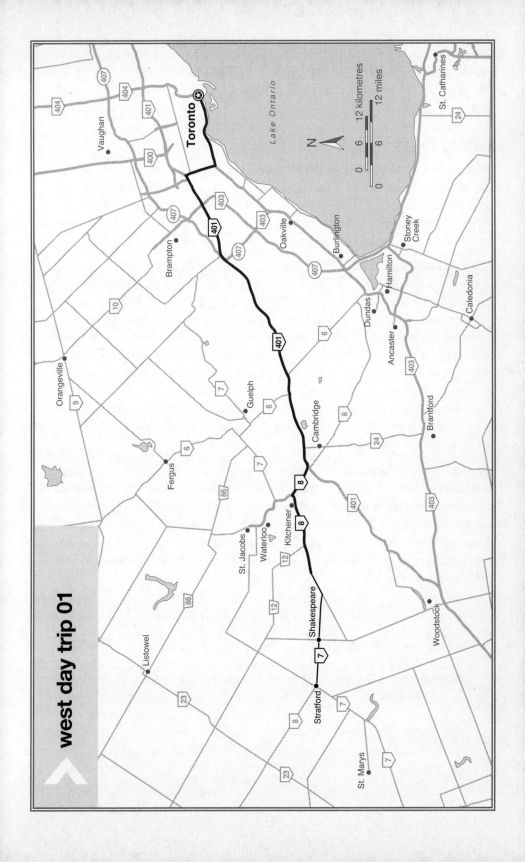

west day trip 01

West. Follow the 401 West to exit 278 for Highway 8 to Kitchener. In Kitchener, turn left and continue on the combined Highway 7/8 to Stratford.

where to go

Shakespearean Garden–Huron Street Bridge, Stratford. This charming garden was designed in the English style by Thomas Orr, a prominent businessman in Stratford. The garden contains herbs, roses and English flowers, many of which are referenced in Shakespeare's plays. The tower in the garden marks the first saw and gristmill in Stratford. There are free tours of the garden Mon and Thurs at 2 p.m. during July and Aug.

Stratford Festival. Main Theatre, 55 Queen St., Stratford; (800) 567-1600; www.stratford festival.ca. One of the most prestigious and popular theatre companies in North America, the Stratford Festival has been producing and presenting the plays of Shakespeare and of other playwrights, including new and emerging Canadian ones, since 1953. While Shakespeare's works form the backbone, the company does musicals like *Jesus Christ Superstar,* and classics like Moliere's *Misanthrope.* There are four different stages, from the classic thrust stage of the Festival Theatre to the intimate, surround-stage design of the Tom Patterson Theatre. Stars like Christopher Plummer, William Shatner, and Maggie Smith have performed here, but it may be that Stratford's newest young star—Justin Bieber—is the one getting all the attention lately. Book your tickets well ahead of time to be sure you get to see the performance you want.

Stratford Summer Music Festival. www.stratfordsummermusic.ca. This annual multi-week festival is set in indoor and outdoor venues throughout Stratford. The festival hosts performances by Canadian and international artists over a three to five week period in July and August. The festival brings a variety of genres to its stages, including jazz, blues, folk, opera, country, innovative instrumental, orchestral, classical and world music. There are even performances held on barges that float down the river. Entrance fees vary. Check the website for performers and times.

for more information

Stratford Tourism Alliance. 47 Downie St., Stratford; (800) 561-7926; www .welcometostratford.com. Stratford Tourism runs a very well-supplied visitors centre in the middle of town, with helpful people and lots of information, maps, brochures, and suggestions for visiting. You can even download podcasts of their walking tours. The centre is open Mon to Fri. The York Street Visitors Kiosk is open 7 days a week from May to Sept.

stratford chefs school

I've been reviewing restaurants and writing about chefs and dining for many years, and many of the chefs who have impressed me the most have been graduates of the Stratford Chefs School.

For 16 weeks from November until March, The Old Prune Restaurant becomes home to approximately 75 students from across Canada attending the Stratford Chefs School. Established as a private, nonprofit educational institution in 1983, the Stratford Chefs School has quickly become a resoundingly successful joint venture of the private sector, the Government of Ontario, and the Government of Canada. The school's uniqueness and special strengths derive from the fact that it is the only culinary institute in the country operated by working restaurant professionals: Eleanor Kane of The Old Prune and James Morris of Rundles Restaurant. The curriculum remains in step with the changing market, developments in the restaurant business, and emerging innovations in cuisine. The graduates have gone out into the restaurants of Ontario and are raising the level of cuisine province-wide.

where to shop

Distinctly Tea Inc. 18 York St., Stratford; (519) 271-9978; www.distinctlytea.com. With an unsurpassed selection of more than 350 quality loose teas from around the world, and a variety of tea accessories, anyone interested in tea should not skip a visit here. Walls lined with green, black, white, Darjeeling, rooibos, oolong, herbal, yerba mate, estate teas, and fruit tisanes, make a quick choice impossible, but you can try any one of them, and have them make your tea elixir to go! (There is a second location in Shakespeare.)

where to eat

Stratford has so many great places to dine that making a choice is difficult. Here are a few highlights:

Church Restaurant. 70 Brunswick St., Stratford; (519) 273-3424; www.churchrestaurant .com. The setting as well as the food inspire reverence. Nestled in a converted church, the restaurant is elegant but not solemn. I tried the "heritage pork belly three ways" when last there—lovely, but also consider the wild coho salmon cooked sous vide, if it is still on the menu. It comes with porcini crusted Qualicum Bay Scallops, wild mushroom galette, asparagus, and a watercress sauce. Closed Sun and Mon. $$$

Country Food Co. 38 Erie St., Stratford; (519) 275-COOK; www.countyfoodco.com. They make great pot pies and focaccia pizzas, but the best thing they do is picnics to go. Just pick out your sandwiches, drinks, dessert, and salad and they package it up in a cool container, all ready for you to head down to the river for a great lunch. Closed Sun and Mon. $$

Old Prune. 151 Albert St., Stratford; (519) 271-5052; www.oldprune.on.ca. The last time I was there I loved the warm salad of sweetbreads with preserved lemon. Try the cider-glazed Perth County pork loin with herbed gnocchi, spring onion, and asparagus ragout. If you can, make a reservation for a table in the glassed-in garden room. Open for dinner Tues to Sun. $$$

Rundles. 9 Cobourg St., Stratford; (519) 271-6442; www.rundlesrestaurant.com. I once took my three kids, teenagers then, to Rundles for lunch before we went to see a production at the Festival Theatre. They still talk about that lunch. This is one of my favourite places in Stratford to dine. The location is perfect, the decor soothing, and the food sublime. Consider the tandoori-spiced pickerel with pea shoots and local green asparagus, and a soy-ginger vinaigrette. All the dishes are inventive, fresh, and dominated by local ingredients. This is not an inexpensive place to dine, but when did you ever have a truly memorable meal that was cheap? Closed Monday. $$$

where to stay

Stratford has an embarrassment of riches when it comes to places to stay too. You can find every type of accommodation, from cosy bed-and-breakfasts to elegant suites.

At 26. 26 Trinity St., Stratford; (519) 272-0022; www.suitesat26.ca. There are 2 self-contained suites, in a convenient location, with kitchenette and patio. $$

Residences at 72. 72 Ontario St., Stratford; (519) 275-3706; www.stratfordluxurysuites .com. These 2-bedroom suites are situated in a downtown historical landmark. They're designer-decorated and furnished, including antiques and artwork. $$$

captain kirk as king lear?

Few who adore Star Trek *and Captain Kirk realize that William Shatner had his early start on the stage at the Stratford Festival playing Shakespearean roles. Not only did he sharpen his talents on the bard's lyrics, one night he had to go on at the last minute without rehearsal to fill in for Christopher Plummer in* Henry V. *While he will always be remembered in the popular imagination as the fearless leader of the* Enterprise, *he has always hankered to play Hamlet.*

XXVIII. 28 Waterloo St. North, Stratford; (519) 272-0841; www.xxviii.ca. This stylish place, with independent 1- and 2-bedroom apartments, strikes me as the perfect place to go for a romantic, and very private, weekend. You get a code by e-mail that opens the door, and you never have to come face to face with anyone! Perfect for a secret getaway. The apartments include Euro-top king beds, self-catering kitchen, large private bath(s), flat screen TVs, and step out veranda. $$$

shakespeare

The town is little more than a crossroads but it has become an antiquing centre. Almost every store here is an antiques store, which makes it a great place for a shopping stop on your way to Stratford. There are also craft stores and quilting centres.

getting there

Shakespeare is just along Highway 7/8 at the intersection with Highway 107, about 12 km (7 miles) before you reach Stratford.

where to stay

Shakespeare Inn. 2166 Highway 7/8, Shakespeare; (519) 625-8050, (888) 396-6355; www.shakespeareinn.com. This is a plain but comfortable 50 room inn that is close enough to the Stratford Festival that it is easy to get there. $$

where to shop

Jonny's Antiques. 10 Shakespeare St., Shakespeare, Ontario. Jonny's is a refined antique store with fine furniture, silver, carpets, statuary, and china. Winter Hours: Wed to Sun 10 a.m. to 5 p.m., Mon and Tues by appointment (or chance), Open daily in summer.

The Quilt Place. 3991 Perth Road 107, Shakespeare; (519) 625-8435. This is a quilt lover's paradise, with everything you could ever need to make great quilts. As well as quilting supplies, there are wonderful quilts for sale, and you can order custom quilts too.

Shakespeare Antique Centre. 2 Fraser St., Shakespeare; (519) 625-8842. This is a barn of a place, stuffed with treasures, and some junk too. It would be easy to spent a few hours browsing for great finds here. Open Tues to Sat from 10 a.m. to 5 p.m. and on Sun from 11 a.m. to 5 p.m.

where to eat

The Harry Ten Shilling Tea Room. 9 Huron St., Shakespeare; (519) 625-8333. Stop in here for high tea, or just for some homemade scones and jam. Open from April to Christmas, Tues through Sun, 11 a.m. to 5 p.m.

day trip 02

west

bonnets & carriages—
the mennonite villages
st. marys, st. jacobs

In the picturesque countryside through the Counties of Waterloo, Perth, and Wellington in Southern Ontario, you'll find some of the most fertile farmland in Ontario. Home to a large community of Mennonites, the counties are full of country roads lined with picture perfect and prosperous farms. Plain black horse-drawn buggies, black suited and black bonneted families are common sights in the town and along the byways. And the markets are some of the best you will ever visit, full of prime produce, local cheeses, preserves, handicrafts, and local foods.

st. marys

St. Marys is another of the limestone villages that are to be found in this section of western Ontario. It is also in the heart of Mennonite country, and it is not uncommon to watch horse-drawn buggies maneuver through the town's streets.

getting there

St. Marys is just over 2 hours (169 km or 105 miles) from Toronto. Take Highway 401 West to exit 278 for Highway 8 West to Kitchener/Waterloo. At Kitchener, turn left and continue on Highway 7/8 to Stratford. In Stratford, turn left on Erie Street and head out on Highway 7 in the direction of London. In about 13 km (8 miles), turn right on County Road 9, which will bring you into St. Marys.

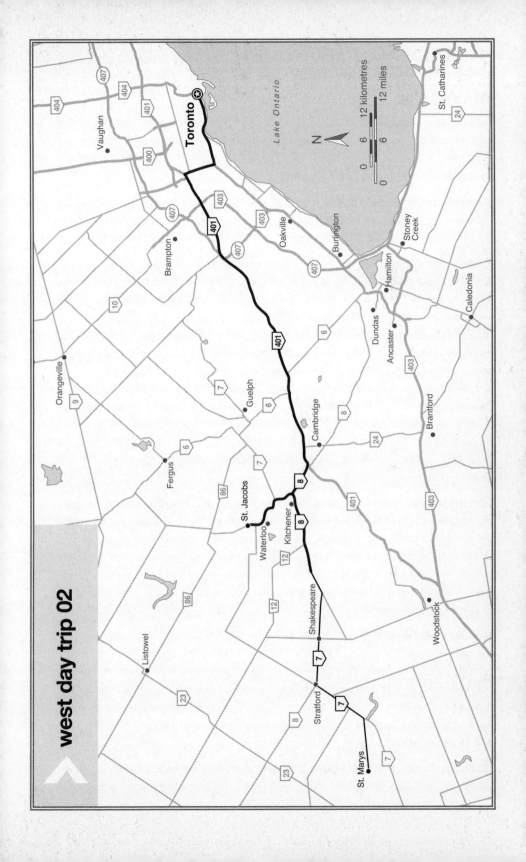

west day trip 02

where to go

Avon Trail. www.avontrail.ca. This is the perfect attraction for those who like to explore an area on foot. The Avon Trail is a 104-km (65-mile) Hiking Trail that runs from St. Marys to Conestogo. It links the Thames Valley Trail, and the Grand Valley Trail. Most of the trail runs through farmland and along small rivers and streams.

Baseball Hall of Fame. 140 Queen St. East, St. Marys; (519) 284-1838; www.baseball halloffame.ca. Housed in a century-old building, the shrine pays homage to inductees who have left their mark on Canadian baseball. Open weekends in May and from June through to Oct.

Explore The Stone Village. St. Marys didn't get the name "the stone town" for nothing. Walk the streets to view the limestone architecture unique to the area and to enjoy the vernacular architecture of 19th-century Ontario. As you walk down the main street, look up to the rooflines, the windows, wood trim, and other features original to many of the structures. Unique to St. Marys are the solid, limestone commercial blocks, built along the main street using local stone. The intersection of Queen and Water has a 19th-century limestone building on each of the four corners. One important building to be sure to see is the Junction Station on Glass Street. It was constructed in 1858, under the supervision of the famous Canadian contractor Sir Casmir Gzowski, as a major station on the Toronto to Sarnia Branch of the Grand Trunk Railway. It is believed to be the only remaining structure in Canada in which the famous inventor Thomas Edison worked while employed with the Grand Trunk.

Farmers' Market. Jones Street, in the parking lot behind the Radio Shack store. Saturday mornings from May to October are market mornings in St. Marys. Visit just for the experience, the fresh coffee and pancakes, or to shop from a wide range of fresh vegetables and herbs, jams, vinegars, and other preserves; pies, cookies, most just hours from the oven; buffalo meat; and fresh fruits. Local artisans are also there—crafters, hand-woven blankets made from hand-spun wool from local sheep and wooden products. All of the vendors are local, and so are the goods.

McCully's Hill Farm. 4074 Perth Line 9, R.R. 2, St. Marys; (519) 284-2564; www.mccullys .ca. Visit McCully's for a taste of rural life. McCully's Hill Farm has been family run for generations and specializes in the production of maple products, natural meats, homemade baking and preserves, and garden fresh produce such as sweet corn, pumpkins, and other vegetables Their large retail store features the fresh produce they grow as well as maple syrup, gift baskets, cheeses, preserves, and baked goods. For the kids, there are goats and roosters and a corn maze.

St. Marys Community Development Department and Information Centre. 5 James St. North, St. Marys; (519) 284-3500, (800) 769-7668; www.town.stmarys.on.ca. The

Information Centre is located in the historic Grand Trunk Station at 5 James St. North and open year-round, excluding statutory holidays, Mon to Fri from 8:30 a.m. to 4:30 p.m. During the summer months, the centre is open Mon to Fri from 8:30 a.m. to 5:30 p.m., and on Sat from 9 a.m. to 5 p.m. Not only will you find a full supply of maps and brochures, but the staff will answer any questions you may have.

St. Marys Museum. 177 Church St. South, St. Marys; (519) 284-3556; www.stmarys museum.ca. The museum is located in an old hilltop home at 177 Church St. South. The building was constructed from locally quarried limestone in 1854. The museum offers changing and permanent exhibits relating to the history of the area. Two outbuildings contain a woodworking shop and displays of farm implements and early methods of transportation. There is also a children's discovery area and resources for research into local history. The early photographs of pioneer family life in the area, in the gallery, are fascinating and an authentic window to the past. Open year-round Mon to Fri, and on weekends in summer. Admission by donation.

where to stay

Stone Willow Inn. 940 Queen St. East, St. Marys; (800) 409-3366; www.stonewillow.com. There are 25 guest rooms in this inn just outside of St. Marys. There is a dining room, and one nice touch is that you can arrange to have your breakfast delivered to your room. $$

Westover Inn. 300 Thomas St., St. Marys; (800) 268-8243; www.westoverinn.com. Originally a limestone Victorian mansion, built in 1867, the hotel has 22 guest rooms, 2 dining rooms, and an outdoor patio. There are extensive and attractive landscaped grounds. $$

st. jacobs

The Mennonites trekked from Pennsylvania in Conestoga wagons and settled in and around St. Jacobs in the late 1700s and early 1800s, making St. Jacobs one of the original Mennonite settlements in Ontario. Today, the rural areas around St. Jacobs Country are populated with many Old Order Mennonite farmers who retain the religion, customs, and lifestyle of their 19th-century forefathers. The area is studded with beautifully maintained farms and large colourful barns, and the town itself is historic. Take a self-guided walking tour (maps are available in the Visitor Centre) to absorb the austere beauty and deep history of the town and its architecture. Shop in the Mill Shops in a renovated stone mill, or search for antiques in the many places along the main street.

getting there

From St. Marys it is about 1 hour (82 km or 51 miles) to St. Jacobs. Follow Highway 9 and then 7 to Stratford and then go along Highway 7/8 all the way to Kitchener. At Kitchener, turn left on Regional Road 85, which will take you to St. Jacobs.

where to go

Maple Syrup Museum. 1441 King St. North, St. Jacobs; (519) 664-1232. Located on the third floor of the Country Mill at the corner of Front Street and King Street, this museum teaches visitors about the history of maple syrup production through artifacts, photographs, and displays. Maple syrup products are available for purchase at the nearby Farm Pantry located at 1386 King St. North, St. Jacobs. Open daily. Admission is free.

Mennonite Farmers' Market. Weber Street and Farmers' Market Road, 3 km (2 miles) south of Village of St. Jacobs. St. Jacobs Farmers' Market is a year-round market, but the best times to visit are in the summer when the local produce is at its best, or in the fall when all the preserves are ready. There is aisle upon aisle of fresh produce, meats, cheese, baking, crafts, home decor, furniture, clothes, tools, and more. You can pick up local delicacies, including summer sausage and pure maple syrup sold by Mennonite farmers who travel to market by horse and buggy. There are often buskers (street musicians) who liven up the experience. Markets are held on Thurs and Sat from 7 a.m. to 3 p.m., with an extra market added in summer on Tues from June to Aug.

Mennonite Story. Visitor Centre, 1406 King St. North, St. Jacobs; (519) 664-3518. Learn about the Mennonite people by visiting *The Mennonite Story.* Take a multi-media journey, beginning with a 13-minute DVD presentation. Then browse through an informative exhibit of photos, artifacts, and displays that describe the history, culture, and religion of the Mennonites yesterday and today. Group visits can be arranged by appointment and group rates include a guided tour. Open daily.

St. Jacobs Quilt Gallery. 1441 King St. North, St. Jacobs; (800) 265-3353. Located adjacent to the Maple Syrup Museum, the St. Jacobs Quilt Gallery showcases exciting examples of quilting excellence. Exhibits change every few months and feature the work of individual artists, as well as groups and guilds. The gallery makes it clear why St. Jacobs is the "quilt capital of Canada." Open daily.

where to stay

Benjamin's Restaurant & Inn. 1430 King St. North., St. Jacobs; (519) 664-3731. This refurbished inn dates back to 1852 and features 9 guest rooms. Breakfast is served in the upstairs veranda overlooking the village. $$

day trip 03

>>> **german country**
kitchener, waterloo, cambridge

Kitchener, Waterloo, and Cambridge were settled by Pennsylvania Dutch and German settlers, and their character is still evident in the area and survives in the Oktoberfest festivals and the Christkindl markets.

kitchener

This small city used to be called Berlin, but the name was changed to commemorate Lord Kitchener instead after World War I, in the face of anti-German sentiment. It was heavily populated by German Mennonites from Pennsylvania in the early 1800s and still retains strong Germanic flavour. The city was also home to William Lyon Mackenzie King, Canada's tenth, and longest serving, prime minister.

getting there

It is about a 1 hour and 10-minute drive (109 km or 68 miles) from Toronto to Kitchener. From Toronto, follow Highway 401 West. Take exit 278 to Highway 8 which will take you into Kitchener.

where to go

Homer Watson House and Gallery. 1754 Old Mill Rd., Kitchener; (519) 748-4377; www .homerwatson.on.ca. The internationally recognized artist Homer Watson was born in the

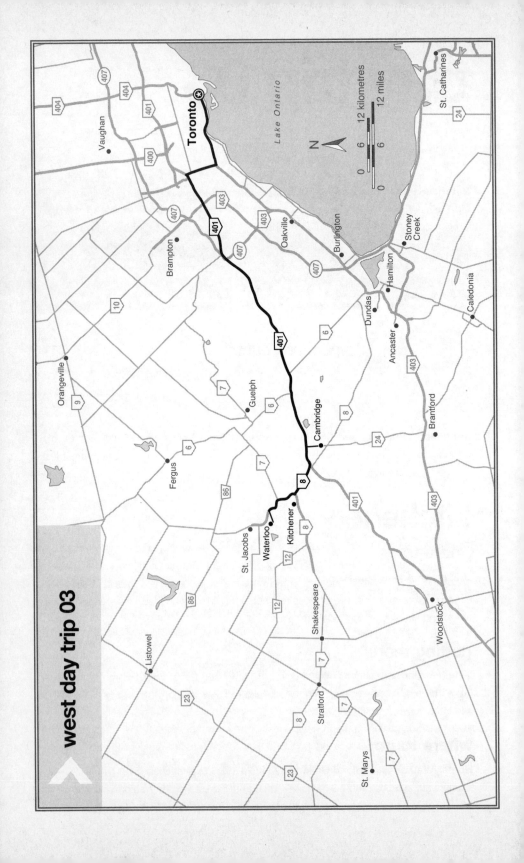

village of Upper Doon in 1855. For 55 years, what is now known as the Homer Watson House was the artist's residence, his studio, and his gallery. Now it acts as a museum of the artist's life and work as well as exhibition space and an active community arts centre. For those who have fallen in love with Watson's landscapes—Queen Victoria owned three of them—this is an important place. Open Tues to Sun. Free.

Waterloo Region Museum and Doon Heritage Village. 10 Huron Rd., Kitchener; (519) 748-1914; www.waterlooregionmuseum.com. The museum building includes more than 20,000 square feet of long-term and temporary gallery space. The museum building acts as the gateway to Doon Heritage Village, a living history museum that re-creates a rural village and two farms, where costumed interpreters welcome you to the year 1914. Over 20 historic buildings, period furnishings, farm animals, heritage gardens, and demonstrations of daily chores help visitors discover an important era of Canadian history. Check for seasonal hours.

waterloo

Waterloo is the home of intellectual capital—blooming in places like the University of Waterloo and the Perimeter Institute, a technology think tank, and of course in the area's most famous business, Research in Motion, makers of the world famous Blackberry.

getting there

From Kitchener, it is a 10-minute drive (16 km or 10 miles) to Waterloo. Take Highway 7 East, which becomes Highway 85. Continue north on Highway 85. Turn left at Highway 57/Univeristy Avenue. Turn right on Albert Street which will take you into Waterloo.

where to go

Brubacher House Museum. c/o University of Waterloo, North Campus, Waterloo; (519) 886-3855. The Brubacher House was built in 1850 in typical Pennsylvania German architectural style. The home provides education about the Pennsylvania German heritage of Waterloo County during the 1850 to 1890 time period. Open Wed to Sat, May to Oct. Admission by donation.

Canadian Clay and Glass Gallery. 25 Caroline St. North, Waterloo; (519) 746-1882; www.canadianclayandglass.ca. The Canadian Clay and Glass Gallery is dedicated to the public education and enjoyment of contemporary clay, glass, stained glass, and enamel art. The gallery features a year-round program of exhibitions, lectures, workshops, tours, and demonstrations, and offers educational opportunities for professionals, schools, and members of the community. Open daily.

RIM Park. 2001 University Ave. East, Waterloo; (519) 884-5363. RIM Park is a city park facility in Waterloo. Key facilities and features include the Manulife Financial Sportsplex and the Healthy Living Centre, the heritage Mennonite Martin farm, and the Grey Silo Golf Course. The eastern edge of the park borders on the Grand River.

where to stay

Walper Terrace Hotel. 1 King St. West, Kitchener; (519) 745-4321; www.walper.com. This historical 79-room hotel is perfectly placed for touring Waterloo; it's in the middle of downtown. The rooms are nicely decorated and fresh. $$

where to eat

Sole Restaurant and Wine Bar. 83 Erb St. West, Waterloo; (519) 747-5622. Situated in a 150-year-old Seagram's building, the restaurant offers items ranging from thin crust pizza, pastas, vegetarian entrees, and steaks. Open daily. $$

cambridge

The ambience and architecture of the historic buildings, the river winding its way through their midst, the old stone and iron bridges, all have a quality of an English or maybe a German village. It is a lovely old town, with some well preserved stone houses and riverside views.

getting there

Cambridge is about a 15-minute drive (17 km or 11 miles) from Kitchener. Take Highway 8 South to Highway 401. Take the 401 East towards Toronto and then in about 6 km (4 miles), take Regional Road 24, on the right, which will take you into Cambridge.

where to go

Cambridge Butterfly Conservatory. 2500 Kossuth Rd., Cambridge; (519) 653-1234; www.cambridgebutterfly.com. A great place for families to visit and learn about butterflies, nature, and conservation. The 25,000-square-foot facility includes a 10,800-square-foot indoor tropical garden featuring thousands of free-flying butterflies from all over the world, tropical plants, waterfalls, streams, reflecting pools, tropical finches, Chinese painted quail, and red-eared slider turtles. There are a cafe and a gift shop. Closed Monday in winter.

Cambridge Farmers' Market. 40 Dickson St., Cambridge; (519) 740-4680 ext. 4252. The market has been in operation since 1830 making it the third oldest market in the country. You can buy fresh meats, fresh baked goods, cheese, cold cuts and sausage, European breads, baked goods, fresh poultry, maple syrup and honey, farm fresh eggs, ethnic foods,

> ## for more information
>
> *Cambridge Visitor Centre. 750 Hespeler Rd., Cambridge; (519) 622-2336, (800) 749-7560; www.visitcambridgeontario.com. The Gateway Cambridge Visitor Centre is an 8,000-square-foot, state-of-the-art facility that provides all the information you will need to explore Cambridge. Open daily.*

as well as homemade crafts and one-of-a-kind items. But it is the farmers and the friendliness that you come for. Open every Sat and Wed from June to Aug.

Fire Hall Museum and Education Centre. 56 Dickson St., Cambridge; (519) 621-1144. Housed in a beautiful heritage building, the old Galt Fire Hall, the museum displays something for everyone—a collection of toy fire engines, a fire truck, hose reels, and even real firefighters to talk to. For the adults the museum has a vast collection of artifacts from around the world. For researchers the museum offers a rich archive filled with thousands of photographs, a vast collection of video tapes, document and computer files, as well as the Cambridge Fire Department library. Open Wed and Sat. Free.

where to shop

Southworks Mall. 64 Grand Ave South, Cambridge; (519) 740-0380 ext. 23; www.south works.ca. This former foundry is now home to Canada's largest antique market and more than 28 outlet stores including Kodiak, Corningware, Corelle Revere, Paderno, Tootsies, Oxford Mills, and Saucony. There are some good bargains to be found here, and it's a place where you can easily pass most of an afternoon. Open daily.

where to stay

Langdon Hall Country House Hotel and Spa. 1 Langdon Dr., Cambridge; (519) 740-2100. This is a Relais & Chateaux property, an elegant country hotel, and a superb place to stay. There are 52 rooms, a full spa, and fine dining. There are comfortable Main House sitting rooms, conservatories, and billiard and games room, an outdoor pool, tennis court, and croquet lawn; 12 km (7 miles) of walking trails; courtesy sports equipment including bicycles; whirlpool and sauna facilities at the spa; indoor exercise room; and Langdon Hall's vegetable and flower gardens. $$$

where to eat

Cambridge Mill. 130 Water St., Cambridge; (519) 624-1828; www.cambridgemill.com. The restaurant had been closed and undergoing a complete renovation, and is scheduled to reopen in spring 2011. Because I love the other restaurants that are owned by the Cian-cones, I am certain that this one will be exceptional too. The same devotion to fresh and local produce, to "Earth to Table" dining, will reign. Be sure to give it a try.

Langdon Hall Country House Hotel and Spa. 1 Langdon Dr., Cambridge; (519) 740-2100. The dining room at Langdon Hall is presided over by the talented Chef Jonathon Gushue. Langdon Hall is the only 2010 Ontario recipient of the Five Diamond Award from AAA/CAA and one of only 5 recipient restaurants in Canada. In 2010 the dining room at Langdon Hall was also named on the prestigious S. Pellegrino 100 World's Best Restaurant list. The food is elegant and beautifully presented, using local producers and herbs and vegetables for the Hall's own gardens in season. Mains like the confit veal tenderloin with garden celeriac, pine mushroom crumble, braised Swiss chard matsutake mushrooms, and truffle jus are superb. Open daily. $$$

southwest

day trip 01

southwest

first nations & early ontario heritage
brantford, woodstock, ingersoll

brantford

Brantford is probably most famous as the birthplace of Wayne Gretzky—the main thoroughfare has been renamed Wayne Gretzky Parkway—and for another famous resident, Alexander Graham Bell which has earned it the nickname "The Telephone City," but there is much more of interest here. The city borders the Grand River and still retains many lovely old historic homes in the residential streets.

getting there

It is about a 1 hour and 15 minute drive (106 km or 66 miles) from Toronto to Brantford. Take the Gardiner Expressway West and then follow along the Queen Elizabeth Way (QEW). When the Highway splits, take Highway 403 to Hamilton and Brantford. Take exit 38 and turn right on Wayne Gretzky Parkway, which will take you into the city.

where to go

Bell Homestead National Historic Park. 94 Tutela Heights Rd., Brantford; (519) 756-6220; www.bellhomestead.ca. The Bell family's first North American residence—known to them as "Melville House"—overlooks the Grand River and presents a window into the life and times of Alexander Graham Bell, the man who changed the world. The home is restored to the 1870s era and is furnished with many of the objects and pieces of furniture

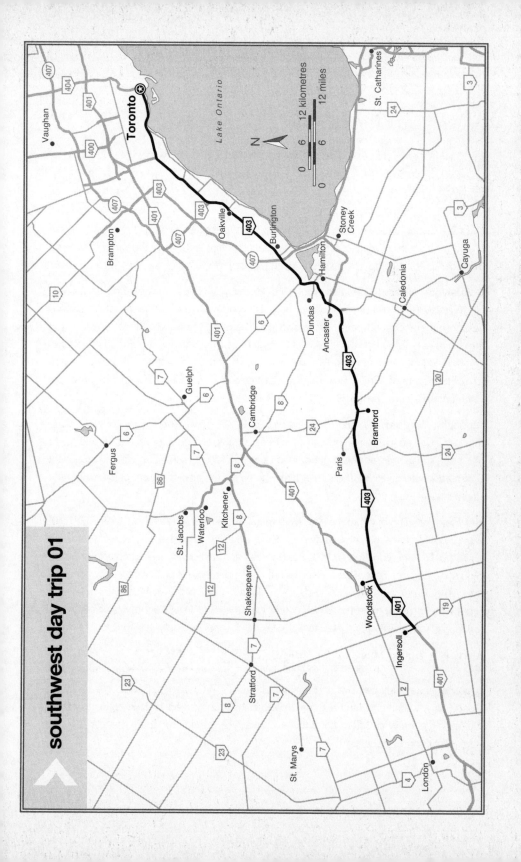

southwest day trip 01

for more information

Brantford Visitor & Tourism Centre. *399 Wayne Gretzky Pkwy.; (519) 751-9900, (800) 265-6299; www.discoverbrantford.com.*

that were owned by the Bell family. Costumed interpreters tell the story of the family. There is also a collection of early and modern telephone equipment. There are picnic places on the grounds, a gift shop, and a cafe. Closed Monday.

Chiefswood National Historic Site. 1037 Highway 54 at Chiefswood Rd., Ohsweken; (519) 752-5005; www.chiefswood.com. Chiefswood was the birthplace of E. Pauline Johnson, the acclaimed poet best known for "The Song My Paddle Sings." Pauline was the daughter of Emily Howells and Chief George H. M. Johnson and was proud of both her English and Mohawk heritages. The Mohawk Chief built this mansion as a wedding present for his English bride, Emily. Built from walnut trees from the estate, it is laid out in a rare plank on plank construction. Open Tues to Sun, daily from May to Dec.

Glenhyrst Gardens. 20 Ava Rd., Brantford; (519) 756-1500. This is Brantford's horticultural park, with annual plantings, specimen trees, shrubs, and outdoor sculptures and public art. It was the former residence of Edmund Lister Cockshutt (1861–1956) of the prominent Brantford industrial family. The former family home is now the Art Gallery of Brant, and the city maintains the gardens. Free.

Her Majesty's Royal Chapel of the Mohawks. 301 Mohawk, Brantford; (519) 756-0240; www.mohawkchapel.ca. Also known as St. Paul's, the chapel is the oldest Protestant church in Ontario, constructed in 1785. Services are held during the summer months on Sun, at 10:30 a.m. Visitors are welcome, but remember that no pictures are allowed inside the chapel. Built by the Crown in 1785, it was given to those Mohawk Indians led by Joseph Brant who had supported the British during the American Revolution. It is a peaceful and inspiring place to visit. Open Wed to Sat, May, June, and Oct, daily July to Sept.

Myrtleville House Museum. 34 Myrtleville Dr., Brantford; (519) 752-3216; www.brant museum.ca. The Myrtleville House Museum is a restored 1837 Georgian-style home with beautiful gardens shaded by hundred-year-old trees. The collections reflect the life of the Good Family who emigrated here from Ireland in 1837 and raised 10 children in this home. It reflects the family and farm life of the era. Open year-round Mon to Fri, daily in July and Aug. Admission by donation.

where to shop

Loon's Call Studio. 5 Pinehill Dr., Brantford; (519) 752-9949; www.loonscallstudio.com. Here you will find some great stained glass pieces that you will love, but also all the glass products a stained glass hobbyist might need. Closed Mon and Tues.

Two Turtle Iroquois Fine Art Gallery. 1110 Highway 54, R.R. 2, Middleport Plaza, Caledonia; (519) 751-2774; www.twoturtlenativeart.com. Arnold Jacobs is an Onandaga artist who over the past 30 years has created works of art that depict the Haudenosaunee culture. His images range from contemporary graphics and realism, to the mystical, but all are reflective of his heritage. He has also created a clothing line, clan jewellery, and framed art cards. Closed Mon in summer, open weekdays only in winter.

where to eat

Cafe Troy. 2290 Highway 5 West, Troy; (519) 647-0606; www.donnzver.com. This is your chance to dine with a famous potter, or at least dine from his artworks. Donn Zver has made all the dishes, and you can buy a whole range of his pottery in the adjacent shop. The decor is an eclectic collection of antiques and stained glass, but it's all comfortable and attractive. The food shows a strong preference for local ingredients. Almost everything on the menu will be from nearby producers. The Tuscan sandwich and smoked chicken penne are excellent. Closed Monday. $$$

mohawk chapel

The year 2010 was the 225th anniversary of the Mohawk Chapel. Its history is fascinating. When four Chiefs of the Sixth Nation Confederacy visited Queen Anne in London England in the early 1700s, they were a sensation. They were called the Four Kings. As a result of their visit, in 1710, the first Royal Chapel was built on Six Nation's land in the Mohawk Valley. Queen Anne sent silver flagons, goblets, and plates for celebrating communion in the new chapel. During the American Revolution, the chapel was burned by the Americans but luckily the Mohawks had buried the Queen Anne silver. When the chapel was rebuilt on the banks of the Grand, the silver was unearthed and returned to the chapel. It is a beautiful chapel to visit. It is the only Royal chapel in North America, and the oldest protestant church in Ontario.

woodstock

Vansittart Avenue (named after Admiral Henry Vansittart, an early settler) in Woodstock's west end has one of the finest residential Victorian streetscapes in the province. This quiet village is a pleasant visit, to walk, hike a nearby trail, enjoy the small town charm, and appreciate the architecture of another time.

getting there

Woodstock is a half hour drive (33 km or 20 miles) from Brantford. Take the Highway 403 West. Take exit 232 for Norwich Avenue toward Oxford Road 59/Delhl/Woodstock. Oxford Road 59 North will take you into Woodstock.

where to go

Old St. Paul's Anglican Church. Huron and Dundas Streets, Woodstock; (519) 537-3912. Old St. Paul's Anglican Church, one of Woodstock's notable buildings, was built in 1833, and the first sermon was held in the rectory on June 29, 1834. Rumour has it that the church tower was once used as a temporary jail during the rebellion of 1837. The church, a beautiful, brick cruciform structure surrounded by Woodstock's oldest cemetery, boasts original box pews and dozens of memorial tablets commemorating prominent Woodstock citizens.

Woodstock Museum National Historic Site. 466 Dundas St., Woodstock; (519) 537-8411; www.woodstockmuseum.ca. The museum is situated in the nationally designated Old Town Hall, and presents an interpretation of the past of Woodstock. As well as artifacts, the museum displays a complete antique barber shop, artifacts from the famous Birchall trial, and the history of the Oxford Rifles. Open Mon to Sat in summer, Tues to Sat in winter.

ingersoll

Ingersoll has always been known as the cheese town. Canada's first cheese factory was built here in 1840. The cheese-making practice was introduced to Canada by English and Scottish immigrants, and most of the cheese was made in farmhouse kitchens, and then the factories were built to meet increasing demand.

getting there

Ingersoll is about 15 minutes (18 km or 11 miles) from Woodstock. Drive west along Highway 401. Exit at Highway 19/Harris Street to the right, and this highway will take you into the town.

ingersoll's "mammoth" cheese

In 1866, at the James Harris Cheese Company in Ingersoll, Ontario, a cheese of mammoth proportions was born! Weighing in at more than 7,300 pounds, the round was created by three local cheese factories as part of a unique promotional campaign to market Oxford County cheddar cheese to England, Paris, and the United States. The cheese travelled to England, where it was displayed in London, then to Paris, and through parts of the US. When the tour was finished, the cheese was returned to Ingersoll and divided up among the cheese factory workers. Because of its exceptional popularity in England, Oxford County went on to export a large portion of its cheese to Britain for well over 50 years. The mammoth cheese was an early example of a clever and successful advertising campaign.

where to go

Ingersoll Cheese Factory Museum. 290 Harris St., Ingersoll; (519) 485-5510, (519) 485-0120. The site consists of a series of 5 unique buildings, which include a replica 20th-century Cheese Factory, the Sherbrooke Barn, a Sports Hall of Fame that features locally inducted athletes, a working blacksmith shop, and the Ingersoll Community Museum. Seasonal hours. Call for details.

where to stay

Elmhurst Inn & Country Spa. 415 Harris St., Ingersoll; (519) 485-5321, (800) 561-5321; www.elmhurstinn.com. There are 49 rooms in this pleasant inn, and an Aveda spa. The Victorian Manor Restaurant has an excellent reputation. In addition to the attractions of Ingersoll, the inn is very close to Stratford and St. Jacobs. $$

day trip 02

southwest

european capitals, ontario style
paris, london

There's very little that these two Ontario cities have in common with their European namesakes, except their names, and a certain cosmopolitan polish. Paris, Ontario is a cobblestoned treat of a place, and London is a fast-paced and prosperous metropolis with a proud history.

paris

Contrary to what you might assume, Paris was not named for the city with the Eiffel Tower, but rather for the nearby deposits of gypsum, used to make plaster of Paris. This attractive small town, sometimes named the prettiest town in Ontario, is also referred to as "the cobblestone capital of Canada" because of the large number of cobblestone houses. There are 14 cobblestone buildings (12 homes, 2 churches).

getting there

Paris is about 1 hour and 10 minutes (111 km or 69 miles) from Toronto. Take the Gardener Expressway West to the Queen Elizabeth way. Follow along, and the QEW turns into Highway 403, which you will follow through Hamilton and on to Brantford. Just past Brantford, take exit 33 to County Road 2/Paris Road. Follow the signs into town.

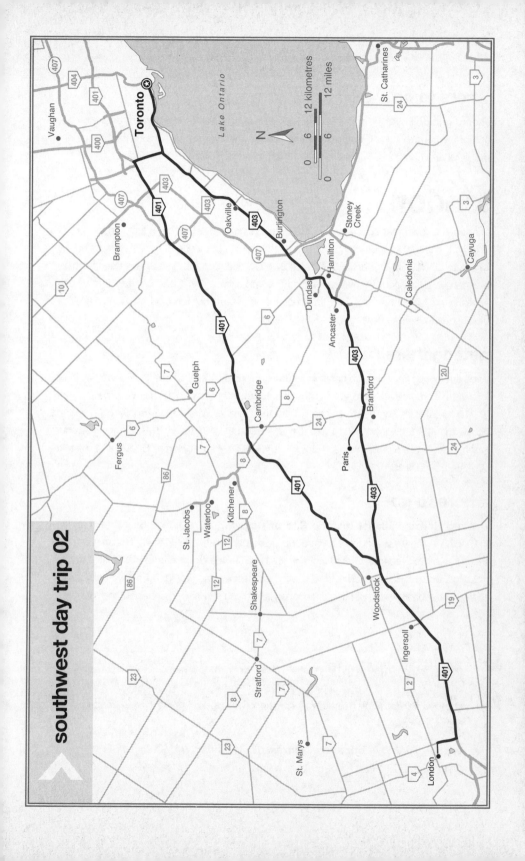

where to go

The thing to do in Paris is to walk. The town is beautiful. Bring your camera or sketch pad and enjoy the great lines, contrasting textures, and refined proportions of the homes and buildings and churches. There are lots of places to stop for a coffee or snack.

london

London is a town that specializes in intellectual pursuits—insurance, education, and technology. It has a vibrant energy, undoubtedly due to the presence of all the young students who attend Western University and Fanshawe College. London has always been a quietly prosperous town, and the historic homes that still survive are a testament to that wealth. The arts are alive here too, with the frequent shows at the John Labatt Centre and the prestigious Museum London.

getting there

If you are driving from Paris to London, return to Highway 403 and drive to Highway 401 and follow the Toronto-to-London directions. It's about a 2 hour and 15 minute drive (191 km or 119 miles) from Toronto to London. Take the Gardner West to the Highway 427 North. Follow the 427 to Highway 401 West. Drive west on the 401 to exit 189, Highbury Avenue North. Turn left at Hamilton Road, which verges slightly left at Horton Street, and will take you into the centre of the city.

where to go

Banting House National Historic Site of Canada. 442 Adelaide St. North, London; (519) 673-1752; www.diabetes.ca/about-us/who/banting-house. Banting House was once the home of Sir Frederick Grant Banting (1891–1941), the discoverer of insulin. It is quite a nostalgic and interesting home, visited often by people who wouldn't be alive and healthy today if it hadn't been for Banting's discovery. Here you can learn more about the man, who

for more information

Dundas Street (Downtown) Information Centre. 267 Dundas St., London. Closed Sunday.

London Tourist Information Centres. 696 Wellington Rd. South, London; (519) 661-5000, (800) 265-2602; www.londontourism.ca. Open daily.

was also a war hero, a possible spy, and painted, quite respectably, with members of the Group of Seven. It is easy to spend an enjoyable half day here. Open Tues to Sat.

Covent Garden Market. 130 King St. (corner of King and Talbot), London; www.covent market.com. Since 1845, this wonderful market has been providing fresh food and vegetables to the people of London. In this bustling and busy place you will find every kind of fresh food—much of it organic, and one of the largest selections of cheeses in Southwestern Ontario. The indoor market is open daily but the outdoor farmers market is on Thurs and Sat.

Eldon House. 481 Ridout St., London; (519) 661-0333; www.eldonhouse.ca. Museum London also operates Eldon House, the oldest single-family residence in the City of London. One of the nicest things to do when visiting London is to tour Eldon House and then have a proper English tea on the veranda overlooking the Thames. The gardens are lovely, and the house is not just full of antiques and treasures—it's full of stories. Eldon House was built in 1834 for John and Amelia Harris and remained in the Harris family for four successive generations. Seasonal hours. Call for details. Admission by donation.

Fanshawe Pioneer Village. 1424 Clarke Rd., London; (519) 457-1296; www.fanshawe pioneervillage.ca. This is an attractive place to spend the day with your family, learning about life in the 19th century at Fanshawe Pioneer Village. The past is brought to life through daily demonstrations of 19th-century trades and farming practices, domestic chores, and social pastimes by costumed interpreters. There's also a general store and a Village Cafe. Open May to Oct. Closed Monday.

Grand Theatre. 471 Richmond St., London; (519) 672-8800, (800) 265-1593; www.grand theatre.com. This grand old lady is an elegant theatre brought back to life by a thoughtful renovation. The theatre has had a lofty past. Some of the famous people who have performed here are: W. C. Fields, Sarah Bernhardt, Michael Redgrave, Donald O'Connor, Sidney Poitier, Jessica Tandy, Hume Cronyn, Maggie Smith, Michael Burgess, William Hutt, Martha Henry, Karen Kain, Victor Garber, Sandra Oh, and Leonard Nimoy. It even has its own ghost. The theatre runs a busy schedule of musicals, plays, and shows. Open daily.

John Labatt Centre. 99 Dundas St., London; (866) 455-2849; www.johnlabattcentre .com. The facility seats 9,000 for hockey and ice events and more than 10,000 for concerts, family shows, and other events. It has been constructed in the heart of downtown London and its exterior design incorporates a replica of the facade of the old Talbot Inn with a state-of-the-art entertainment and sports facility. The facility has been designed to accommodate touring Broadway shows and attracts some of the biggest names in the business. I enjoyed a Rod Stewart concert here, and found it a wonderful venue for music.

Museum London. 421 Ridout St. North, London; (519) 661-0333: www.museumlondon .ca. The museum is impressive. It overlooks the river and its collection includes more than

> ## the mystery of ambrose small

There are those who claim to have seen a ghostly presence sitting in the royal box of the newly refurbished Grand Theatre in London, Ontario. There are stories of odd sounds, strange happenings, and unexplained lights. Everyone blames it on Ambrose Small, a Toronto entrepreneur who built the theatre and operated it until his mysterious disappearance on December 2, 1919. That day, Mr. Small deposited $1 million in a Toronto bank account, lunched with his wife, and was never seen again. Weeks after his disappearance, the night watchman swore he saw Mr. Small entering The Grand Theatre. Despite this lead, police were never able to close the file. Many believe that Mr. Small's ghost still keeps a watchful eye on his beloved theatre.

5,000 regional and national works and more than 25,000 artifacts that reflect the history of the City of London. There are works by Paul Peel, Greg Curnoe, and many others. Closed Monday. Admission by donation.

Royal Canadian Regiment Museum. Wolseley Hall, 750 Elizabeth St., London; (519) 660-5102; www.theroyalcanadianregiment.ca/thercrmuseum/thercrmuseum.htm. A visit here is very affecting—tours are often led by veterans, and their passion and knowledge are formidable. You can follow the timeline of the history of the Royal Canadian Regiment, view the memorials honouring the Regiment's actions, and see medals awarded to soldiers of the Regiment. It is somehow a deeply personal museum, and well worth a visit. Closed Monday. Admission by donation.

where to eat

Aroma Mediterranean Restaurant. 717 Richmond St., London; (519) 435-0616; www .aromarestaurant.ca. The highlight of this breezy bistro is the open courtyard and the great entertainment, including Fado. The food is excellent too, with some nice riffs on Mediterranean specialties. The Aroma Calamari is calamari stuffed with seasoned bread crumbs, mushrooms, and chorizo topped with Andalucian sauce, and it is different and delicious. There's an extensive and attractive wine cellar. Open daily. $$

Tru Restaurant and Lounge. 45 King St., London; (519) 672-4333; www.trurestaurant .ca. Crab fitters, house-made gnocchi, and "five mushroom three onion risotto" are just some of the delicious dishes at this sophisticated New York-style restaurant that is housed in one of the oldest buildings in the core. Closed Sunday. $$$

where to stay

Idlewyld Inn. 36 Grand Ave., London; (519) 433-2891; www.idlewyldinn.com. The inn was once a private mansion, and is now an elegant place to stay, with a cosy old world charm. Each room is different, and the dining room is excellent. $$

where to shop

Jonathon Bancroft-Snell Gallery. 258 Dundas St., London; (519) 434-5443, (866) 229-5244; www.jonathons.ca. This place is known to every important glass collector in Canada, and probably in North America. Jonathon's is Canada's largest contemporary Canadian ceramic gallery and also features early career painters and Canada's leading silversmiths in the 4,500-square-foot showroom. The shop is huge, and each room is more compelling than the next. Great place for the true collector. Closed Sunday.

appendix: festivals & celebrations

january

What better reason to visit London than to explore new tastes and discover the latest culinary trends at **The London Wine and Food Show!** This mid-Jan show promises high-end food, wine, cheese, spirits, and beer. (519) 438-7203; www.westernfair.com.

Experience glass art in a glass house in Jan at Burlington's Royal Botanical Garden's Mediterranean Garden. **The Annual Glass Under Glass Exhibition & Sale** includes an expanded display of glass art created by Ontario artists. (905) 527-1158; www.rbg.ca.

For three weekends Niagara celebrates one of Canada's most cherished products, Ontario Icewine. Enjoy gala evenings, outdoor tastings, and activities to wine pairings along the famed Niagara Wine Route during the **Niagara Icewine Festival** in St. Catharines and various spots in Niagara. (905) 688-0212; www.niagarawinefestival.com.

For more adventures in wine in Jan, visit the **Twenty Valley Winter WineFest** in Jordan. (905) 562-3636.

Celebrate Cobourg's culinary delights and take advantage of prix fixe offers at a variety of Cobourg's restaurants during the Jan **Savoury Celebrations.** There are special menus for each of the restaurants. (905) 372-5481; www.cobourgtourism.ca.

Hosted at Deerhurst Resort in Huntsville in late Jan with 24 pond hockey rinks scattered on 2.4 hectares (6 acres) of open ice, the **Canadian National Pond Hockey Championships** are an amazing way to experience Canada's favourite pastime in beautiful Muskoka. www.canadapondhockey.ca.

february

Experience the Winter Carnival and enjoy winter with great activities at Burlington's **Celebrate Winter.** Workshops, an interactive ice sculpture, and recreational skating with BurBear are just some of the Feb events held over two weekends. (905) 335-7766; www.burlington.ca.

Join the **Lowville Winter Games** on the first Sun in Feb for wagon rides, log sawing competitions, a winter hike along the Bruce Trail, entertainment, and more. There will be outdoor skating, tobogganing, and snowshoe demos. (905) 335-7600.

For winter fun for the whole family, try the **Barrie Winterfest and Festival of Ice.** Grab your mittens and enjoy wagon rides, snow slide, dog sled rides, lumberjack show, ice sculptures, polar bear swim, and much more. Indoor activities too! (705) 739-4285; www .barrie.ca.

Consider a family trek to Canada's best known national park for the **Algonquin Outfitters Winter Family Fun Day** at Oxtongue Lake. This annual winter fun day will get you excited about winter! (705) 789-4771; www.algonquinoutfitters.com.

Penetanguishene Winterama is one of Ontario's longest running, community winter celebrations! The combination of a winter parade, children's activities, competitions, music entertainment, wagon rides, and hearty food is irresistible on a chilly day. Hours vary based on activity. (705) 549-7453; www.penetanguishene.ca.

If you are beginning to dream about spring, **Seedy Saturday** is the perfect activity. Swap or buy seeds, participate in a workshop or take part in a demonstration at Burlington's Royal Botanical Gardens. Full of seed vendors featuring heritage and specialty seeds as well as supplies for home. (905) 527-1158; www.rbg.ca.

A Taste of Burlington allows visitors to experience the eclectic styles and flavours of the world at various restaurants that offer prix fixe lunch and/or dinner menus at great savings. The food celebration lasts from late Feb into mid Mar. (905) 634-5594; www.tasteof burlington.ca.

march

Expect the unexpected on a whimsical visit through the looking glass at **Wonderland at Whitehern** in Hamilton. The lovely historic home will host activities and games, as well as a Mad Hatter Tea Party. (905) 546-2018; www.hamilton.ca/museums.

Take part in the oldest footrace in North America during the **Around the Bay 30K Road Race,** in Mar in Hamilton. (905) 574-8982.

Get your sugar-fix at the **Sugarbush Maple Syrup Festival,** Vaughan and Stouffville. (416) 661-6600.

The past will come to life with fun and exciting hands-on activities for the whole family during **A Monumental March Break** at Battlefield House in Stoney Creek. The event runs Mon to Fri during March Break. (905) 662-8458; www.hamilton.ca/museums.

april

Can't think of a more charming way to usher in spring than by attending the **Annual Swan Parade,** in Stratford, when the gaggle of swans is marched down to the Avon River and gleefully take to the water. The event takes place on the first Sun in Apr. (519) 271-5140.

Explore the province's heritage sites during **Doors Open Ontario,** a collection of province wide community events that run from Apr to Oct. This is an opportunity to explore some historic homes and gardens that are otherwise never open to the public, as well as tour, for free, many of the province's most notable historic buildings and museums. (416) 325-5000, (800) ONTARIO; www.doorsopenontario.on.ca.

Bring your sweet tooth for **Maple Syrup Day** at the Ganaraska Forest Centre in Port Hope. Tour the sap collecting route, visit the sugar shack, enjoy a campfire and pancakes. (905) 797-2721; www.porthopetourism.ca.

The season begins for the renowned **Stratford Shakespeare Festival.** This is North America's leading repertory theatre with four stages on which magical theatre is performed. From Shakespeare to musicals, be moved and entertained. (519) 273-1600; www.stratford shakespearefestival.com.

Another season begins for the only theatrical festival in the world devoted to the works of George Bernard Shaw and his contemporaries. The **Shaw Festival** in Niagara-on-the-Lake runs brilliant plays and musicals through to Oct. (800) 511-7429; www.shawfest.com.

If you love collectibles and old things, don't miss this auction in the town made famous by its antiques stores. The **Port Hope Antiques & Artifacts Auction** starts with a preview and tag sale, followed by the auction. (905) 885-7929; www.acoporthope.ca.

Visit the Easter Bunny, have your face painted, enjoy an Easter puppet show and live magician, go on a wagon ride, and see farm animals during weekends at the **Downey's Farm Easterfest** in Caledon. (905) 838-2990; www.downeysfarm.com.

Scare yourself silly during the **Historic Ghost Walks** in St. Catharines, happening on the full moon every month through the summer. (905) 685-8424; www.mydowntown.ca.

may

Here's something for the budding engineer in the family. Catch a ride on coal-burning steam-powered miniature trains, enjoy demonstrations of radio-controlled model boats, and discover the Canadian Modeling Association for Mecanno and Allied Systems at the **Golden Horseshoe Live Steamer Days.** At the Park & Meccano Weekend at the Hamilton Museum of Steam & Technology, Hamilton. (905) 546-4797; www.hamilton.ca/museums.

Attend **IlluminAqua in Welland** and enjoy a blend of art, culture, elements of fire and water. Pods of fire float in a laid-out design along the Recreational Waterway, while music fills the air. (905) 735-1700; www.illuminaqua.com.

This is a sight to take your breath away. The **Lilac Celebration** at the Royal Botanical Gardens in Burlington is spectacular—the gardens possess the largest collection of lilacs in the world. Weekends include guided tours. (905) 527-1158; www.rbg.ca.

You can bid for one of the spectacular handmade quilts and also contribute to a good cause at the **New Hamburg Mennonite Relief Sale & Quilt Auction,** New Hamburg. (519) 745-8458.

Long Point Carolinian Nature Fest in Port Rowan is a celebration of local nature and features a weekend of birding, wildflower identification walks, salamander monitoring, frog walks, tree identification, kids activities, and more. (519) 410-8878; www.longpoint biosphere.com.

Prepare to spend the day—there are picnic facilities—at the **Christie Classic Antique Show** in Dundas, one of the largest antiques markets in the country. It stretches for miles, and is full of treasures and collectibles. (905) 628-3060.

june

The single largest event in the Hills of Headwaters region is the **Orangeville Blues & Jazz Festival,** one of the most highly-respected events of its kind in Canada, featuring live blues and jazz, a classic car cruise, antique motorcycles, and more. (519) 941-9041; www.objf.org.

Ladies, gentlemen, and children of all ages step right up to 3 days of nonstop laughter and family fun! It's organized pandemonium, uncontrollable laughter, nonstop chaos, and abso-lute family fun at the **Dundas International Buskerfest.** (905) 528-9113; www.downtown dundas.ca.

The **Streetsville Founders' Bread & Honey Festival** is a fun-filled family festival featur-ing a huge parade, live entertainment on two stages, a petting zoo, pony rides, children's inflatables, crafts, souvenirs, and much more. (905) 816-1640; www.breadandhoney.com.

Build, decorate, and fly a kite! Or bring your own at the **Burlington Kite Festival.** (905) 335-7600; www.burlington.ca.

The one-day celebration of the arts along the banks of the Grand River is known as the **Cambridge Grand Riverfest.** It features live music, dance, art demonstrations, family art-making activities, and more than 100 specialty food purveyors and craftspeople. (519) 740-4681; www.cambridgeriverfest.com.

Find fun for all ages at the **33rd Ancaster Heritage Days.** The Old Mill Road Race starts events, followed by parade, soapbox derby, craft market, kids world, battle of teen bands, and fireworks. (905) 546-3196; www.ancasterheritagedays.com.

Get to see and tour some of the beautiful gardens for which Niagara-on-the-Lake is famous during the **Shaw Garden Tour,** Niagara-on-the-Lake. (800) 511-7429.

The **Cambridge Tour de Grand** is a recreational cycling event for the novice to elite rider with various routes from 10 km (6 miles) to the "Tour 160 k." Set along the scenic Grand

River with refreshments and rest areas along the way. (519) 622-1087; www.cambridge tourdegrand.com.

From the Grower of the Year's Tailgate Party to exploring the Wine Route with the Discovery Pass, the **New Vintage Niagara Celebration** in St. Catharines celebrates the newly released vintages. Experience the finest in wine and cuisine across Niagara. (905) 688-0212; www.niagarawinefestival.com.

June is strawberry season and there are strawberry socials everywhere. Try the **Annual Strawberry Festival** in Niagara-on-the-Lake where there are many activities as well as the strawberries. (905) 468-1950.

Another salute to the strawberry is the **Beamsville Strawberry Festival** with a day of fun and entertainment for the whole family. Crafters, vendors, food, charity bed race, La-Z-Boy recliner race, Strawberry Idol contest, and a Kidz Zone are all part of the all-day activities. (905) 562-5191; www.strawberryfest.ca.

Hendrie Gardens is the site of the famous **Rose Celebration** in the massive rose gardens in the Burlington Royal Botanical Gardens. Spend a day enjoying the variety of collections, eat lunch on the patio, and enjoy the gardens or bring a picnic and lounge in the shade. (905) 527-1158; www.rbg.ca.

july

There are Canada Day Celebrations all over the country, and some of the most joyous ones can be found within the Toronto environs. Oakville, for example, holds its **Annual Canada Day** lakeside with a national holiday festival attracting more than 50,000 people. It's a family friendly event with music, food, fun for all ages. (905) 825-3258, www.brontevillage.net.

The **Waterfront Festival** in Cobourg is held on the first weekend in July and is one of the city's largest annual events. Each year Victoria Park and the Waterfront is turned into one of the largest annual outdoor art and craft shows in Canada. The Canadian Forces Snowbirds Airshow is proudly presented by the Cobourg Rotary Club each year during the Waterfront Festival activities. There is also an outdoor flea market. www.waterfrontfestival.ca.

Showcasing culinary samplings from Niagara's best chefs and caterers and complimented by Niagara finest wines are the main purposes of the **Flavours of Niagara Festival** in Port Colborne. Features include picnic areas, beer garden, and a lively entertainment line up. (905) 834-1668; www.portcolborne.ca.

National and international artists feature in the **Huntsville Festival of the Arts.** There are evening concerts in the Algonquin Theatre and outdoor and fringe events throughout the month. (705) 789-4975; www.huntsvillefestival.on.ca.

Celebrate peace, and the wonder of the longest undefended border in the world with **Hands Across the Border in Fort Erie.** Come and be a part of this giant human handshake. www.friendshipfestival.com.

Sit in the gardens and enjoy **Red-Hot Jazz and Cool Blues** at the Royal Botanical Gardens in Burlington. Bring your own picnic or purchase dinner from the on-site restaurant. Every Wed in Aug. (905) 527-1158; www.rbg.ca.

Taste foods from many cultures at the **Brantford International Villages Cultural Festival,** during 4 days of wonderful food. (519) 756-8767; www.brantfordvillages.ca.

On Wed, bring your lunch and enjoy the garden during the **Wednesdy at Whitehern** events. Sip all-you-can-drink tea or lemonade while listening to live music. (905) 546-2018; www.hamilton.ca/museums.

TD Sunfest is a London festival of global arts. It features more than 30 top world music and dance and jazz ensembles, complemented by more than 250 food and craft exhibitors. (519) 672-1522; www.sunfest.on.ca.

The **Elora Festival** features concerts of classical, chamber, jazz, choral, and world music, to suit every taste. (888) 747-7550; www.elorafestival.com.

Visit downtown **Bracebridge for Art in the Heart,** a juried art show that takes place in the alleys and public spaces in the downtown's heart. New and emerging visual artists display and offer their craft for sale. (705) 645-5264; www.artintheheartbracebridge.com.

When you attend the **Lakefield Jazz, Art and Craft Festival,** you will have the chance to enjoy a wide variety of jazz music and colourful works for sale by artisans and crafters, interesting foods, and ice cold beverages on the shores of Lakefield's scenic Otonabee River. (705) 292-7034; www.lakefieldjazzfest.com.

Car enthusiasts from across Ontario showcase their cars with more than 50 trophies available to be won at the **15th Annual Antique and Classic Car Show** in Peterborough, at the Lang Pioneer Village Museum. (705) 295-6694; www.langpioneervillage.ca.

Get in touch with your inner Scottie at the **Cambridge Highland Games** featuring traditional Highland games, pipe band competition, massed marches, and tug of war events. There are sheepdog demos, a Scottish dance competition, children's games, clan avenue, and Scottish food vendors. (519) 222-2447; www.cambridgehighlandgames.org.

Fiesta Buckhorn in Peterborough is an event for anyone who likes wine, food, jazz music, and relaxing with friends. (705) 742-2201; www.fiestabuckhorn.com.

With the 200-year anniversary approaching, there is much interest in the War of 1812. Watch the **1812 Reenactment at Fort George** in Niagara-on-the-Lake; (905) 468-6621.

CayugaFest, in Cayuga, is a grand event with something for everyone! Parade, river activities, live entertainment, family events, artisans, vendors, food, and more. (905) 912-6641; www.cayugafest.com.

While this is not for everyone, if you are a fan of Elvis or love the music, don't miss the **Collingwood Elvis Festival.** It's a community music festival celebrating the life and career of Elvis Presley. www.collingwoodelvisfestival.com.

Meet the artists and visit them in their studios on the **22nd Annual Seguin Regional Art Tour,** in Parry Sound. (705) 732-1985.

august

There are 5 days of activities and entertainment for the entire family at the **Turkey Point Summerfest.** (519) 426-1022; www.turkeypoint.ca.

Celebrate a unique way of cooking at the **JerkFest (Jerk Food Festival)** in Mississauga. A wide variety of meats are slow cooked at the foot of the picturesque ski hills of Centennial Park. (416) 993-5123; www.jerkfestival.ca.

The **Cobblestone Theatrical Festival** in Paris aims to promote the Cobblestone Legacy that exists in Paris through theatre. With 12 homes and 2 churches, Paris is proud to be the Cobblestone Capital of Canada. (519) 442-6324; www.cobblestonefestival.ca.

The largest Scottish Festival and Highland Games outside of Scotland is the **Fergus Highland Games and Scottish Festival** held in Fergus in Aug. Listen to the bagpipes, or watch traditional Scottish dancing, and athletes in kilts competing in the traditional caber toss, hammer throw, and tug-of-war. www.fergusscottishfestival.com.

Come to see the elegant vehicles of a past era on the lawn in front of the Wellington County Museum in Fergus. **The Antique & Classic Car Show** is on the last Sun of Aug. Antique and classic cars are exhibited and admired. www.wcm.on.ca.

For something really different, try the **Expressions in Chalk Street Painting Festival** in London, Ontario. The Imadon Street Painting Performance Group puts on the festival with public performances and special events, teaching street painting to attendees. The festival takes place on Talbot Street between King and Dundas in front of the John Labatt Centre. www.imadon.org.

Enjoy music, artists, and a food marketplace and unique Canadian entertainment at the annual **Festival of Friends** in Hamilton. The festival has moved to the **Ancaster Fair Grounds.** (905) 546-2666; www.tourismhamilton.com.

The largest summer railway show in Ontario is the **Muskoka Model Railway Show,** in Bracebridge. Check out the operating layouts, modelling clinics, train vendors, and manufacturers. (705) 645-5264; www.muskokamodelrailwayclub.com.

Build your own castle at **Oakville's Harbour Days.** Watch the National Sandcastle builder competition at the beach, watch some live entertainment, and enjoy some Tall Ship Cruises, concerts, food, and family fun. (905) 825-3258; www.brontevillage.net.

Cowapolooza in Woodstock promises food, a beer garden, crafters, rides, exhibits, strongman/women competition, soapbox derby, and 2 open-air concerts. (519) 539-1291; www.city.woodstock.on.ca.

Race your boat in the **Thunder on the Grand Boat Races** in Dunnville. (905) 774-3183; www.dunnvillechamberofcommerce.

Peach season is definitely something to celebrate and one of the longest running ones is the **Winona Peach Festival.** (905) 643-2084; www.winonapeach.com.

The **Dundas Cactus Festival** is a 3-day festival with lots of free attractions for all ages. (905) 627-0926; www.dundascactusfest.ca.

The popular **Port Dover Summer Festival** features 100 juried arts and crafts vendors, antique market, book fair, and local musicians in downtown Port Dover. Bonus sidewalk sales run at the local businesses. (519) 583-2136; www.portdoversummerfestival.com.

Animal lovers shouldn't miss this one. **Pawlooza—London's Festival for Dogs—**is one of North America's largest festivals for dog lovers. Bring your dog! Thousands of dogs and 15,000+ people shop from hundreds of vendors and join in on dozens of demos and fun events. (519) 439-0352; www.pawlooza.com.

To celebrate Sir Allan MacNab's Scottish ancestry, Hamilton has **A Scottish Celebration at Dundurn National Historic Site.** It is a day of 19th-century children's games, workshops, and music by the Royal Hamilton Light Infantry and Argyll and Sutherland Highlanders. (905) 546-2872; www.hamilton.ca/museums.

september

The first **Western Fair** was held in September 1868 in downtown London and has been an annual event ever since. It is Canada's seventh largest fair. The fair runs for 10 days every Sept and includes exhibits, concerts, and animals. www.londonkiosk.ca/london-events/western-fair.php.

The **Fergus Fall Fair** is held at the Fergus and District Community Centre. www.fergus fallfair.ca.

People come from across the province for this indulgent festival. It's Canada's Largest **Ribfest** held by the lake in Burlington. There's great music, fun for the kids, and of course, some of the best tasting ribs in Canada. (905) 332-3513; www.canadaslargestribfest.com.

Say farewell to summer at the **Summer Sundown** in Blue Mountain. Experience live bands, fireworks, street performers, beach volleyball, hiking, biking, scenic gondola rides, and The Apple Pie Trail. (705) 445-0231; www.villageatblue.com.

How many ways can you cook with mustard? Find out at the **14th Annual Mustard Festival.** (800) 263-8590; www.tourismhamilton.com.

There are hundreds of Fall Fairs in Ontario. One big one is the **Bracebridge Fall Fair & Horse Show.** There's old fashioned fall fair fun with horse pulls, antique garden and tractor pulls, culinary and fiber arts, horticultural displays, youth and junior exhibits, entertainment, and midway rides. (705) 645-4223; www.bracebridgefair.com.

Fall is harvest time for grapes and that means it's time for the **Niagara Wine Festival** in St. Catharines and other venues throughout Niagara. For 2 weeks in Sept experience premium wine tastings, local culinary, and live entertainment. (905) 688-0212; www.niagarawine festival.com.

If you love chili, don't miss the **Downtown Cobourg Harvest Festival Featuring the Chili Cook-Off.** There's a farmers' market, live bands, children's activities and contests, merchant displays, a chili cook-off, apple pie contest, and more. (905) 377-8024; www .downtowncobourg.ca.

Visit the artists' studios during the **Elora Fergus Studio Tour.** The tour takes place over 2 weekends; (877) 242-6353; www.elorafergusstudiotour.ca.

In a town that is famous for its restaurants, you know that the culinary festival is going to be special. **Savour Stratford Perth County Culinary Festival** is a foodie's paradise. (519) 271-5140.

The **Word on the Street Festival** in Kitchener promotes the importance of literacy with free exhibits, performances, readings, and hands-on activities. (519) 745-3536; www.the wordonthestreet.ca.

Enjoy the best of the season, and some interesting history at the **Applefest Fall Fair** at historic Ireland House in Burlington. (905) 332-9888.

This is one of the province's longest running fairs, the **Caledonia Fair,** approaching its 140th year. There's livestock, crafts, food, and the midway combined with continuous entertainment and a popular demolition derby. (905) 318-5932; www.caledoniafair.ca.

There's good eating at the **Niagara Food Festival** in Welland. There are more than 40 wineries and many food vendors showcasing their finest delights. There's also entertainment all weekend long. (905) 735-1700; www.niagarafoodfestival.com.

october

The long running **Norfolk County Fair & Horse Show,** held in early Oct features agricultural displays, craft exhibits, food vendors, art demonstrations, talent competitions, midway rides, free grandstand entertainment, and many added special attractions. (519) 426-7280; www.norfolkcountyfair.com.

Dundas is an artsy town, and you'll be amazed at the talent you'll see on the **Dundas Studio Tour.** (905) 379-7353.

In Penetanguishene, **The Bay Studio Tour** includes locally based artists from Penetanguishene, Tiny, and Midland featuring a variety of locations from home studios, local businesses, and the Penetanguishene Centennial Museum. (705) 549-1060; www.penetanguishene.ca.

The **Scarlet Maple Tour,** in the Lanark Highlands, is a free self-guided driving tour showcasing beautiful scenery, heritage buildings, and stunning products produced by local businesses and artisans. (613) 259-2398; www.lanark-highlands.com/scarletmapletour.html.

This is Canada's tribute to all things German—the popular **Kitchener-Waterloo Oktoberfest.** The "Tapping of the Keg" signifies the opening and the celebrations continue with music, beer tents, great German food, and plenty of *gemütlich.* (519) 570-4267; www.oktoberfest.ca.

Rockton World's Fair has old-fashioned country fun, and one of the largest combined heavy horse shows in Canada. There are beef/dairy cattle, demo derby, family entertainment, and a midway. (519) 647-3899; www.rocktonworldsfair.com.

Fall colours and spectacular landscapes are the attraction at the **Fall into Nature Festival** in Milton. There are chairlift rides, guided hikes, live performances (music, First Nations Dancers), demonstrations, and family-fun activities. (905) 336-1158; www.fallintonature.ca.

Love to go to the movies? You'll appreciate the **Vintage Film Festival** in Port Hope that features classic films from the 1920s to 1940s. www.capitoltheatre.com.

Parents are invited to bring their children to a safe trick-or-treating experience at the **Muskoka Heritage Place Great Pumpkin Trail** in Huntsville. Heritage homes are decorated for the kids to enjoy going door to door in a safe, traffic-free area. (705) 789-4771; www.huntsvillelakeofbays.on.ca.

november

Niagara Falls really knows how to celebrate Christmas. **The Winter Festival of Lights** is spectacular, with light sculptures, fireworks, live concerts, and the Falls themselves bathed in coloured lights. (800) 563-2557; www.wfol.com.

Enjoy an old-fashioned Christmas at **Christmas in Bayfield**. There are special shops, charming atmosphere, friendly service, leisurely dining, festive music, holiday decor, "tree lighting festival," and much more. (519) 556-5549; www.villageofbayfield.com.

Enjoy 3 days of shopping at local studios, stores, and home-based businesses throughout the Port Rowan area during the **Festival by the Bay.** There are special offers, entertainment, and goodies. (519) 586-8555; www.portrowan-longpoint.org.

The **McQuesten's Childhood Christmas at Whitehern Historic House & Garden,** in Hamilton will show you how one family celebrated the holiday. The table is set with the china they used for Christmas and New Years from the 1850s to the 1930s. (905) 546-2018; www.hamilton.ca/museums.

december

In keeping with the city's German character, Kitchener presents the **Christkindl Market** (Festival of German Christmas) at Kitchener City Hall. In addition to traditional foods, there are bands, choirs, dancers, railway display, Christkindl, organ grinder, *Kinderecke* (crafts), and more than 70 vendors. (519) 741-2387; www.christkindl.ca.

Bring your skates and make your mark during the **First Skate** of the season on The Rotary Centennial Pond. Skating performances, music, and dignitaries help launch the season. www.burlington.ca.

Lang Pioneer Village in Peterborough presents a historic Christmas at their **Christmas by Candlelight** Festival. www.langpioneervillage.ca.

Take a walk along the waterfront to enjoy the **Burlington Lakeside Festival of Lights,** then head to the Centennial Pond for a skate. (905) 333-9868; www.burlingtonfestivalof lights.com.

The **Santa's Village Candlelight Stroll,** centered around Centennial Square at Niagara Falls City Hall, includes horse-drawn wagon rides, Victorian carolers, hot chocolate, and roasted chestnuts. (905) 374-1616; www.wfol.com.

Can you think of a more impressive place to ring in the New Year than at the Falls? Share the countdown with **New Year's Eve in Niagara Falls,** including a fireworks display over the Falls and musical entertainment. (877) 642-7275; www.niagaraparks.com.

Oshawa rings in the New Year with a free event at the annual **Legends Centre, Oshawa Celebrates.** There are free skating, a swimming entertainment act, and New Year's countdown at 9 p.m. for younger folks, and those who may not be able to stay awake until midnight. (905) 436-3892; www.oshawa.ca.

index

INSIDERS' GUIDE®

The acclaimed travel series that has sold more than 2 million copies!

Discover: Your Travel Destination.
Your Home. Your Home-to-Be.

Albuquerque

Anchorage &
  Southcentral
  Alaska

Atlanta

Austin

Baltimore

Baton Rouge

Boulder & Rocky Mountain
  National Park

Branson & the Ozark
  Mountains

California's Wine Country

Cape Cod & the Islands

Charleston

Charlotte

Chicago

Cincinnati

Civil War Sites in
  the Eastern Theater

Civil War Sites in the South

Colorado's Mountains

Dallas & Fort Worth

Denver

El Paso

Florida Keys & Key West

Gettysburg

Glacier National Park

Great Smoky Mountains

Greater Fort Lauderdale

Greater Tampa Bay Area

Hampton Roads

Houston

Hudson River Valley

Indianapolis

Jacksonville

Kansas City

Long Island

Louisville

Madison

Maine Coast

Memphis

Myrtle Beach &
  the Grand Strand

Nashville

New Orleans

New York City

North Carolina's
  Mountains

North Carolina's
  Outer Banks

North Carolina's
  Piedmont Triad

Oklahoma City

Orange County, CA

Oregon Coast

Palm Beach County

Palm Springs

Philadelphia &
  Pennsylvania Dutch
  Country

Phoenix

Portland, Maine

Portland, Oregon

Raleigh, Durham &
  Chapel Hill

Richmond, VA

Reno and Lake Tahoe

St. Louis

San Antonio

Santa Fe

Savannah & Hilton Head

Seattle

Shreveport

South Dakota's
  Black Hills Badlands

Southwest Florida

Tucson

Tulsa

Twin Cities

Washington, D.C.

Williamsburg & Virginia's
  Historic Triangle

Yellowstone
  & Grand Teton

Yosemite

**To order call 800-243-0495
or visit www.Insiders.com**

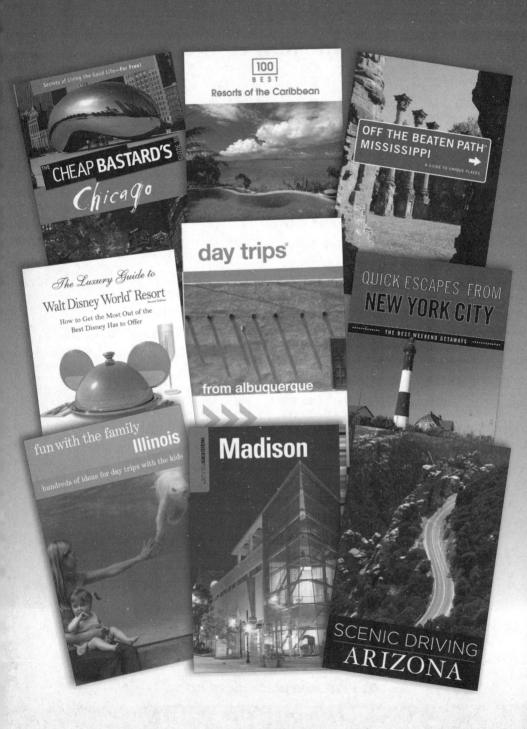